The Differend: Phrases in Dispute

Theory and History of Literature
Edited by Wlad Godzich and Jochen Schulte-Sasse

For other books in the series, see p. 209

The Differend
Phrases in Dispute

Jean-François Lyotard

Translation by Georges Van Den Abbeele

Theory and History of Literature, Volume 46

University of Minnesota Press, Minneapolis

The University of Minnesota gratefully acknowledges translation
assistance for this book by the French Ministry of Culture and the
Georges Lurcy Charitable and Educational Trust.

Published by the University of Minnesota Press
111 Third Avenue South, Suite 290, Minneapolis, MN 55401-2520
http://www.upress.umn.edu
Printed in the United States of America on acid-free paper
Ninth printing 2014

Library of Congress Cataloging-in-Publication Data

Lyotard, Jean François.
  [Différend, English]
  The differend : phrases in dispute / Jean-François Lyotard :
translation by Georges Van Den Abbeele
      p.   cm. – (Theory and history of literature : v. 46)
  Translation of: Le différend.
  Bibliography: p.
  Includes indexes.
  ISBN 978-0-8166-1611-4 (pbk.)
  1. Philosophy. I. Title. II. Series.
B29.L913 1988   88-4780
190–dc19

For further information on publishing history, see p. vi.

The University of Minnesota
is an equal-opportunity
educator and employer.

aAMma

Preface: Reading Dossier

Title

As distinguished from a litigation, a differend [*différend*] would be a case of conflict, between (at least) two parties, that cannot be equitably resolved for lack of a rule of judgment applicable to both arguments. One side's legitimacy does not imply the other's lack of legitimacy. However, applying a single rule of judgment to both in order to settle their differend as though it were merely a litigation would wrong (at least) one of them (and both of them if neither side admits this rule). Damages result from an injury which is inflicted upon the rules of a genre of discourse but which is reparable according to those rules. A wrong results from the fact that the rules of the genre of discourse by which one judges are not those of the judged genre or genres of discourse. The ownership of a literary or artistic work can incur damages (as when the moral rights of the author are assailed); but the very principle that one ought to treat a work as an object of ownership may constitute a wrong (as when it is not recognized that the "author" is its hostage). The title of this book suggests (through the generic value of the definite article) that a universal rule of judgment between heterogeneous genres is lacking in general.

Object

The only one that is indubitable, the phrase, because it is immediately presupposed. (To doubt that one phrases is still to phrase, one's silence makes a phrase).

Or better yet, phrases: because the singular calls forth the plural (as the plural does the singular) and because the singular and the plural are together already the plural.

Thesis

A phrase, even the most ordinary one, is constituted according to a set of rules (its regimen). There are a number of phrase regimens: reasoning, knowing, describing, recounting, questioning, showing, ordering, etc. Phrases from heterogeneous regimens cannot be translated from one into the other. They can be linked one onto the other in accordance with an end fixed by a genre of discourse. For example, dialogue links an ostension (showing) or a definition (describing) onto a question; at stake in it is the two parties coming to an agreement about the sense of a referent. Genres of discourse supply rules for linking together heterogeneous phrases, rules that are proper for attaining certain goals: to know, to teach, to be just, to seduce, to justify, to evaluate, to rouse emotion, to oversee. . . . There is no "language" in general, except as the object of an Idea.

Question

A phrase "happens." How can it be linked onto? By its rule, a genre of discourse supplies a set of possible phrases, each arising from some phrase regimen. Another genre of discourse supplies another set of other possible phrases. There is a differend between these two sets (or between the genres that call them forth) because they are heterogeneous. And linkage must happen "now"; another phrase cannot not happen. It's a necessity; time, that is. There is no non-phrase. Silence is a phrase. There is no last phrase. In the absence of a phrase regimen or of a genre of discourse that enjoys a universal authority to decide, does not the linkage (whichever one it is) necessarily wrong the regimens or genres whose possible phrases remain unactualized?

Problem

Given 1) the impossibility of avoiding conflicts (the impossibility of indifference) and 2) the absence of a universal genre of discourse to regulate them (or, if you prefer, the inevitable partiality of the judge): to find, if not what can legitimate judgment (the "good" linkage), then at least how to save the honor of thinking.

Stakes

To convince the reader (including the first one, the A.) that thought, cognition, ethics, politics, history or being, depending on the case, are in play when one phrase is linked onto another. To refute the prejudice anchored in the reader by centuries of humanism and of "human sciences" that there is "man," that there is "language," that the former makes use of the latter for his own ends, and that if he does not succeed in attaining these ends, it is for want of good control over language "by means" of a "better" language. To defend and illustrate philosophy in its differend with its two adversaries: on its outside, the genre of economic discourse (exchange, capital); on its inside, the genre of academic discourse (mastery). By showing that the linking of one phrase onto another is problematic and that this problem is the problem of politics, to set up a philosophical politics apart from the politics of "intellectuals" and of politicians. To bear witness to the differend.

Context

The "linguistic turn" of Western philosophy (Heidegger's later works, the penetration of Anglo-American philosophies into European thought, the development of language technologies); and correlatively, the decline of universalist discourses (the metaphysical doctrines of modern times: narratives of progress, of socialism, of abundance, of knowledge). The weariness with regard to "theory," and the miserable slackening that goes along with it (new this, new that, post-this, post-that, etc.). The time has come to philosophize.

Pretext

The two thoughts which beckon to the A.: the Kant of the third *Critique* and the historical-political texts (the "fourth Critique"); the Wittgenstein of the *Philosophical Investigations* and the posthumous writings. In the context imagined by the A., they are epilogues to modernity and prologues to an honorable postmodernity. They draw up the affidavit ascertaining the decline of universalist doctrines (Leibnizian or Russellian metaphysics). They question the terms in which these doctrines thought they could settle differends (reality, subject, community, finality). They question them more rigorously than does Husserl's "rigorous science," which proceeds by eidetic variation and transcendental evidence, the ultimate expedient of Cartesian modernity. At the opposite pole, Kant says that there is no such thing as intellectual intuition, and Wittgenstein that the signification of a term is its use. The free examination of phrases leads to the (critical) dissociation of their regimens (the separation of the faculties and their conflict in Kant; the disentanglement of language games in Wittgenstein). They lay the ground for the thought of dispersion (diaspora, writes Kant) which, according to the A., shapes our context. Their legacy ought to be relieved today of its cumbersome debt to anthropomorphism (the notion of "use" in both, an anthropomorphism that is transcendental in Kant, empirical in Wittgenstein).

Mode

The book's mode is philosophic, reflective. The A.'s only rule here is to examine cases of differend and to find the rules for the heterogeneous genres of discourse that bring about these cases. Unlike a theoretician, he does not presuppose the rules of his own discourse, but only that this discourse too must obey rules. The mode of the book is philosophical, and not theoretical (or anything else) to the extent that its stakes are in discovering its rules rather than in supposing their knowledge as a principle. In this very way, it denies itself the possibility of settling, on the basis of its own rules, the differends it examines (contrary to the speculative genre, for instance, or the analytic). The mode is that of a metalanguage in the linguist's sense (phrases are its object) but not in the logician's sense (it does not constitute the grammar of an object-language).

Genre

In the sense of poetics, the genre is that of Observations, Remarks, Thoughts, and Notes which are relative to an object; in other words, a discontinuous form of the Essay. A notebook of sketches? The reflections are arranged in a series of numbers and grouped into sections. The series is interrupted on occasion by Notices, which are reading notes for philosophical texts, but the whole is to be read in sequence.

Style

The A.'s naive ideal is to attain a zero degree style and for the reader to have the thought in hand, as it were. There sometimes ensues a tone of wisdom, a sententious one, which should be disregarded. The book's tempo is not that of "our time." A little out of date? The A. explains himself at the end about the time of "our time."

Reader

A philosophical one, that is, anybody on the condition that he or she agrees not to be done with "language" and not to "gain time." Nevertheless, the present reading dossier will allow the reader, if the fancy grabs him or her, to "talk about the book" without having read it. (For the Notices, a little more professional a reader.)

Author

Announced the present reflections in the "Prière de désinsérer" of *Rudiments païens* (1977) [*Pagan Rudiments*] and in the Introduction to *The Postmodern Con-*

dition (1979). Were he not afraid of being tedious, he would confess that he had begun this work right after the publication of *Economie libidinale* (1974). Or for that matter . . . These reflections could not in the end have seen the light of day without an agreement reached between the University of Paris VIII (Vincennes in Saint-Denis) and the C. N. R. S. , and without the obliging help of Maurice Caveing and Simone Debout-Oleszkiewicz, researchers at the C. N. R. S. The A., if not the reader, thanks them for this.

Address

So, in the next century there will be no more books. It takes too long to read, when success comes from gaining time. What will be called a book will be a printed object whose "message" (its information content) and name and title will first have been broadcast by the media, a film, a newspaper interview, a television program, and a cassette recording. It will be an object from whose sales the publisher (who will also have produced the film, the interview, the program, etc.) will obtain a certain profit margin, because people will think that they must "have" it (and therefore buy it) so as not to be taken for idiots or to break (my goodness) the social bond! The book will be distributed at a premium, yielding a financial profit for the publisher and a symbolic one for the reader. This particular book, along with others, belongs to the last of last year's line [*fin de série*]. Despite every effort to make his thought communicable, the A. knows that he has failed, that this is too voluminous, too long, and too difficult. The promoters have hidden away. Or more exactly, his timidity kept him from "contacting" them. Contented enough that one publisher (condemned also by this very act) has agreed to publish this pile of phrases.

Philosophers have never had instituted addressees, which is nothing new. The reflection's destination is also an object of reflection. The last of last year's line has been around a long time. So has solitude. Still there is something new: the relation to time (I am tempted to write the "use of time") that reigns today in the "public space." Reflection is not thrust aside today because it is dangerous or upsetting, but simply because it is a waste of time. It is "good for nothing," it is not good for gaining time. For success is gaining time. A book, for example, is a success if its first printing is rapidly sold out. This finality is the finality of the economic genre. Philosophy has been able to publish its reflections under the guise of many genres (artistic, political, theological, scientific, anthropological), at the price, of course, of misunderstandings and grave wrongs, but still . . .
—whereas economic calculation seems fatal to it. The differend does not bear upon the content of the reflection. It concerns (and tampers with) its ultimate presuppositions. Reflection requires that you watch out for occurrences, that you don't already know what's happening. It leaves open the question: *Is it happening?* [*Arrive-t-il?*] It tries to keep up with the now [*maintenir le maintenant*] (to use

a belabored word). In the economic genre, the rule is that what happens can happen only if it has already been paid back, and therefore has already happened. Exchange presupposes that the cession is canceled in advance by a counter-cession, the circulation of the book being canceled by its sales. And the sooner this is done, the better the book is.

In writing this book, the A. had the feeling that his sole addressee was the *Is it happening?* It is to it that the phrases which happen call forth. And, of course, he will never know whether or not the phrases happen to arrive at their destination, and by hypothesis, he must not know it. He knows only that this ignorance is the ultimate resistance that the event can oppose to the accountable or countable [*comptable*] use of time.

The Differend: Phrases in Dispute

The Differend

1. You are informed that human beings endowed with language were placed in a situation such that none of them is now able to tell about it. Most of them disappeared then, and the survivors rarely speak about it. When they do speak about it, their testimony bears only upon a minute part of this situation. How can you know that the situation itself existed? That it is not the fruit of your informant's imagination? Either the situation did not exist as such. Or else it did exist, in which case your informant's testimony is false, either because he or she should have disappeared, or else because he or she should remain silent, or else because, if he or she does speak, he or she can bear witness only to the particular experience he had, it remaining to be established whether this experience was a component of the situation in question.

2. "I have analyzed thousands of documents. I have tirelessly pursued specialists and historians with my questions. I have tried in vain to find a single former deportee capable of proving to me that he had really seen, with his own eyes, a gas chamber" (Faurisson in Pierre Vidal-Naquet, 1981: 81). To have "really seen with his own eyes" a gas chamber would be the condition which gives one the authority to say that it exists and to persuade the unbeliever. Yet it is still necessary to prove that the gas chamber was used to kill at the time it was seen. The only acceptable proof that it was used to kill is that one died from it. But if one is dead, one cannot testify that it is on account of the gas chamber. — The plaintiff complains that he has been fooled about the existence of gas chambers, fooled that is, about the so-called Final Solution. His argument is: in order for

3

a place to be identified as a gas chamber, the only eyewitness I will accept would be a victim of this gas chamber; now, according to my opponent, there is no victim that is not dead; otherwise, this gas chamber would not be what he or she claims it to be. There is, therefore, no gas chamber.

3. Can you give me, says an editor defending his or her profession, the title of a work of major importance which would have been rejected by every editor and which would therefore remain unknown? Most likely, you do not know any masterpiece of this kind because, if it does exist, it remains unknown. And if you think you know one, since it has not been made public, you cannot say that it is of major importance, except in your eyes. You do not know of any, therefore, and the editor is right. — This argument takes the same form as those in the preceding numbers. Reality is not what is "given" to this or that "subject," it is a state of the referent (that about which one speaks) which results from the effectuation of establishment procedures defined by a unanimously agreed-upon protocol, and from the possibility offered to anyone to recommence this effectuation as often as he or she wants. The publishing industry would be one of these protocols, historical inquiry another.

4. Either the Ibanskian* witness is not a communist, or else he is. If he is, he has no need to to testify that Ibanskian society is communist, since he admits that the communist authorities are the only ones competent to effectuate the establishment procedures for the reality of the communist character of that society. He defers to them then just as the layperson defers to the biologist or to the astronomer for the affirmation of the existence of a virus or a nebula. If he ceases to give his agreement to these authorities, he ceases to be a communist. We come back then to the first case: he is not a communist. This means that he ignores or wishes to ignore the establishment procedures for the reality of the communist character of Ibanskian society. There is, in this case, no more credit to be accorded his testimony than to that of a human being who says he has communicated with Martians. "There is therefore nothing surprising in the fact that the [Ibanskian] State regards opposition activity in general as a criminal activity on the same level as robbery, gangsterism, speculation and so on . . . It is a nonpolitical society" (Zinoviev, 1977: 600–601). More exactly, it is a learned State (Châtelet, 1981), it knows no reality other than the established one, and it holds the monopoly on procedures for the establishment of reality.

5. The difference, though, between communism, on the one hand, and a virus or a nebula, on the other hand, is that there are means to observe the latter — they are objects of cognition — while the former is the object of an idea of historical-

---

*The term is from Alexander Zinoviev's satirical novel *The Yawning Heights*, set in a fictitious locale — Ibansk — whose name is a derivative of Ivan, the stereotypical Russian name.-tr.

political reason, and this object is not observable (Kant Notice 4 §1). There are no procedures, defined by a protocol unanimously approved and renewable on demand, for establishing in general the reality of the object of an idea. For example, even in physics, there exists no such protocol for establishing the reality of the universe, because the universe is the object of an idea. As a general rule, an object which is thought under the category of the whole (or of the absolute) is not an object of cognition (whose reality could be subjected to a protocol, etc.). The principle affirming the contrary could be called totalitarianism. If the requirement of establishing the reality of a phrase's referent according to the protocol of cognition is extended to any given phrase, especially to those phrases that refer to a whole, then this requirement is totalitarian in its principle. That's why it is important to distinguish between phrase regimens, and this comes down to limiting the competence of a given tribunal to a given kind of phrase.

6. The plaintiff's conclusion (No. 2) should have been that since the only witnesses are the victims, and since there are no victims but dead ones, no place can be identified as a gas chamber. He should not have said that there are none, but rather that his opponent cannot prove that there are any, and that should have been sufficient to confound the tribunal. It is up to the opponent (the victim) to adduce the proof of the wrong done to him or her!

7. This is what a wrong [*tort*] would be: a damage [*dommage*] accompanied by the loss of the means to prove the damage. This is the case if the victim is deprived of life, or of all his or her liberties, or of the freedom to make his or her ideas or opinions public, or simply of the right to testify to the damage, or even more simply if the testifying phrase is itself deprived of authority (Nos. 24–27). In all of these cases, to the privation constituted by the damage there is added the impossibility of bringing it to the knowledge of others, and in particular to the knowledge of a tribunal. Should the victim seek to bypass this impossibility and testify anyway to the wrong done to him or to her, he or she comes up against the following argumentation: either the damages you complain about never took place, and your testimony is false; or else they took place, and since you are able to testify to them, it is not a wrong that has been done to you, but merely a damage, and your testimony is still false.

8. Either you are the victim of a wrong, or you are not. If you are not, you are deceived (or lying) in testifying that you are. If you are, since you can bear witness to this wrong, it is not a wrong, and you are deceived (or lying) in testifying that you are the victim of a wrong. Let p be: you are the victim of a wrong; *not p*: you are not; Tp: phrase p is true; Fp: it is false. The argument is: either p or *not p*; if *not-p*, then Fp; if p, then *not-p*, then Fp. The ancients called this argument a dilemma. It contains the mechanism of the *double bind* as studied by

the Palo Alto School*, it is a linchpin of Hegelian dialectical logic (Hegel Notice, § 2). This mechanism consists in applying to two contradictory propositions, *p* and *not-p*, two logical operators: exclusion (*either . . . , or*) and implication (*if . . . , then*). So, at once [(*either p or not-p*) and (*if p, then not-p*)]. It's as if you said both, *either it is white*, or *it is not white*; and *if it is white, it is not white.*

Protagoras

1. "A story is told of the time Protagoras demanded his fee (*misthos*) from Euathlus, a pupil of his. Euathlus refused to pay, saying, 'But I haven't won a victory yet' (*oudèpô nikèn nenikèkà*). Protagoras replied, 'But if I win this dispute (*ègô mèn an nikèsô*), I must be paid because I've won (*oti ègô énikèsa*), and if you win it I must be paid because you've won' " (Diels and Kranz, 1952, 80 A1, A4; Capizzi, 1955, 158). As is proved by the frequency of its occurrences in various guises (Capizzi: Apuleius, Aulus-Gellius, Ammonius, Diogenes Laërtius, Lucian), the fable has a didactic value. It contains several paradoxes (Mackie, 1964; Burnyeat, 1976).

The master and the pupil have concluded a contract: the former will be paid only if the latter has been able to win, thanks to the teaching he receives, at least one of the cases he will plead before the tribunals during the period of said teaching. The alternative is simple and the judgment easy: if Euathlus has won at least once, he pays; if not, he is absolved. And since he has not won, there is nothing to pay. In its brachylogical conciseness, Protagoras' reply transforms the alternative into a dilemma. If Euathlus has won at least once, he must pay. If he never won, he still won at least once, and must pay.

How can it be affirmed that Euathlus won when he always lost? It suffices to include the present litigation between him and Protagoras among the series of litigations to be considered in order to decide whether he always lost. In every previous litigation, he lost. Therefore, in the case against Protagoras who maintains that he won one time, he triumphs by ascertaining that he never won. But, if he thereby prevails in a litigation against Protagoras, he has indeed won at least once.

2. The paradox rests on the faculty a phrase has to take itself as its referent. I did not win, I say it, and in saying it I win. Protagoras confuses the modus (the declarative prefix: Euathlus says that) with the dictum, the negative universal that denotes a reality (Euathlus did not win once). It is in order to prohibit this kind of confusion that Russell introduced the theory of types: a proposition (here, the verdict in the litigation between master and pupil) that refers to a totality of propositions (here, the set of prior verdicts) cannot be a part of that totality. Or else, it ceases to be pertinent with regard to negation (that is, to the principle of non-contradiction). It is not decidable in terms of its truth value.

The phrase whose referent is *all phrases* must not be part of its referent. Otherwise, it is "poorly formed," and it is rejected by the logician. (This is the case for the Paradox of the Liar in the form *I lie.*) The logician has nothing but scorn for the sophist who ignores

---

*The foremost member of which was, of course, Gregory Bateson. –tr.

this principle; but the sophist doesn't ignore it, he unveils it (and in laughter, while Ibanskian power makes one weep) (No. 4).

The Russellian axiom of types is a rule for forming logical phrases (propositions). It delimits a genre of discourse, logic, in terms of its finality: deciding the truth of a phrase. Protagoras' argument is not acceptable within logic because it bars coming to a decision. Is it acceptable within another genre?

3. The totality upon which the argument bears is serial: there are n litigations, the "current" litigation between master and pupil is added to the preceding ones, $n + 1$. When Protagoras takes it into account, he makes $n = n + 1$. It is true that this synthesis requires an additional 'act': $(n + 1) + 1$. This act corresponds to Protagoras' judgment. That is why he phrases his decision using the aorist (*enikèsa*), the tense for the indeterminate: *If you win, then I'm the winner.* The seriality of totality introduces the consideration of time, which is excluded from the genre of logic. There are, though, logics of time that at least allow for this aspect of the litigation to be made evident.

From this aspect, Euathlus' affirmation wouldn't be: *None of my pleas is a winning one* (a negative universal, which we can designate by *not-p*); but: *None of my pleas was a winning one.* Expressed in a logic of time (Gardies, 1975), this last phrase could be written: *For all times prior to now, it is true during that time that not-p.* The pinpointing of the true is axed on the "now." It is thus not ruled out for Protagoras to say: *There exists at least one time and that time is now or later, and it is true during that time that p.*

Now is indeed the same temporal-logical operator, even though in Protagoras' phrase it is not in the same place in the series as is Euathlus' now. If we situate them in relation to an arbitrary origin t_0, the latter is called t_1 and Protagoras' now t_2. But the arbitrary origin t_0 is precisely what one calls now.

In this respect, Protagoras has done nothing more than use the faculty given him by the temporal deictic "now" for it to be both the origin of temporal series (before and after) and an element in these series (Schneider, 1980). Aristotle encounters and elaborates the same problem when he analyzes the dyad before/after in its relation to the now (Aristotle Notice). The paradoxical phrase cannot be eliminated here simply for its poor formulation. The genre of discourse which ought to accept it is not logic, but "physics," whose referent is not the phrase, but all moving objects (including phrases). Generalized relativity will confer upon that phrase citizenship rights in the physics of the universe.

4. Phrases form a physical universe if they are grasped as moving objects which form an infinite series. The phrase referring to this universe is therefore by hypothesis part of that universe: it will become part of it in the following instant. If we call history the series of phrases considered in this way (physically), then the historian's phrase "will become part" of the universe to which it refers. The difficulties raised by historicism and dogmatism stem from this situation. The former declares that his phrase is part of its referent, history; the latter that his phrase is not part of it.

In the solution to the antinomies of pure reason (*KRV*), Kant writes that the question of the series resumes in itself all the conflicts that are raised by cosmological Ideas. The "last" phrase synthesizes the preceding ones. Is it or is it not part of their set? Dogmatism answers no, empiricism yes. Criticism remarks that the series is never given (*gegeben*), but only proposed (*aufgegeben*), because its synthesis is always deferred. The phrase that synthesizes the series (the judgment actually born upon the set of Euathlus' pleas) is not part of the series when it "takes place" (as an occurrence), but it is inevitably destined to become part of the series synthesized by the following phrase. The series formed by the world, in particular the world of human history, is neither finite or infinite (we can argue either one indifferently), but the synthesis of the series, for its sake, is "indefinite" (*KRV*, pp. 455–548).

5. Protagoras' argument is an *antistrephon*. It is reversible. In the version given by Aulus-Gellius, the dispute between master and pupil takes place before a tribunal. It could be retranscribed as follows: Protagoras: If you win (against me), you will have won; if you lose (against me), even if you say you always lose (against others), then you will still have won. The judges are perplexed. Euathlus: If I lose (against you), I will have lost; if I win (against you), even if I say I always lose, then I will still have lost. The judges decide to put off their pronouncement until later. The history of the world cannot pass a last judgment. It is made out of judged judgments.

9. It is in the nature of a victim not to be able to prove that one has been done a wrong. A plaintiff is someone who has incurred damages and who disposes of the means to prove it. One becomes a victim if one loses these means. One loses them, for example, if the author of the damages turns out directly or indirectly to be one's judge. The latter has the authority to reject one's testimony as false or the ability to impede its publication. But this is only a particular case. In general, the plaintiff becomes a victim when no presentation is possible of the wrong he or she says he or she has suffered. Reciprocally, the "perfect crime" does not consist in killing the victim or the witnesses (that adds new crimes to the first one and aggravates the difficulty of effacing everything), but rather in obtaining the silence of the witnesses, the deafness of the judges, and the inconsistency (insanity) of the testimony. You neutralize the addressor, the addressee, and the sense of the testimony; then everything is as if there were no referent (no damages). If there is nobody to adduce the proof, nobody to admit it, and/or if the argument which upholds it is judged to be absurd, then the plaintiff is dismissed, the wrong he or she complains of cannot be attested. He or she becomes a victim. If he or she persists in invoking this wrong as if it existed, the others (addressor, addressee, expert commentator on the testimony) will easily be able to make him or her pass for mad. Doesn't paranoia confuse the *As if it were the case* with the *it is the case*?

10. But aren't the others acting for their part as if this were not the case, when it is perhaps the case? Why should there be less paranoia in denying the existence of gas chambers than in affirming it? Because, writes Leibniz, "nothing is simpler and easier than something"(Leibniz, 1714: § 7). The one who says there is something is the plaintiff, it is up to him or her to bring forth a demonstration, by means of well-formed phrases and of procedures for establishing the existence of their referent. Reality is always the plaintiff's responsibility. For the defense, it is

sufficient to refute the argumentation and to impugn the proof by a counter-example. This is the defense's advantage, as recognized by Aristotle (*Rhetoric* 1402 b 24-25) and by strategists. Likewise, it cannot be said that a hypothesis is verified, but only that until further notice it has not yet been falsified. The defense is nihilistic, the prosecution pleads for existents [*l'étant*]. That is why it is up to the victims of extermination camps to prove that extermination. This is our way of thinking that reality is not a given, but an occasion to require that establishment procedures be effectuated in regard to it.

11. The death penalty is suppressed out of nihilism, out of a cognitive consideration for the referent, out of a prejudice in favor of the defense. The odds that it is not the case are greater than the odds that it is. This statistical estimation belongs to the family of cognitive phrases. The presumed innocence of the accused, which obligates the prosecution with adducing the proof of the offense, is the "humanist" version of the same playing rule of cognition. − If the rules of the game are inverted, if everyone accused is presumed guilty, then the defense has the task of establishing innocence while the prosecution has only to refute the argumentation and to impugn the proofs advanced by the defense. Now, it may be impossible to establish that the referent of a phrase does not have a given property, unless we have the right to resort to a refutation of the phrase in which the referent does have that property. How can I prove that I am not a drug dealer without asking my accuser to bring forth some proof of it and without refuting that proof? How can it be established that labor power is not a commodity without refuting the hypothesis that it is? How can you establish what is not without criticizing what is? The undetermined cannot be established. It is necessary that negation be the negation of a determination. − This inversion of the tasks expected on one side and on the other may suffice to transform the accused into a victim, if he or she does not have the right to criticize the prosecution, as we see in political trials. Kafka warned us about this. It is impossible to establish one's innocence, in and of itself. It is a nothingness.

12. The plaintiff lodges his or her complaint before the tribunal, the accused argues in such a way as to show the inanity of the accusation. Litigation takes place. I would like to call a *differend* [*différend*] the case where the plaintiff is divested of the means to argue and becomes for that reason a victim. If the addressor, the addressee, and the sense of the testimony are neutralized, everything takes place as if there were no damages (No. 9). A case of differend between two parties takes place when the "regulation" of the conflict that opposes them is done in the idiom of one of the parties while the wrong suffered by the other is not signified in that idiom. For example, contracts and agreements between economic partners do not prevent − on the contrary, they presuppose − that the laborer or his or her representative has had to and will have to speak of his or her work as though it were the temporary cession of a commodity, the "service," which he

dom to use can be revoked by a threat. This is not false, it is a way of talking about language, humanity; and their interrelations which obeys the rules of the family of certain cognitive phrases (the human sciences). The phrase, "Under threat, under torture, in conditions of incarceration, in conditions of 'sensory deprivation,' etc. , the linguistic behavior of a human being can be dictated to him or to her," is a well-formed phrase, and examples can, alas, be presented for which the scientist can say: here are some cases of it. But the human and linguistic sciences are like the juries of labor arbitration boards.

20. Just as these juries presuppose that the opponents they are supposed to judge are in possession of something they exchange, so do the human and linguistic sciences presuppose that the human beings they are supposed to know are in possession of something they communicate. And the powers that be (ideological, political, religious, police, etc.) presuppose that the human beings they are supposed to guide, or at least control, are in possession of something they communicate. Communication is the exchange of messages, exchange the communication of goods. The instances of communication like those of exchange are definable only in terms of property or propriety [*propriété*]: the propriety of information, analogous to the propriety of uses. And just as the flow of uses can be controlled, so can the flow of information. As a perverse use is repressed, a dangerous bit of information is banned. As a need is diverted and a motivation created, an addressor is led to say something other that what he or she was going to say. The problem of language, thus posited in terms of communication, leads to that of the needs and beliefs of interlocutors. The linguist becomes an expert before the communication arbitration board. The essential problem he or she has to regulate is that of sense as a unit of exchange independent of the needs and beliefs of interlocutors. Similarly, for the economist, the problem is that of the value of goods and services as units independent of the demands and offers of economic partners.

21. Would you say that interlocutors are victims of the science and politics of language understood as communication to the same extent that the worker is transformed into a victim through the assimilation of his or her labor-power to a commodity? Must it be imagined that there exists a "phrase-power," analogous to labor-power, and which cannot find a way to express itself in the idiom of this science and this politics? — Whatever this power might be, the parallel must be broken right away. It can be conceived that work is something other than the exchange of a commodity, and an idiom other than that of the labor arbitrator must be found in order to express it. It can be conceived that language is something other than the communication of a bit of information, and an idiom other than that of the human and linguistic sciences is needed in order to express it. This is where the parallel ends: in the case of language, recourse is made to another family of phrases; but in the case of work, recourse is not made to another family of work, recourse is still made to another family of phrases. The same goes for every

differend buried in litigation, no matter what the subject matter. To give the differend its due is to institute new addressees, new addressors, new significations, and new referents in order for the wrong to find an expression and for the plaintiff to cease being a victim. This requires new rules for the formation and linking of phrases. No one doubts that language is capable of admitting these new phrase families or new genres of discourse. Every wrong ought to be able to be put into phrases. A new competence (or "prudence") must be found.

22. The differend is the unstable state and instant of language wherein something which must be able to be put into phrases cannot yet be. This state includes silence, which is a negative phrase, but it also calls upon phrases which are in principle possible. This state is signaled by what one ordinarily calls a feeling: "One cannot find the words," etc. A lot of searching must be done to find new rules for forming and linking phrases that are able to express the differend disclosed by the feeling, unless one wants this differend to be smothered right away in a litigation and for the alarm sounded by the feeling to have been useless. What is at stake in a literature, in a philosophy, in a politics perhaps, is to bear witness to differends by finding idioms for them.

23. In the differend, something "asks" to be put into phrases, and suffers from the wrong of not being able to be put into phrases right away. This is when the human beings who thought they could use language as an instrument of communication learn through the feeling of pain which accompanies silence (and of pleasure which accompanies the invention of a new idiom), that they are summoned by language, not to augment to their profit the quantity of information communicable through existing idioms, but to recognize that what remains to be phrased exceeds what they can presently phrase, and that they must be allowed to institute idioms which do not yet exist.

24. It is possible then that the survivors do not speak even though they are not threatened in their ability to speak should they speak later. The socio-linguist, the psycho-linguist, the bio-linguist seek the reasons, the passions, the interests, the context for these silences. Let us first seek their logic. We find that they are substitutes for phrases. They come in the place of phrases during a conversation, during an interrogation, during a debate, during the *talking* of a psychoanalytic session, during a confession, during a critical review, during a metaphysical exposition. The phrase replaced by silence would be a negative one. Negated by it is at least one of the four instances that constitute a phrase universe: the addressee, the referent, the sense, the addressor. The negative phrase that the silence implies could be formulated respectively: *This case does not fall within your competence, This case does not exist, It cannot be signified, It does not fall within my competence.* A single silence could be formulated by several of these phrases. − Moreover, these negative formulations, which deny the ability of the referent, the ad-

dressor, the addressee and the sense to be presented in the current idiom, do not point to the other idiom in which these instances could be presented.

25. It should be said by way of simplification that a phrase presents what it is about, the case, *ta pragmata*, which is its referent; what is signified about the case, the sense, *der Sinn*; that to which or addressed to which this is signified about the case, the addressee; that "through" which or in the name of which this is signified about the case, the addressor. The disposition of a phrase universe consists in the situating of these instances in relation to each other. A phrase may entail several referents, several senses, several addressees, several addressors. Each of these four instances may be marked in the phrase or not (Fabbri and Sbisa, 1980).

26. Silence does not indicate which instance is denied, it signals the denial of one or more of the instances. The survivors remain silent, and it can be understood 1) that the situation in question (the case) is not the addressee's business (he or she lacks the competence, or he or she is not worthy of being spoken to about it, etc.); or 2) that it never took place (this is what Faurisson understands); or 3) that there is nothing to say about it (the situation is senseless, inexpressible); or 4) that it is not the survivors' business to be talking about it (they are not worthy, etc.). Or, several of these negations together.

27. The silence of the survivors does not necessarily testify in favor of the nonexistence of gas chambers, as Faurisson believes or pretends to believe. It can just as well testify against the addressee's authority (we are not answerable to Faurisson), against the authority of the witness him- or herself (we, the rescued, do not have the authority to speak about it), finally against language's ability to signify gas chambers (an inexpressible absurdity). If one wishes to establish the existence of gas chambers, the four silent negations must be withdrawn: There were no gas chambers, were there? Yes, there were. — But even if there were, that cannot be formulated, can it? Yes, it can. — But even if it can be formulated, there is no one, at least, who has the authority to formulate it, and no one with the authority to hear it (it is not communicable), is there? Yes, there is.

Gorgias

In its form, the argumentation establishing reality follows the nihilist reasoning of Gorgias in *On Not-Being*: "Nothing is; and even if it is, it is unknowable; and even if it is and is knowable, it cannot be revealed to others" (Anonymous 979 a 12).

The framework of the argumentation (its *taxis*) rests on the concession granted the opponent. Let's call him *x*. *X* says: there is something. — Gorgias: there is nothing at all. *X* answers: there is something, and that something is apprehensible. — Gorgias: if there were something, that something would not be apprehensible (*akatalèpton anthropô*, writes Sextus, 65). *X* continues: this something which is and which is apprehensible is able to be conveyed to others. —Gorgias: it is not able to be conveyed to others (*anexoiston hét-érô*, writes Sextus, 83; *oistos*, the verbal adjective of *phero*, to carry; for his part, the Anonymous text says: "even if they [realities] were knowable, how, he says, could some-one make them manifest to another?").

It is a matter of logical retreat (concession), as in — what Freud calls — the "piece of sophistry" about the kettle. The plaintiff *x* declares that he lent to the accused (Gorgias) an undamaged kettle which was returned to him with a hole in it. The dialectical argumen-tation is: *x:* borrowed. — Gorgias: not borrowed. *x:* borrowed undamaged. — Gorgias: borrowed with a hole in it already. *x:* borrowed undamaged and returned with a hole in it. — Gorgias: returned undamaged (Freud, 1905: 62). Even if there is a reality (bor-rowed), it is not predicable (undamaged/with a hole in it); and if it is, the case correspond-ing to the attribute cannot be shown (returned with a hole in it/returned undamaged). The logical retreat, absurd when it is isolated from the course of the prosecution's argumenta-tion, unveils the rules for the family of cognitive phrases: determination of the referent (kettle borrowed or not), attribution of a predicate to the subject of the utterance (borrowed with a hole in it or not), display of a case which proves conclusively (returned with a hole in it or not). Note that, in this trial, Gorgias pleads for the defense.

Barbara Cassin has shown that he is "defending" the thesis of Parmenides. He tries to make an argument for it instead of sticking to its divine revelation by the goddess, and he thereby ruins the thesis: "It is possible (*ouk esti*) neither to be nor not to be." This is his conclusion, and here is how it is reasoned: "For if Not-Being is Not-Being [which is what Parmenides writes], just as much as the existent, then the non-existent would be: in fact, the non-existent is non-existent as the existent is existent, such that actual things (*ta pragmata*) are, no more than they are not" (979 a 25ff.). He adds: "But then if Not-Being is, its opposite, Being, is not. In fact, if Not-Being is, it makes sense that Being is not. " So nothing would be, either because Being and Not-Being are the same thing, or because they are not. If they are, it is because Being is Not-Being; if they are not, it is because Being is not Not-Being, and is only affirmed through a double negation.

Gorgias thus anticipates Hegel's argumentation in the first chapter of the *Science of Logic*. What Hegel calls "becoming" in order to name the *Resultat* immanent to his ar-gumentation, Gorgias calls "neither Being nor Not-Being." He "ignores" the rule of the re-sult (Hegel Notice) which is the mainspring of speculative dialectics. This rule presup-poses the finality of a Self (a sort of Aristotelian god), who could not hold out against the Gorgian refutation.

In constructing itself, the *logos*, the argument, ruins the demonic phrase, the revelation upon which Parmenides' poem opens. This argument does not refute that phrase, it turns it into a family of phrases. Ontology, poesis, is permitted, it is a genre. This genre does not have the same rules as the dialectical genre (in the Greek sense). Specifically, the god-dess is not an interlocutor subject to the rules of refutation. It suffices for Parmenides to indicate two paths available to thought, that of *Being* and that of *Not-Being*, for Gorgias to turn them into a thesis and an antithesis argued by partners in a dialectic from which the goddess is absent and to have them refute each other. The duality of paths is intolerable to ontology, it implies contrariness and authorizes a negative dialectic.

The dialectic obeys rules. (Aristotle gave himself the task of establishing them, espe-cially in the *Topics* and the *Sophistical Refutations*.) Whatever they may be, and no matter how hard it is to establish them, however, these rules presuppose in themselves a kind of metaprinciple. Barbara Cassin (who calls it arch-origin) disengages it from the anonymously reported Treatise by offering an original interpretation of a disputed phrase: "If nothing is therefore, then demonstrations say everything without exception (*ei mén oun oudén, tas apodeixeis légein hapanta*)" (980 a 9). It is from this simultaneously nihilistic and logological standpoint that we receive and study the question of reality. Reality is not bestowed by some goddess at the tip of her index finger, it has to be "demonstrated," that is, argued and presented as a case, and, once established, it is a state of the referent for cognitive phrases. This state does not preclude that, simply put, "nothing is."

Just as for Wittgenstein, color serves Gorgias as a paradigm for the question of reality. Phrases like "To begin with, he does not say a color but a saying" (980 b 5), or "There is neither a conceiving (*dianoesthai*) nor a seeing of color, no more than there is of sound, there is only hearing" (980 b 6) are to be placed next to "For looking does not teach us anything about the concepts of colors"; or "Imagine a tribe of color-blind people, and there could easily be one. They would not have the same color concepts as we do. For even assuming they speak, e. g., English, and thus have all the English color words, they would still use them differently than we do and would *learn* their use differently. Or if they have a foreign language, it would be difficult for us to translate their color words into ours." Or: "We do not want to establish a theory of color (neither a physiological one nor a psychological one), but rather the logic of color concepts. And this accomplishes what people have often unjustly expected of a theory" (Wittgenstein, 1950–51: I 72, I 13, I 22).

28. To establish the reality of a referent, the four silences must be refuted, though in reverse order: there is someone to signify the referent and someone to understand the phrase that signifies it; the referent can be signified; it exists. The proof for the reality of gas chambers cannot be adduced if the rules adducing the proof are not respected. These rules determine the universes of cognitive phrases, that is, they assign certain functions to the instances of referent, addressor, addressee, and sense. Thus: the addressor presumably seeks to obtain the addressee's agreement concerning the referent's sense: the witness must explain to the addressee the signification of the expression, *gas chamber*. When he or she has nothing to object to the explicative phrase, the addressee presumably gives his or her agreement to the addressor: one either accepts or does not accept the signification, that is, the explanation given by the addressor. If one does not accept it, one presumably proposes another explanation for the expression. When agreement is achieved, a well-formed expression becomes available. Each one can say: we agree that a gas chamber is this or that. Only then, can the existence of a reality which might suit as a referent for that expression be "shown" by means of a phrase in the form: *This or that is a case of a gas chamber.* This phrase fills an ostensive function, which is also required by the rules of the cognitive genre.

29. But is this really so in the sciences? It seems doubtful (Feyerabend, 1975).
— The question does not even need to be answered unless this is not so, for then the game played with regard to the phrase in question is not scientific. This is what

Latour (1981) affirms when he says that the game is rhetorical. But to what game does this last phrase, in its turn, belong? This, rather, is what should be answered: it's up to you to supply the proof that it is not so, but that it is otherwise. And this will be done according to the minimal rules for adducing a proof (No. 65), or it will not be done at all. To say that it is not really so in the sciences is to set about establishing what really happens, and that can be done only according to the rules of scientific cognitives, which allow for the reality of a referent to be established. If the phrase affirming that science is really a rhetoric is scientific, we have one of two things: either this phrase is itself rhetorical because it is scientific, and it can bring forth the proof neither for the reality of its referent nor for the truth of its sense. Or else, it is declared scientific because it is not rhetorical. It is an exception then to what it nonetheless affirms to be universal, and it should not be said that science is rhetoric, but that some science is rhetoric.

30. Why say a "well-formed expression" rather than a "meaningful phrase"? The former is subject to rules for forming cognitive phrases, in which truth and falsehood are at stake. In turn, these rules are the object of studies in formal logic, and, insofar as the phrases bear upon domains of reference, they are the object of axiomatic studies. With respect to their good formation, it is not pertinent whether the phrases obeying these rules are meaningful or not, in the sense of their meaning in ordinary language. Transcribed into ordinary language, they may appear absurd. Conversely, phrases from ordinary language may appear "meaningful" in that language and be poorly formed or at least equivocal with respect to the rules for cognitive phrases. *X* calls up his friend *Y* whom he hasn't seen for a long time and says to him: *I can come by your place* (Nos. 137, 139, 140). In a critical situation, a highly placed bureaucrat orders his subordinates to *Disobey*. The first phrase is equivocal, the second poorly formed, but both are accepted as meaningful by their addressees. Similarly, the phrase *The garbage pail is full* does not induce for the logician or the scholar the nonetheless common response: *Okay, I'll be right there* (Fabbri, c. 1980). The "restrictions" placed on phrases acceptable in the sciences are necessary in order for the verification or falsification of these phrases to be effective: they determine effectible procedures whose reiterable effectuation authorizes the consensus between addressor and addressee.

31. These are not really "restrictions." On the contrary, the more you specify rules for the validation of phrases, the more you can distinguish different ones, and conceive other idioms. The ballgame is not the same if the rule states that the ball must never touch the ground, or that it may touch the ground once only per return for each player, or only once per team for a serve, or once per team for a return, etc. It is as if the conditions of sense were changing. Vidal-Naquet quotes Lucien Febvre quoting Cyrano de Bergerac: "We must not believe everything about a man, because a man can say everything. We must believe only what

is human about him" (1981: 93). The historian asks: "What is human? What impossible? The question we must answer is: Do these words still have a meaning?" Shouldn't we believe the inhumanity reported by the testimonies of Auschwitz? — *Inhuman* means incompatible with an Idea of humanity. This sense is pertinent for the ethical, the juridical, the political, and the historical families of phrases, where this Idea is necessarily at stake. In cognitive phrases, *human* predicates an event which relates to the human species, and for which cases can be shown. The victims, the executioners, and the witnesses at Auschwitz enter into the class of human beings; the messages we receive from them are meaningful and offer material for verification, even if they are incompatible with any Idea of humanity. Voyager II's messages about Saturn can almost be said to be inhuman in the second sense, because most humans understand nothing in them and could not vouch for them, but they are human at least in the first sense to the extent that they would not take place were they not required by the Idea of a humanity progressing in its knowledge.

32. Even if the verification procedures are specified as they should be, how does the addressor know that the addressee correctly understands what he or she wants to say, and that, like the addressor, the addressee desires that the truth about which they speak be established? — The addressor presupposes it. He or she believes that it is so. He or she also believes that the addressee believes the same thing about the addressor. Etc. — Here you are in the act of doing "human sciences," of probing the meanings (*vouloir-dire*), the desires, the beliefs that you presuppose to be the property of these entities, human beings. You presuppose by the same token that they use language for certain ends. Psychology, sociology, pragmatics, and a certain philosophy of language have in common this presupposition of an instrumental relation between thoughts and language. This relation follows a technological model: thought has ends, language offers means to thought. How can the addressee discern the addressor's ends from the means of language put to work in the message? For questions of language, the pertinence of the ideas of Homo, of Homo faber, of will, and of good will, which belong to other realms, appears not to raise any doubts!

33. It remains that, if Faurisson is "in bad faith," Vidal-Naquet cannot convince him that the phrase *There were gas-chambers* is true. The historian bitterly notes that, in an analogous fashion, "there are still anti-Dreyfusards" (1981: 93). Consensus may be missing even in a case, such as that of the falsehoods fabricated by Colonel Henry*, whose reality has been established as much as the procedures for establishing reality will permit. Thus bad will, or bad faith, or a blind belief

---

*The author of a phony document injurious to Dreyfus's case written after the initial trial and designed as part of a cover-up by the French military to prevent a re-opening of the investigation. Subsequent to the revelation of the document's inauthenticity, Henry committed suicide.–tr.

(the ideology of the League for the French Fatherland*) can prevent truth from manifesting itself and justice from being done. − No. What you are calling bad will, etc., is the name that you give to the fact that the opponent does not have a stake in establishing reality, that he does not accept the rules for forming and validating cognitives, that his goal is not to convince. The historian need not strive to convince Faurisson if Faurisson is "playing" another genre of discourse, one in which conviction, or, the obtainment of a consensus over a defined reality, is not at stake. Should the historian persist along this path, he will end up in the position of victim.

34. But how can you know that the opponent is in bad faith as long as you haven't tried to convince him or her and as long as he or she has not shown through his or her conduct a scorn for scientific, cognitive rules? − One "plays the game" permitted by these rules; and the addressee's rejoinder shows that he or she does not observe them. − But, what if the opponent strives to hide that he or she does not observe the rules of cognition, and acts as if he or she were observing them? I would need to know his or her intentions. . . . − Either way, it comes down to the same thing: the phrases, whose addressor he or she is, satisfy or do not satisfy the rules. They cannot be equivocal on this score, since equivocalness is what the rules exclude. − But you can simulate that they satisfy the rules, that they are univocal; you can invent convicting evidence. In the Dreyfus case, the French high command did not hesitate. − Of course, but it is up to the defense to refute the argument, to object to the witness, to reject the proof, as much as needed and up until the accusation is withdrawn. Then you'll see that the accuser was playing another game. − Undoubtedly, but is it not possible to evade the differend by anticipating it? − This seems to be impossible. What would distinguish such an anticipation from a prejudice, whether favorable or unfavorable, bearing upon the person of your opponent, or upon his or her way of phrasing? Now, prejudging is excluded by the rules of scientific cognitives. − But what about those who establish these rules, aren't they prejudging their competence to establish them? How, indeed, could they not prejudge it as long as the rules have not been established and as long as they therefore lack the criteria by which to distinguish competence?

Plato

1. Strong and weak.
Meletus, says Socrates, has just brought a charge against me before the tribunal. For

---

*An extreme right-wing organization, many of whose members were notorious for their anti-Semitism, egregiously supportive of the verdict against Dreyfus−even after the proof of his innocence had become manifest−in order to protect the "sanctity" and "authority" of France's military, judicial and political institutions.-tr.

a long time, though, rumors have preceded him and I fear them even more: I would have made suspicious investigations into what is below the earth and in heaven; I would know how to turn the weaker argument into the stronger argument; I would teach to disbelieve in the gods (*Apology* 18 b, 19 b-c, 23 d). These are, in effect, the principal counts of indictment leveled against Socrates, twenty-five years earlier, by Aristophanes in the *Clouds*. The comedian also attacked the sexual inversion of the Socratics.

The trial takes aim at an inversion in the way of speaking, an impious genre of discourse. It is to Protagoras and to Corax that Aristotle imputes the art of turning the weaker argument into the stronger (*Rhetoric* II 24: 1402 a 23); it is to Protagoras that Eusebius, Sextus, Diogenes Laërtius, Philostratus, Hesychius, Plato, and Cicero (DK 80 B4, A12, A1, A2, A3, A23) attribute the declaration that for lack of time and demonstrable proof, it cannot be known whether the gods exist or not, nor what they are if they do exist. Diogenes, Philostratus, and Eusebius also report that Athens had Protagoras' books seized and burned, and Sextus adds that he fled to escape prosecution for impiety (DK 80 A1, A2, A4, A12). Except for the flight, the names of Socrates and of Protagoras are mutually substitutable under the inculpating charge of some logical reversal.

Solving the question of impiety is one of the stakes of the Platonic opus. It is a matter of confirming the decline of the *ontologos,* and of defining the rules for the new *logologos.* The phrase that comes down to us from Parmenides is the one he heard from a divine mouth. As a genre of discourse, ontology presupposes this obscure illumination: what it phrases, Being, is also what is phrased through its mouth; the referent is also the addressor. "Being and thinking are the same." The ontological phrase is above all a received phrase, and the thinker of Being is an addressee, a witness. Thereupon, the rhetor and the sophist call the witness to the stand and ask that he exhibit his proofs. He doesn't have any; either because there is no referent at all, or because it is not apprehensible, or finally because it is not communicable. What Gorgias says about Being and Not-Being, Protagoras says about the gods. The former and the latter have become referents, instances to be established. It is on this account that the new discourse is declared impious; it does not invoke revelation, it requires refutation ("falsification") with a view to establishing the referent's reality. Impiety resides in the addressor and addressee instances having charge of the argumentation. The word *logos* changes meaning. It is no longer speak-welcome, it is speak-argue.

For Plato, it is a question of establishing argumentative rules prohibiting the weaker argument from winning over the stronger, with all the accompanying effects of persuasion (of enchantment, of *goéteia* [*Menexenus* 234 c-235 a]). These effects are described in *Menexenus* with regard to the genre of funeral oration, under the cover of a pastiche (Loraux, 1974: 172–211; 1981: 267–332). Socrates pinpoints the displacements of instances operated by funeral oration. The *logos epitaphios*, a kind of epideictic genre, has as its instituted addressor an orator proposed by the Council, as its addressee the Assembly of citizens, as its referent the citizens dead in combat for the fatherland. Its instituted sense is praise for the latter. Its effect on the addressee is a "charm" (the hearer believes himself transported to the Islands of the Blessed).

To this feeling there corresponds a sequence of displacements of names on instances: death in combat is a "beautiful death"; a beautiful death implies a "fine" life; Athenian life is fine; the Athenian living this life is fine; you are fine. The situations of the names upon the instances in the manifest universe presented by the epitaphios are: I, the orator, am telling you (the Assembly) that those dead in the field of honor are fine. In the copresented (latent) universe, the situations are as follows: I am telling you that you are fine. Or even, by taking note of the final prosopopeia (where the dead heroes begin to speak) through his (the orator's) mediation, we (the dead heroes) are telling us (the living citizens) that we (the living and the dead) are fine. The addressee in the first universe also occupies the place of referent in the second. The referent of the first universe also becomes the addressor in the second (Nos. 156, 160).

It is not expected of the Assembly that it should take the floor, that it should debate, nor even that it should judge. The epideictic is not dialectics, nor is it even forensic or deliberative rhetoric; it leans rather toward poetics. It is a matter of arousing in the addressee not phrases but those quasi-phrases, which are silent feelings. If phrases took place, they would sooner or later remove the equivocation from the pathos and dissipate the charm. (It can be observed here that certain phrase families − the poetic ones − are staked upon the addressee's silence as the signal of feeling.) The silence of pathos, the vertigo described by Socrates, proceeds from the ubiquity of the situations of names upon instances: the addressee hears what is said about him as if he were not there, thus simultaneously alive as addressee and dead as referent, immortal. (This ubiquity could be called the fulfillment of desire, but that appellation is metaphysical.)

This group of paralogical operations is in the Platonic lexicon called *métabolè, mimèsis, peithô*. It presupposes in the addressee a passibility, a *patheia*, an ability to be affected, a metamorphic ability (whose symbol is the cloud); in the addressor is presupposed a dissimulation, an occultation, the apocrypt (it's not me, it's the gods or the heroes who are phrased through my mouth: prosopopoeia of the dead, prosopopoeia of the Parmenidian goddess).

2. Impiety.

How does this group of operations relate to impiety? First of all, the gods are taken for addressees. "No man who believes in gods as the law would have him believe can of his own free will do unhallowed deed or let slip lawless discourse. If a man acts thus, it is because he is the victim of an affection (*paschôn*), of which there are three kinds. Either, as I say, he does not believe, or again, he believes that they are, but are heedless of mankind, or lastly, that they are lightly to be won over by the cajoling of offerings and prayers" (*Laws* X 885 b). Three impieties. Either the gods are not addressees for our phrases, or, if they are, they do not answer them, and are not interlocutors; or else, if they answer them, they are subject to corruption and passion, and are not just. Thus: they are not; if they are, they are mute; if they speak, they say what they are made to say. Transcribed into the second person, the one indicating the addressee instance, that is to say, addressed to the gods, the impious phrases can respectively be formulated thus: you do not exist; you do not speak; you say what I make you say. In all of the cases, you are less strong than I, who exists, speaks, and says what I want to say. Impiety consists in this reversal of the relation of forces. The gods are traditionally called "the strongest ones" (*kreittonès*), in particular by Aristophanes and Plato (*Des Places* I, 299–300).

One can still be impious, no longer by speaking to the gods, but by speaking about them. They are then in the situation of referent in phrases exchanged between men. This is the case for many traditional narratives, the *muthoi*: the gods would be the causes of evil as well as of good, and they would metamorphose themselves (they would therefore lie), two symptoms of feebleness accredited by the *mythopoiétés* and also by the *logopoioi,* that is, by the poets and by the rhetors and sophists (*Republic* II, 376 cff.). The canonical phrase for these genres of discourse is: I tell you that they are as feeble as you and me. That is why these makers of phrases are kept out of the ideal city (*Republic*) and condemned to the worst in the real city (*Laws*).

Finally, impiety could consist in betraying the veracity of the gods. They are situated here as the addressor of phrases. The impiety is in making them say: We lie, we deceive you, we say this even though it is that. Here, the Platonic critique (*Republic* III, 392 c-398 b) mainly attacks the procedure which consists in making the gods speak rather than attacking what they are made to say, the *lexis* rather than the *logos.* The procedure is mimetic: by situating the god in the addressor instance, the addressor "properly" called, who is in principle the narrator, is occulted. Theater is the pure case of mimetic poetics: the author does not appear on stage, he remains hidden, apocryphal. The dithyramb, on the contrary, is a direct writing, which conserves the traces of the "authentic" addressor. Homeric epic mixes mimesis with diegesis (*Ibid.*).

In principle, mimesis must be rejected. It creates a second nature, it favors impropriety by multiplying disguises and *metabolai* (*Republic* III, 395 d, 397 b). It's still okay for the carpenter to be to the bed as the god is to the idea of the bed. That's the dual, miserable, but ontological organization of appearance and existence. But when the painter adds the image of the bed to this, we have a pitiful artefact that does no more than double the ontological misery by doubling the most infirm and the most sensible existent.

Still, Socrates uses this same artefact in *Republic* VIII. Having to explain that the sun is to objects as the good is to ideas, he doubles the analogy by an analogue of the most mimetic sort: as fire, he says, placed at the entrance to a cave is to the fabricated objects whose shadows it projects. Socrates draws on the following accommodation: one ought to forbid mimesis but one cannot. In fact, things themselves are not grasped, only their images. If things were grasped, there would be no need to phrase. Or else, if we didn't phrase, there would be no need to mime. Phrasing takes place in the lack of being of that about which there is a phrase. Language is the sign that one does not know the being of the existent. When one knows it, one is the existent, and that's silence (*Letter* VII, 342 a-d). One can thus only compromise with mimesis.

The simulacrum is deceitful as idol (*eidolon*); but, taken as *eikos* (verisimilar), it is also a signpost on the path to the true, to the "proper" (*Phaedrus* 261 ff.). The similar must be regulated. There needs to be good *typoi,* good print keys that give appropriate simulacra (*eoikota*) (*Republic* II, 377 e-379 a). A sign that imitation is necessary, language came to us through the stories that nurses and mothers told us when we were small (*Ibid.,* 377b). How can you avoid it? You can merely improve the imprint. The canonical phrase of Platonic poetics would be in sum: I deceive you the least possible.

3. Dialogue.

It is within this problematics of the loss or decline of the referent's reality that rules are instituted, which are proper to allow a consensus between partners concerning a phrase that identifies its referent as it should. A new species of discourse is needed in the very heart of the dialectical genre. The quest for consensus is not the regulating ideal of eristics, which aims to win at any cost, nor of sophistics, which is a venal eristics, nor even of peirastics, or the dialectic of experimentation, which seeks to test out opinions (Aristotle, *Sophistical Refutations* 2, 8, 11). The rules for forming and linking phrases and the adducing of proofs are far from established and far from being the object of a consensus even for those who seek the true through discussion. Discussion is often interrupted by a *that's not fair*. The establishment of these rules likewise forms the object of the *Topics*, of the *Sophistical Refutations*, and of the *Rhetoric*.

To Polus Socrates objects (*Gorgias* 471 e-472 b, 474 a ff., 475 d-476 a) that the debate they are having is not of the genre of forensic or political rhetoric, but of *dialegesthai*. We are not before the tribunal, "I am no politician." The lawyer and the tribune think they can sway the decision by calling many witnesses to the stand. "This genre of refutation," states Socrates, "is worthless toward discovering the truth." The only testimony that matters to him is that of his opponent, Polus. For Polus and he to come to an agreement (*homologia*) concerning a phrase is the mark of the true. The requirement must be reciprocal: Socrates' agreement is all that Polus ought to wish. The third party, the witness, turns out therefore to be impugned: the only acceptable testimony about the referent is that of those who, in disputing over the referent, pass all of the testimony about it through the sieve of refutation.

In the *Republic* (I, 348 a-b), Socrates proposes to eliminate the other kind of third party who intervenes on the courtroom floor and in the assembly, namely the judge. He describes the antilogical genre to Thrasymachus: one argument is set up against another, each person replies in turn, it is then necessary to count up and evaluate the arguments, and a judge is therefore needed to decide between (*diakrinôn*) them. But, "if we examine things together with a view toward bringing us to an agreement [*anomologoumenoi*, which also means: even if not in agreement], then we shall be ourselves both judges and pleaders [*rhètorés*]."

This double rejection (or double condensation) frees dialogue from rhetorics and dialectics that are not axed upon the identification of the referent. An institution takes shape, removed from public places. In its heart, the stakes are not that of vanquishing but of coming to an agreement. The *agôn* between phrases is the rule of deliberative politics (Nos. 210–215) and of political life. But inside the Academy, the rule is, as far as it can be judged, analogous rather to the rule observed by the *mathématikoi*, those initiated into Orphic and Pythagorian circles, right down to demonic revelation (Detienne, 1963). To the *politikoi*, the mathemes are taught without any elaboration.

The difference in the relation to knowledge between the esoteric seminar and the exoteric exposition cuts across the difference between the oral dialogue and the book. The written signifies the death of dialogue: it is not its own addressor and cannot defend itself unaided (*Phaedrus* 275 d); it cannot choose its readers as the man of dialogue chooses his partners (275 e); through the use of written signs it calls upon a formal and mechanical mnemotechnics and not as voice does upon the active anamnesia of contents (275 a); learning through writing occurs in a simulated (short) time, like the growth of plants in those artificial gardens named after Adonis, while insemination through living speech requires the time of dialogue, which is long and slow, perhaps interminable (276 b-277 a).

That part of the written that is mourning governs politics: if laws need to be written, it is as one writes medical ordonnances, in order to be able to govern oneself in the absence of the one who knows, the doctor, the "kingly man" who is the living legislator (*Statesman*

293 a-295 c). The disappointed Pythagorean carries out his ontological and political mourning: it is necessary to write, to govern through the written, to teach through the written, to concede to imitation ("the terrible thing about writing is its resemblance to painting," *Phaedrus* 275 d), and to grant institutional status to that addressee unworthy of dialogue who is called the *politikos*, the reader. As a counterpoint to oral dialogical phrases, there will need to be written pedagogical ones.

4. Selection

Not just anybody can be allowed to participate in the living dialogue. "Socrates" comes up against this obstacle of the partner: what if he is an idiot, or is in bad faith? It is never doubted that the final *homologia* can take place, it is the object of an idea, of an end that does not need to be realized in order to stay an end. Rather, it has a need not to be realized, which is perhaps why the time of the living dialogue is infinite. What is required, though, by the institution of the dialogue is at least an agreement between the partners concerning the stakes, that is concerning the quest for an agreement. Alexander Aphrodisiensis calls *koinologia* the consensus on method: if the theses are to be identical at the end, it is then necessary that the idioms at least of the two parties and the use they make of them be common right from the start. Imagine a candidate for the dialogue who would be a bumpkin, or a fool, or a trickster. He would have to be eliminated. Socrates asks the Stranger from Elea according to what procedure he intends to argue, whether by long discourses or by questions and answers. The Stranger: "When the other party to the conversation is tractable [*euènios* from *ènia*, bit] and gives no trouble, to address him is the easier course; otherwise, to speak by oneself" (*Sophist* 217 c-d). For instance, one can dialogue with the friends of forms, they are better "domesticated" (tamed, *hèmérôteroi*) (*Ibid.*, 246 c) than the materialists who reduce everything to the body. The latter would have to be "civilized" (*nômimôteron*) before they could be admitted to dialogue. But in fact (*ergô*), there is no question of this. One will act as if (*logô*) they were civilized: one speaks in their place, one reinterprets (*aphermèneué*) their theses (246 d), one makes them presentable for dialogue.

In fact, it is not just a question of eliminating a few, infirm brutes who claim to dialogue, but also of attracting and of taming those recalcitrant ones who don't want to dialogue. The simulated dialogue serves to lure them in. The materialist does not enter upon the scene of the dialogue, but he is represented in it. Good mimesis is to engage in imitating the *koinologia, logô* evidently, even if it does not exist *ergô*. The procedure is described with care by the Athenian in the *Laws* (X, 892 d ff.). Suppose, he says to Clinias and Megillus, before engaging a debate about the priority of the soul to the body, suppose we have to cross a river with a strong current. I am more athletic and experienced than you. Let me try to cross and see if it is passable for you. If it is not, the risk will be for me alone. Isn't that reasonable? "Well it is even so with the waters of discourse which confront us now; the current is strong, and the passage perhaps too much for your strength," you are not used to answering questions, you will lose your footing. "I propose that I should act in this same fashion now: I will first put certain questions to myself while you listen in safety, and then once more give the answers to them myself. This plan will be followed throughout the argument" (*Ibid.*). And in passing straight to the act: "If put to the proof, then, on such a subject, the safest course, I take it, is to meet the following questions with the following answers [etc.]? — Of course, I shall reply, some are [etc.]." There ensues a simulated dialogue (893 b-894 b) which ends with: "Perhaps, my friends, we have now [etc.]?"

Who are these friends? The interlocutors simulated by the Athenian in his one-voice dialogue, or his "real" interlocutors, Megillus of Sparta and Clinias the Cretan? In any case, Clinias goes ahead and links onto the "my friends," whether fictive or "real," with a question. He has thus crossed the torrent. The poetician calls this turn a metalepsis (Genette, 1972: 234), a change in the level of one's take on the referent. Aristotle examines the use of the *translatio disputationis* which is a metalepsis (*Topics* II, 111 b 31), but the take whose change he describes is exerted upon the argument, not upon the partners. What Genette has to say and the examples that he cites give a different import to metalepsis: it is the crossing of a "shifting but sacred frontier between two worlds, the world in which one tells, the world of which one tells" (236). He points out some cases, innocent in Balzac or Proust, more audacious in Sterne, Diderot, Pirandello, and Genet.

He sees the archetype of metalepsis in the preamble to the *Theaetetus*. Euclides reports to Terpsion a debate between Theaetetus, Theodorus, and Socrates, reported to him by Socrates himself. In order, though, to avoid the tedious repetition of narrative markings such as *he said, he answered, I said*, or *he agreed*, Euclides, who wrote down the conversation from memory, suppressed such formulas from the book. Terpsion and we, Euclides' readers, therefore read Socrates' dialogue with Theaetetus and Theodorus as if he (Terpsion) and we were listening to them with no intermediary informant. This is a case of perfect mimesis: recognizable by the writer's effacement, by Euclides' apocryptism. The Athenian in the *Laws* retained at least the marks of the simulation in his monologued dialogue. Now, the writer Plato similarly effaces himself from the dialogues we read (and attribute to him). He thereby violates, to all appearances, the poetic legislation decreed by Socrates in the *Republic*, and runs the risk, by his form if not by his thesis, of being accused of impiety.

However, the preambles to most of the dialogues bear upon the marks of the stagesetting: *x* says to *y* that he encountered *z* who told him that . . . The most important shifts in level (Genette, 1972: 227ff.) vary here: one shift in level for the *Laws:* (Plato) → the Athenian and his interlocutors; two shifts in the *Republic:* (Plato) → (Socrates) → Socrates and his interlocutors; four levels in the *Theaetetus:* (Plato) → Euclides, Terpsion → Euclides, Socrates → Socrates, Theodorus, Theaetetus (in writing). Moreover, the variations in person and distance (Genette, 1972: 243, 161) should be examined in the *proimia*. The proliferation of levels increases the addressee's (the reader's) distance from the referent. Thus, in our passage from the *Laws*, Clinias and Megillus are sent out from the stage into the pit, where they listen to the Athenian's fictive dialogue with himself. As readers of the dialogues written by "Plato," we undergo the same fate. Pushed back into the distance by the stagesetting operations, our identification with the partners in the dialogue seems delayed.

These operators of narrative distanciation play, within Platonic poetics, a role analogous to the exclusions that strike the third party in the "Socratic" dialogue. We readers can be neither more nor less admitted to the written dialogue than the Cretan and the Spartan are to the simulated dialogue. Like them, we are too feeble or, like the materialists, we are vulgar and recalcitrant. We are incapable of coming to an agreement concerning the rules of the dialogue, whose principal rule is that the agreement concerning the referent ought to be obtained for ourselves by ourselves. We believe in the decision of the third party in matters of reality. We think that success in the eyes of the third party is the sign of the true. We believe in agonistics. We allow the lesser argument to prevail, under the right conditions.

5. Metalepsis

There is a differend, therefore, concerning the means of establishing reality between the partisans of agonistics and the partisans of dialogue. How can this differend be regulated? Through dialogue, say the latter; through the *agôn*, say the former. To stick to this, the differend would only perpetuate itself, becoming a sort of meta-differend, a differend about the way to regulate the differend about the way to establish reality. On this score, the principle of agonistics, far from being eliminated, still prevails. It is in order to defuse the threat of this recurrence that "Plato" stages the metalepsis of the partner, which is perhaps the kernel of pedagogy.

The paradox of this staging is the following. By its principle, dialogue eliminates recourse to a third party for establishing the reality of the debate's referent. It requires the partners' consensus about the criterion for this reality, this criterion being a consensus over a single phrase regarding this reality. The elimination of third parties takes place upon a scene which is already that of dialogue. But this scene calls upon third parties, those who are in the audience, the spectators, who are the same as those who have been eliminated from the scene of dialogue. They are dedicated to agonistics, that is, to three-way games, the traditional rhetorics, dialectics, and poetics (in particular theatrical poetics). Placed in the position of third party in relation to the scene of dialogue, they are led to witness or to judge whether a given reply, episode, or sequence is or is not dialogical. If this is so, however, then dialogue remains a three-way game, and poetical and rhetorical agonistics remain its principle. Over and above Thrasymachus' head, "Socrates" has in view an audience attending the conversation, a public of readers who will decide who is the stronger. It is necessary then that at the very moment they think they're intervening as a third party, they cease to be third parties, or spectators, witnesses and judges of the dialogues, and take their place as partners in the dialogue. Metalepsis constitutes this change of take on the debate. By accomplishing it, they are no longer the addressees of the staged dialogue, they become the addressees of "Socrates" or of the Athenian at the flanks of Thrasymachus or Clinias, just as we, readers initially, become the addressees of "Plato" dialoguing.

Need we admit a dynamics of dialogue which would absorb differends through metalepses and which would lead, if not to a consensus concerning the referents, then at least to a common language? It would have to be admitted on that account then that the One is stronger than the multiple, that consensus is sought and won in the midst of dissensions. No proof can be adduced for phrases having a value of principle such as these. It is thus never certain nor even probable that partners in a debate, even those taken as witness to a dialogue, convert themselves into partners in dialogue. It is certain only that this is a genre of discourse different from traditional dialectics. It simultaneously institutes and seeks to institute the rules for what we call scientific cognition.

35. But the one who stands as witness, the addressor of the phrase *There is this*, the accuser in short, isn't he or she at least subject to criteria of competence, of morality (*ethos* in Aristotle), of sincerity or of truthfulness which allow it to

be decided if the testimonial is or is not admissible? — Vidal-Naquet questions his own authority to testify in favor of the reality of gas chambers. He feels himself wavering between two motives: to preserve memory from oblivion, to carry out revenge. The first motive subjects the witness only to the rules of scientific cognitives: to establish the facts of the human past. The second is different. The historian finds its archetype in this phrase from Chateaubriand: "In the silence of abjection, when the only sounds to be heard are the chains of the slave and the voice of the informer; when everything trembles before the tyrant and it is as dangerous to incur his favor as to deserve his disfavor, this is when the historian appears, charged with avenging the people" (1981: 94). Such was, he says, for a long time his conception of the historian's task. But now, "the war is over," the tragedy has become secularized, "the people," in any case the Jewish people, are no longer divested of the means to make themselves heard and to obtain reparations. They have ceased to be victims. We would be in case 4 (Nos. 26 and 27) where silence is imposed because the witness lacks the authority to testify or in case 2 where there is no referent, here no victim, for whom to bear witness. The historian would be left then only with the authority of knowledge, his task would be "de-sublimated" (White, 1982: 126).

36. "There are no more victims" (No. 35). Now, to say that the Jews are no longer victims is one thing, but to say that there are no more victims at all is another. A universal cannot be concluded from a particular. Whence the phrase: *There are no more victims* (which is tautological with the phrase: There are no more differends) is not a cognitive phrase and can neither be verified nor refuted by means proper for establishing and validating cognitives. For example, the referent *labor-power* is the object of a concept, but to speak like Kant, it does not give rise to an intuition nor consequently to controversy and to a verdict before the tribunal of knowledge. Its concept is an Idea (Kant Notice 3: §2 and 3). Here is another example: a Martinican is a French citizen; he or she can bring a complaint against whatever impinges upon his or her rights as a French citizen. But the wrong he or she deems to suffer from the fact of being a French citizen is not a matter for litigation under French law. It might be under private or public international law, but for that to be the case it would be necessary that the Martinican were no longer a French citizen. But he or she is. Consequently, the assertion according to which he or she suffers a wrong on account of his or her citizenship is not verifiable by explicit and effective procedures. These are examples of situations presented in the phrase universes of Ideas (in the Kantian sense): the Idea of nation, the Idea of the creation of value. These situations are not the referents of knowledge phrases. There exist no procedures instituted to establish or refute their reality in the cognitive sense. That is why they give rise to differends. The

formulation of these differends is paradoxical, at least in regard to the rules for the family of cognitive phrases.

37. Let us admit your hypothesis, that the wrong comes from the damages not being expressed in the language common to the tribunal and the other party, and that this gives birth to a differend. But how can you judge that there is a differend when, according to this hypothesis, the referent of the victim's phrase is not the object of a cognition properly termed. How can you (No. 1) even affirm that such a situation exists? Because there are witnesses to it? But why do you grant credence to their testimony when they cannot, by hypothesis, establish the reality of what they affirm? Either the differend has an established reality for its object and it is not a differend but a litigation, or, if the object has no established reality, the differend has no object, and there is simply no differend. − So speaks positivism. It confuses reality and referent. Now, in many phrase families, the referent is not at all presented as real: *O'er all the hilltops/ Is peace,** 2 X 2 = 4, Get out, At that time, he took the path toward . . . , That's very beautiful.* This does not prevent these phrases from taking place. (But is *to take place* the same thing as *to be real?*) (No. 131.)

38. Some feel more grief over damages inflicted upon an animal than over those inflicted upon a human. This is because the animal is deprived of the possibility of bearing witness according to the human rules for establishing damages, and as a consequence, every damage is like a wrong and turns it into a victim *ipso facto.* − But, if it does not at all have the means to bear witness, then there are not even damages, or at least you cannot establish them. − What you are saying defines exactly what I mean by a wrong: you are placing the defender of the animal before a dilemma (No. 8). That is why the animal is a paradigm of the victim.

39. But if phrases belonging to different regimens or genres, such as those of cognition and those of the Idea, encounter each other to the point of giving rise to differends, then they must have certain properties in common and their "encounter" must take place within a single universe, otherwise there would be no encounter at all! − The universe you are thinking of would be a universe prior to the phrases and where they would encounter each other; but it is your phrase that presents it. It presents it as being there before all phrases. That is the paradox that in general signals reality as that which is, even when there is no validatable testimony through cognitive procedures (Nos. 37, 47). − No, I am not saying that this universe is reality, but only that it is the condition for the encounter of phrases, and therefore the condition for differends. − The condition of the encounter is not this universe, but the phrase in which you present it. It is a transcendental and not an empirical condition. Regarding this universe, it can just as easily

---

*The opening line of Goethe's famous short poem *Uber allen Gipfeln ist Ruhe.* −tr.

be said that it is the effect of the encounter as its condition (the two expressions are equivalent). Similarly, the linguist's phrase is the transcendental condition of the language to which it refers. This does not prevent language from being the empirical condition of the linguist's phrase. *Transcendental* and *empirical* are terms which do no more than indicate two different phrase families: the critical (criticizing) philosophical phrase and the cognitive phrase. Finally: phrases from heterogeneous regimens or genres "encounter" each other in proper names, in worlds determined by networks of names (Nos. 80, 81, 60).

40. Why these encounters between phrases of heterogeneous regimen? Differends are born, you say, from these encounters. Can't these contacts be avoided? − That's impossible, contact is necessary. First of all, it is necessary to link onto a phrase that happens (be it by a silence, which is a phrase), there is no possibility of not linking onto it. Second, to link is necessary; how to link is contingent. There are many ways of linking onto *I can come by your place* (Nos. 137, 139, 140). − But some are pertinent, and others inconsistent. Eliminate the latter, and you escape the differend. − Let's agree to this, but how can you know that some are pertinent? By trying out many ways of linking, including the inconsistent ones. − But there exist genres of discourse (Nos. 147, 179, 180) which fix rules of linkage, and it suffices to observe them to avoid differends. − Genres of discourse determine stakes, they submit phrases from different regimens to a single finality: the question, the example, the argument, the narration, the exclamation are in forensic rhetoric the heterogeneous means of persuading. It does not follow that differends between phrases should be eliminated. Taking any one of these phrases, another genre of discourse can inscribe it into another finality. Genres of discourse do nothing more than shift the differend from the level of regimens to that of ends. − But because several linkages are possible does that necessarily imply that there is a differend between them? − Yes it does, because only one of them can happen (be "actualized") at a time (Nos. 184, 186).

41. It is necessary to link, but the mode of linkage is never necessary. It is suitable or unsuitable. *I can come by your place? How is the dollar?* Or: *It's a crisis of overcapitalization.* −*Did you brush your teeth?* Or: *Help! Help!* −*For whom?* −Or: *either p or q; if p, then not-q.* −*Did you know that she had arrived?* −Or: *Close the door!* −*You are saying to close the door.* These unsuitabilities are so many damages inflicted upon the first phrase by the second. Would you say that these damages become wrongs from the fact that the first phrase cannot link on with a view toward its validation? −It is not even that. Validation is a genre of discourse, not a phrase regimen. No phrase is able to be validated from inside its own regimen: a descriptive is validated cognitively only by recourse to an ostensive (*And here is the case*). A prescriptive is validated juridically or politically by a normative (*It is a norm that* . . .), ethically by a feeling (tied to the *You ought to*), etc.

42. "The victim's vengeance alone gives the authority to bear witness" (No. 35). — The word authority is equivocal. The victim does not have the legal means to bear witness to the wrong done to him or her. If he or she or his or her defender sees "justice done," this can only be in spite of the law. The law reserves the authority to establish the crime, to pronounce the verdict and to determine the punishment before the tribunal which has heard the two parties expressing themselves in the same language, that of the law. The justice which the victim calls upon against the justice of the tribunal cannot be uttered in the genre of juridical or forensic discourse. But this is the genre in which the law is uttered. The authority that vengeance may give ought not then to be called a right of law. The plea is a demand for the reparation of damages, addressed to a third party (the judge) by the plaintiff (addressor). The avenger is a justice-maker, the request (the cry) is addressed to him or her (the addressee) as to a judge. It is not transferable to a third party, even for its execution (idiolect), its legitimacy allows for no discussion, it is not measured distributively because its referent, the wrong, is not cognizable.

43. All the same, vengeance authorizes itself on account of the plea's having no outcome. Since one is not able to obtain reparation, one cries out for vengeance. — This is still psychology or socio-psychology. In any case, it is to accept unquestioningly that a teleological principle regulates the passage from one genre of discourse (the cognitive) to another (the phrase of the Idea). But what proof do we have that there is a principle of compensation between genres of discourse? Can it be said that since I don't succeed in demonstrating this, then it is necessary that I be able to tell it? To begin with, the referent is not the same when the phrase referring to it is not from the same family. The damages are not the wrong, the property to be demonstrated is not the event to be told, and I understand this even in the case when they bear the same name. Moreover, why must this referent necessarily be the object of a "second" phrase? The only necessity is to link onto it, nothing more. Inside a genre of discourse, the linkings obey rules that determine the stakes and the ends. But between one genre and another, no such rules are known, nor a generalized end. A classical example is that of the linking of a prescriptive onto a cognitive: simply because a referent is established as real it does not follow that one ought to say or do something in regard to it (Obligation Section). Conversely, on the basis of one prescriptive, several sorts of phrases are possible. "We say: 'The order orders *this* —' and do it; but also: 'The order orders this: I am to . . . ' We translate it at one time into a proposition, at another into a demonstration, and at another into action" (Wittgenstein, *Ph U:* § 459). Or into an evaluation: the officer cries *Avanti!* and leaps up out of the trench; moved, the soldiers cry *Bravo!* but don't budge.

44. Vengeance has no legitimate authority, it shakes the authority of the tribunals, it calls upon idioms, upon phrase families, upon genres of discourse (any which one) that do not, in any case, have a say in the matter. It asks for the

revision of competences or for the institution of new tribunals. It disavows the authority of any tribunal of phrases that would present itself as their unique, supreme tribunal. It is wrong to call "rights of man" that which vengeance calls upon against the law. *Man* is surely not the name that suits this instance of appeal, nor *right* the name of the authority which this instance avails itself of (No. 42). *Rights of the other* is not much better. *Authority of the infinite* perhaps, or *of the heterogeneous*, were it not so eloquent.

45. One defers to the "tribunal of history," Hegel invokes the "tribunal of the world. " These can only be symbols, like the last judgment. In what genre of discourse, in what phrase family would the supreme tribunal be able to render its judgment upon the pretensions to validity of all phrases, given that these pretensions differ according to the families and genres to which they are attached? A convenient answer is found in the use of citation (metalanguage), which makes all phrases pass under the single regimen of cognitives. Instead of the order: *Open the door*, the tribunal has for its cognizance the descriptive: *It was ordered that the door be opened*; instead of the question: *Is this lipstick?*, the tribunal has for its cognizance the descriptive: *It was asked if this is lipstick*. Instead of the descriptive: *The wall is white*, the tribunal has for its cognizance the descriptive: *It was declared that the wall is white*. After which, the question asked by the tribunal is: Has it effectively been asked if this is lipstick, effectively been declared that the wall is white? *Effectively* signifies: does the cited phrase (order, question, description) well present the traits we say it does (was it indeed an order, etc. ?)? Did it indeed take place (was it indeed the case?)? Now, these two questions are pertinent when it is a matter of validating a cognitive phrase (like: *This wall is white*). But can we validate an order like: *Stop singing*, or an appraisal like: *What a beautiful aria!* by means of these questions? Rather, the validation of the order would seem to be for the addressee to stop singing, and the validation of the appraisal for the addressee to partake in the addressor's emotion (No. 149).

46. Citation submits the phrase to an autonymic transformation. The phrase was: *Open the door*. When cited, it becomes: *The /open the door/*. It is said that it loses its character as a current phrase [*phrase actuelle*]. But what is "current"? It is more conceivable if we say: when one waits after an order for the effectuation of what it prescribes (rather than for a commentary or an appraisal), one can say that it is "current." And the autonymic transformation of the order consists, first of all, in not expecting its effectuation. The soldiers autonymized the *Avanti!* of the lieutenant who drew them to the attack when they linked onto it by shouting *Bravo!* So much so that the currentness of a phrase would depend upon the following phrase's mode of linkage. *The meeting is adjourned* is a current or actual performative only if the following phrases not only cease to refer to the meeting's agenda but also cease to situate their addressors and addressees primarily in terms of the question of that referent's sense.

The Referent, The Name

47. How can the reality of the referent be subordinated to the effectuation of verification procedures, or even to the instructions that allow anyone who so wishes to effectuate those procedures? This inverts the idea of reality we spontaneously have: we think something is real when it exists, even if there is no one to verify that it exists; for example, we say that the table is real if it is always there, even if there are no witnesses to the place it occupies. — Or again: imagine a relay race. Reality would be that object called the "baton" [*témoin*] that the relay runners transmit to each other. The runners do not make this object exist by sheer force of running. Likewise, interlocutors do not make what they discuss in argument real. Existence is not concluded. The ontological argument is false. Nothing can be said about reality that does not presuppose it.

48. The refutation of this common idea of reality (No. 47) is identical in form to the dilemma presented in No. 8. The annihilation of the reality of gas chambers conforms to the annihilation of the referent's reality during verification procedures. The historian Vidal-Naquet calls Faurisson a "paper Eichmann": the latter's "attempt at extermination on paper runs relay for the actual extermination" (1981: 81). This is because there is no reality except as testified on "paper." Clément Rosset would add that this is through a double of the reality (Rosset, 1976). Vidal-Naquet notes that the "revisionists" (of the Final Solution) use a "non-ontological" proof in their inquiry into the question of the gas chambers. But in this, at least, they are like you or me when we have to refute a thesis about reality. This is what the West has done since Parmenides and Gorgias.

49. "I was there, I can talk about it." This same principle governs Faurisson's argument: "to have really seen, with his own eyes" (No. 2). The eyewitness's entire authority proceeds from what one historian calls *autopsy* (Hartog, 1980: 271–316). To Faurisson, it can be answered that no one can see one's own death. To every realism, it can be answered that no one can see "reality" properly called. That would be to suppose that reality has a proper name, and a proper name is not seen (Kripke, 1980: 44). Naming is not showing. Jean says to Jacques: *I assure you that Louis was there.* Jacques asks where. Jean tells him: *Well, at the concert I was telling you about!* It can be supposed that Jacques is able to name the concert hall in question. *But where in the concert hall, and on which day?* Jean must situate the *where* and the *when* of what he is talking about within a system of cross-references which is independent of the space-time presented by his first phrase, if he wants the reality of Louis's presence to be admitted. He says: *In the back, on the right-hand side, looking toward the stage,* and: *the Saturday before Christmas.* Through recourse to chronological, topographical, toponymic, and anthroponymic systems, Jean gives Jacques the means to verify the reality of the referent of this phrase, but these names do not imply that Jean himself "was there."

50. Deictics relate the instances of the universe presented by the phrase in which they are placed back to a "current" spatio-temporal origin so named "I-here-now." These deictics are designators of reality. They designate their object as an extra-linguistic permanence, as a "given." Far from constituting a permanence in itself, however, this "origin" is presented or co-presented with the universe of the phrase in which they are marked. It appears and disappears with this universe, and thus with this phrase (Hegel, 1806: 150–53; Gardies, 1975: 88). *It's my turn* = it's the turn (to do something, here unspecified) of whoever is in the situation of addressor (*I*) when this phrase "takes place." *What did you go imagine?* = it is asked of whoever is in the situation of addressee (*you*) when this phrase "takes place" what unreal sense he or she gave (to a referent here unspecified) at a time prior to when this phrase "takes place." The "subject of the uttering" [*sujet de l'énonciation*] is the addressor instance in the universe presented by the current phrase. This instance may be marked (by a proper name or a pronoun) (*I swear it to you, What do I know?**) or left unmarked (*The solution is incorrect, Halt!*). It suffers the same fate as other instances marked by other deictics.

51. I am explaining to the reader of these lines that *here, now,* and *I* refer to an "origin" which is in the universe presented by the "current" phrase. My reader understands that the words *here, now,* and *I* should not be taken according to their "current" deictic value as in *I am explaining,* or *these lines,* up above, but according to their sense (that is, their usage) as deictics in general in any given phrase.

---

*"Que sais-je?": Montaignes's famous motto in celebration of his skepticism. –tr.

The reader makes a difference between now and *now* (or the now). When I say *"Now" is self-referential*, *"now"* is taken as an image of itself, it is taken in terms of its autonymic value. This is not the case when, in response to the question *When are you leaving?*, I answer, *Now*. In the phrase *"Now" is self-referential*, *now* is not self-referential, because it is situated upon the referent instance of the universe presented by this phrase, it is the "subject of the utterance" [*sujet de l'énoncé*]. In *I am leaving now*, *now* marks the situation of the referent (the act of my leaving) in relation to the time when the phrase "takes place." It is not itself the referent of the phrase as it is in the preceding phrase.

52. When I speak of the "subject of the uttering" in a phrase (No. 51), the addressor instance of this phrase is placed in the situation of the referent instance of the current phrase (mine). Each bears the same proper name (if they are named). The two phrase universes are not equivalent, however. For example, I relate that Kant writes of the French Revolution that it aroused the enthusiasm of its spectators. "Kant" is the "subject of the uttering" in the phrase *The French Revolution aroused the enthusiasm of its spectators*, but he is the referent (or "subject of the utterance") in the phrase (in which "I" am the "subject of the uttering"): *Kant states that the French Revolution (etc.)*. If Kant were not the subject of the utterance in "my" phrase (the second one), how could I say that he is the subject of the uttering in the first? The name he bears is a received one (though not necessarily from "me"), and it may be that every proper name must be a received one.

53. The conversion of a proper name from the position of "subject of the uttering" to that of "subject of the utterance" is equivalent to its displacement from the situation of addressor in the universe of a current phrase p to that of referent in the universe of a current phrase q. "Kant" writes something about the French Revolution in universe p, and someone else ("I") writes something about "Kant" in universe q. This conversion requires at least two phrases, and these seem like they should be successive. The someone else can bear the same name. For example, the author of *The Conflict with the Faculty of Law* signs the phrase about the French Revolution with the name "Kant." Phrase (1) is: *The French Revolution aroused the enthusiasm of peoples*; the signature-phrase (2) is: *Kant states that the French Revolution (etc.)*. It is observed that the addressor of phrase (2) remains unnamed: who speaks? It could be "Kant" or someone else, but there needs to be a phrase (3) to name him (of the type: *Kant (or x) states that Kant states that the French Revolution* (etc.). In any case, what seems important is that at least two phrases be linked together, such that the second assigns to the first an addressor left unnamed in the first and placed in the situation of referent in the second.

54. The displacement undergone by the "subject of the uttering" when, through naming, it becomes the subject of the utterance, presents no particular obscurity.

It is a case of the transformation of a current phrase into a cited phrase, such as Frege studied in relation to sense, but here applied to the addressor (Frege, 1892: 56–78; Descombes, 1977: 175–78). Just as the sense (*Sinn*) of *p* becomes the referent of *q*, so the addressor of *p* becomes the referent of *q* when he is named. —Russell wants "concepts" (Frege's *Sinne*) to be immutable like Platonic ideas, and thus independent of their place in a phrase. He is concerned about the transformation associated with citation which by placing the "concept" of phrase *p* in the position of "term" (referent) in phrase *q* turns it into a determined "object" and amputates it from its universal value. He sees in this the threat of Hegelian dialectics (1903: § 49). But for Frege, the sense (*Sinn*) of a phrase is what it is independently of the context and of the interlocutor. The transformation of phrase (1) into phrase (2) does not alter the sense of (1); it encases it into the sense of (2) and modifies its referential value (*Bedeutung*). The procedures directed toward validating the phrase by establishing a reality presentable through an ostensive phrase (of the type: *Here is a case of it*) no longer apply to the sense of phrase (1) but to the sense of phrase (2). What needs to be validated is no longer that the Revolution aroused the enthusiasm of peoples, but that Kant thought that this was the case. But the sense of (1) remains identical as such, whether Kant did or did not think it. —The addressor's name also remains identical throughout the citations (the encasements) and throughout the accompanying transformations of the referent, but for a different reason. There is no question of validating the truth of a name: a name is not a property attributed to a referent by means of a description (a cognitive phrase). It is merely an index which, in the case of the anthroponym, for example, designates one and only one human being. The properties attributed to the human being designated by this name could be validated, but not his or her name. The name adds no property to him or her. Even if initially many names have a signification, they lose it, and they must lose it. A denominative phrase like *This I call x* (baptism), or *That is called y* (training) is not a cognitive phrase. Nor is it an ostensive one (Nos. 62, 63).

Antisthenes

A pupil of Gorgias, a friend and admirer of Socrates, and according to the doxography a founder of Cynicism along with Diogenes the Dog (Caizzi), Antisthenes maintained two paradoxes, as reported by Aristotle. The first one bears upon error and contradiction. Aristotle is seeking to establish rules for dialectics. He calls dialectical thesis an assertion contrary to the opinion (*paradoxos*) upheld by someone important in philosophy. By way of an example, he gives Antisthenes' thesis: "that contradiction is impossible" (*Topics* 104 b 21). Drawing up a catalogue of notions in *Metaphysics* V, he examines the notion of falsehood: "A false phrase (*logos*) is one that refers to non-existent objects, in so far as it is false. Hence every phrase is false when applied to something other than that of which it is true, e.g. the phrase that refers to a circle is false when applied to a triangle. In a sense there is one phrase for each referent, i.e., the phrase that refers to its 'what its being was' [*ce qu'était qu'être*] [Aubenque, 1966: 462], but in a sense there are many, since the referent itself and the referent itself modified in a certain way [with some property] are somehow the same, e.g., *Socrates* and *musical Socrates*. The false phrase is not the phrase of anything, except in a qualified sense. Hence Antisthenes foolishly claimed that nothing could be described except by its own phrase (*oikeiô logô*), —one phrase to one referent; from which it followed that there could be no contradiction, and about that one could not be misled" (*Metaphysics* 1024 b 27–34).

Plato puts in the mouth of Euthydemus an argument so similar that Ctesippus' partner has been considered to be a double of Antisthenes. We will see that the misunderstanding (and the scorn) that this argument has elicited in the doxography right down to the present stems from the amphibology of the Greek verb *legein*: to say something, or to talk about something, to name something?

"Do you believe that one can be misled? —Yes indeed, unless I am out of my senses. —When one talks about the thing (*pragma*) to which the phrase (*logos*) refers, or when one does not? —When one talks about it. —And one who talks, talks about the thing which one talks about, and no other? —Obviously. —And the thing one talks about is a distinct thing, existing apart from other things? —Certainly. —And one who talks about that thing talks about something that exists? —Yes. —And one who talks about that which exists and about things that exist, says the truth. And therefore Dionysodorus, if he talks about things that exist, says the truth and does not mislead you in any way" (*Euthydemus* 284 a).

I have decided here to give to *ti legein* its referential value, "to talk about something, to refer to something," and to disregard its semantic value, "to say something, to want to say." Both are possible. However, the version I chose seems to impose itself on account of Euthydemus' first question, which is unequivocal: ". . . the thing to which the phrase refers [*to pragma péri hou an ho logos è*, to which the phrase presumably refers]."

As for the impossibility of contradicting, here is the argument by which Dionysodorus, who runs relay for Euthydemus, brings his partner to silence: "When neither of us says the *logos* of the thing, how can we be in contradiction? —Ctesippus assented. —But when I say the *logos* of the thing, will we then be in contradiction? I am talking about the thing [*lego to pragma*], but you are not at all talking about it: how can not talking [about it] [*ho mè legôn*] contradict talking [about it]?"

To clear up the paradox, it is sufficient to understand *ti legein* (to talk about something) here as if it were saying "to name something," a reading allowed by *legein*. For everything one talks about, there is a proper denomination, which is also the only proper one. And conversely, one and only one referent answers to every denomination. If then, you disagree with someone while thinking you're talking about the same thing, it is because you and your interlocutor are speaking about two different things. For, if you were talking about the same thing, you would give it the same name, and would therefore be saying the same thing about it. The *hèn eph ' hènos* [one for each one] attributed to Antisthenes by Aristotle should be understood as a name by designate and vice-versa. And, if there is no error, it is because there is no Not-Being: the referent of a false phrase is not a nothingness, it is an object other than the one referred to.

The two sophists of the *Euthydemus* pass through the breach inscribed in Parmenides' poem between Being and saying, a breach already opened wide by Gorgias upon the "neither Being nor Not-Being" of what is talked about (Gorgias Notice). What can be said about the referent? "Before" knowing whether what one says or will say about it is true or false, it is necessary to know what one is talking about. But how can it be known which referent one is talking about without attributing properties to it, that is, without already saying something about it? Antisthenes, like certain Megarans and like the Stoics later on, asks whether signification precedes or is preceded by designation. The thesis of nomination gets him out of the circle. The referent needs to be fixed; the name, as Kripke says, is a rigid designator that fixes the referent.

Designation is not, nor can it be, the adequation of the *logos* to the being of the existent. Antisthenes has no reason to maintain the thesis that the name is derived from or motivated by the named, the thesis Plato attributes to Cratylus, although the author of the Cratylus confuses the issue as if by pleasurable design (*Cratylus* 429 c - 430 a). This motivation cannot, in truth, be described, unless the essence of the named is already known independently of its name, which is an absurdity. This mimetology that Genette calls an "eponymy of the name" (1976: 11-37) is at the furthest remove from Antisthenes' nominalism. Nomination is an active designation, a *poiein* (*Euthydemus* 284 c) which isolates singularities in the undetermined "neither Being nor Not-Being" (Gorgias Notice).

The second paradox cited by Aristotle concerns determination and proceeds from the same conception of the *logos* as designator. Aristotle shows that by the term *house* one cannot understand merely the bricks, its matter, without also understanding the final form of their disposition, which turns them into a shelter. By sticking to the elements, the substance (*ousia*) of the house is not attained. But then, how can the element itself be determined? "Therefore the difficulty which was raised by the school of Antisthenes and other such uneducated people has a certain appropriateness. They stated that the 'what it is' [*ce que c'est*] (*to ti esti orisasthai*) cannot be defined (for the definition so called is a long phrase (*makros logos*)); but of what 'sort' [*comme quoi c'est*] a thing, e.g. silver, is they thought it possible to explain, not saying what it is but that it is like tin. Therefore one kind of substance (*ousia*) can be defined and phrased (*horon kai logon*), i.e. the composite kind, whether it be the object of sense or of reason; but the primary elements of which this consists cannot be defined, since a definatory phrase (*ho logos ho horistikos*) predicates something of something, and one part of this definition must play the part of matter and the other that of form (*Metaphysics* VIII 1043 b 23-32).

The concession made to the thesis of nomination is considerable despite the show of scorn: simples are not defined, they are named. It clarifies the sense to be given the *oikeios logos*. The latter is not a definition, which is a "long phrase" because it entails at least two constituents, subject and predicate, or matter and form according to Aristotle. It is a short phrase, a phrase with only one place, hence a single word. If it is "proper," it is not because it conforms to the essence of its referent (a logically prior problem, as it were), but because it exclusively designates a referent "different from the others," as "Euthydemus" would say. That word, whatever its grammatical nature, thus has the value of a name. The problem raised by Antisthenes, if it is retranscribed in Aristotelian terms, would be the following: one can perhaps say the "what its being was" of a referent, but this referent would first have to be named "before" any predication is made about it. The simple or the elementary is not a component of the object, it is its name and it comes to be situated as referent in the universe of the definitional phrase. It is a simple — hence prelogical — logic which by itself is not pertinent with regard to the rules of truth (Wittgenstein, *PhU*: § 49).

55. A metaphysical exigency and illusion: names must be proper, an object in the world must answer without any possible error to its call (appellation) in language. Otherwise, says Dogmatism, how would true cognition be possible? Wittgenstein calls "objects" (*TLP* : 2. 02) simples that bound together form states of *things* (2. 01). These are "configurations of objects" (2. 0272) which are unstable, while "objects" are "unalterable and subsistent" (2. 0271). In a "picture" (*Bild*),which is to say at this point, in cognitive language, "elements" correspond to these objects (2. 13). These elements are simple signs (3. 201) which, employed in propositions, are called "names" (3. 202). The "object" is the *Bedeutung* or referent, in the Fregian sense, of the name (3. 203). Concomitantly, "in a proposition a name is the representative [*vertritt*] of an object" (3. 22). Objects can thus only be named (3. 221) without their being known. Between simples and elements, there are certain kinds of feelers (*Fühler*) (2. 1515). Their fixity allows for the cognition of what is unstable, the compounds of objects. −Nevertheless, cognition requires more than the lexical correspondence between the language of elements and the world of simples. It is further necessary that the rule for the composition of elements in language and for that of simples in the world be a "common" one (2. 17, 2. 18). The picture's form, its propositional form when the picture is a logical one, constitutes a kind of standard of measurement (*Masstab*) which comes to be laid against (*angelegt*) reality (2. 1512). It can do this only if reality is shaped the same way as the picture. But how can this conformity or communality be proved? The form of presentation (*Form der Darstellung*) or of representation (*der Abbildung*) cannot be presented or represented (2. 173) without presupposing it (*petitio principii*). Now this presupposition also commands lexical theory: there is supposed to be a biunivocal "correspondence" (through feelers) between names and simple objects. But since the simple is not an object of cognition, it cannot be known whether the denomination of a simple object is true or false.

56. Reality is "given" in the universe of Jean's first phrase (No. 49). This at least is what is indicated by the presence of the deictics *there* and *then*. The marks, though, that the referent is "given" to the addressee of the current phrase, the deictics, do not suffice to turn the referent into a reality. Objections can be found in dreams, hallucinatory deliria, sensory errors, and idiolects in general. Reality has to be established, and it will be all the better established if one has independent testimonies of it. These testimonies are phrases having the same referent, but not immediately linked to each other. How can it be known that the referent is the same? *The same* signifies at least that it is locatable at the same place among common and accessible cross-references. This is what the names of chronology, of topography, of anthroponymy, etc. permit us to do. Once placed in these systems, the referent loses the marks of a current "given": *there, at that very moment*. The place and the moment where it was given can become the object of as many vali-

dations as one would like. *There* and *then* cannot be repeated for the same referent, but *in the last row on the right-hand side of Pleyel hall* and *December 23, 1957* seem able to be.

57. "It is not how the speaker thinks he got the reference, but the actual chain of communication [*l'enchaînement*] which is relevant" (No. 53). Kripke explains his idea of the "chain": "a baby is born; his parents call him by a certain name. They talk about him to their friends. Other people meet him. Through various sorts of talk the name is spread from link to link as if by a chain. . . . A certain passage of communication reaching ultimately to the man himself does reach the speaker" (1980: 91–93). What is important is that "his parents call him by a certain name. They talk about him to their friends." The addressor who signs the name "Kant" was formerly the addressee of 'I baptize you Kant' and the referent of "Kant has grown a lot this week." The proper name is a designator of reality, like a deictic; it does not, any more than a deictic, have a signification, it is not, any more than a deictic, the abridged equivalent of a definite description or of a bundle of descriptions (*Ibid.*). It is a pure mark of the designative function. But unlike deictics, this mark is independent of the "current" phrase. In the case of proper names, the independence of the mark in relation to the current phrase comes from the fact that it remains invariable from one phrase to the next even though what it marks is found sometimes in the position of addressor, sometimes in the position of addressee, sometimes in the position of referent (occasionally even in the position of grammatical predicate: "It's a Kant"). Its rigidity is this invariability. The name designates the same thing because it remains the same. The other "possible universes" (Nos. 18, 25) the proper name traverses without being altered are not merely those in which the descriptions that can be attached to it are different : *Kant, the author of the* Critique of Pure Reason; *Kant, the author of the* Critique of Judgment; *Kant, whose dying days are recounted by Thomas de Quincey* . . . They are above all those phrase universes in which the proper name inhabits different situations among the instances: *I name you Kant; Dear brother, I embrace you, signed Kant; It sounds like Kant; Kant was then writing the* Observations on the Feelings of the Beautiful and the Sublime.

58. Names transform *now* into a date, *here* into a place, *I, you, he* into Jean, Pierre, Louis. Even silences can refer to gods (Kahn, 1978). Names grouped into calendars, cartographical systems, genealogies and civil statutes are indicators of possible reality. They present their referents, dates, places, and human beings as givens. A phrase, otherwise deprived of deictic marks, presents *Rome* instead of *over-there*. The name Rome acts like a deictic: the referent, the addressor, and the addressee are situated in relation to an "as-if right here" [*comme-si ici*]. This quasi-deictic, because it is a name, remains fixed throughout a sequence of phrases. This is not the case for a deictic (in a correspondance, the here of phrase *p* can be the there of phrase *q*). *Rome* is an "image" of many here's actualized in

many phrases (the here Livy talks about . . . , the here where our friends the B's live). This fixed image becomes independent when the universe presented by the phrase in which it "currently" has its place is named.

59. The rigidity of nominal designators spreads to their relations. Between the "as-if here" that is Rome and the "as-if there" that is Bologna, another phrase fixes the gap, in time or in distance. The gap can be ascertained by a "voyage," that is, by the succession of different place-names leading up to the place *here,* and of the different moments leading up to the place of *now.* The measurement of the gap cannot be ascertained, however. It also presupposes a fixed designator: a unit of measure, the foot, the league, the mile, the meter, units of time. This designator traverses the phrase universes without any possible alteration because it is a name (Wittgenstein, *PhU:* § 50; Kripke, 1980: 53–54). We say *This is a meter* as we say *This is Rome,* "after" which we ask what it is and try to define what is named. — It may be that the logic of colors should be examined from the aspect of the referential function of the names of colors (Gorgias Notice). These names, too, are received. They too do not supply any knowledge about what they name. Is this to say that *This is red* is more enigmatic than to say *This is Rome*?

60. Networks of quasi-deictics formed by names of "objects" and by names of relations designate "givens" and the relations given between those givens, that is to say, a world. I call it a world because those names, being "rigid," each refer to something even when that something is not there; and because that something is considered to be the same for all phrases which refer to it by its name; and also because each of those names is independent of the phrase universes that refer to it, and in particular of the addressors and addressees presented in those universes (No. 56). This is not to say that something which has the same name in several phrases has the same meaning. Different descriptions can be made of it, and the question of its cognition is opened and not closed by its name. Cognition can lead one to abandon a name, to replace it by others, to admit or to create new names. Names are subject to the principle attributed to Antisthenes: one name per referent, one referent per name. If the description for "Morning Star" is the same as for "Evening Star," a single name is given to their referent (conversely in the case of homonyms). — But how can one know that there is only one referent when it is shown in different places and at different times? — Because reality is not established by ostension alone. The properties established by descriptions allow one to explain differences in ostension (the hypothesis of the earth's movement); the ostensions testify to these properties (this is the case); and finally, if it can be known that the ostensions themselves are different, it is because the deictics have been replaced by calendar names, by distances to already named stars, etc., which situate what is shown no longer in relation to the "current" ostensive phrase, but in relation to a world of names independent of ostensions.

61. A cognitive phrase is validated thanks to another phrase, an ostensive one or one which displays. This is formulated as *Here's a case of it*. In every phrase, *of it* refers to the cognitive phrase. It is a question of showing a reality that is an example for which the cognitive phrase is true. The ostension should be relieved of deictics and should present the referent (the case) in systems independent of "I-here-now," so that the addressee can repeat the ostension thanks to the cross-references supplied by these systems. The phrase *Here is a red flower* is transformed into two phrases, a cognitive phrase or definition: "Red corresponds to wavelengths in the spectrum from 650 to 750 millimicrons of the radiation emitted by an object"; and an ostensive phrase: "The color of this flower here is a case of it." It is still necessary to relieve the latter of its deictic, "here," and to substitute for it a cross-referencing by systems independent of the current phrase ("the flower observed by *y* in the botanical laboratory of Institute *x* on April 17, 1961).

62. Once the marks of the self-referential universe (the deictics) have been eliminated, any given "red flower" other than the one presented as referent in the initial phrase can come to occupy the referent instance of the ostensive phrase, on the condition that it can validate the cognitive phrase defining red. Henceforth, all flowers whose radiation is emitted between the wavelengths of 650 and 750 millimicrons can serve as examples to validate the cognitive phrase. Obviously, this possibility is never effectuated, since it concerns a totality, that of red flowers. Reality succumbs to this reversal: it was the given described by the phrase, it became the archive from which are drawn documents or examples that validate the description. – The document, though, still entails a cross-referencing by quasi-deictics: red in a chromonymic catalog. Nor is the descriptive phrase itself exempt from this, on account of the term *millimicron* which belongs to the lexicon of metrynymics, it too purely referential. Description cannot free itself from denomination, reference cannot be reduced to sense (Tarski, 1944: 344). For denomination to have only a referential function is to open description (cognition) up to the course of an endless refinement. But what does it open reality up to?

63. – But doesn't one distinguish easily between a name whose referent is real and a name whose referent is not? We do not put in the same category Bonaparte and Jean Valjean, the island of Utopia and Terra America. No one has ever met Jean Valjean, except for the characters in *Les Misérables* (in a system of names that constitute the "world" of that book), no one has ever set foot in Utopia (Raphael Hythloday forgot to give us the geographical coordinates of the island). The name "rigidly" designates across phrase universes, it is inscribed in networks of names which allow for the location of realities, but it does not endow its referent with a reality. If *phlogiston* and *hydrogen* are names, it remains that the second has a real referent, but not the first. – But "to meet" Valjean, "to set foot in Utopia" are not tests of reality. Let us recapitulate. "This is Caesar" is not an ostensive phrase, it is a nominative phrase. Now it "takes place" just as well in

front of a portrait of Caesar as in front of Caesar (Marin, 1981: 279–84): this is because to name the referent is not the same as to show its "presence." To signify is one thing, to name another, and to show still another.

64. To show that an *x* is a case of the cognitive phrase *x is P* is to present *x* as real. Because the ostensive phrase presents its referent as given, it can validate a description with cognitive pretensions. For something to be given means both that its referent is there and that it is there even when it is not shown. It would exist even without its being phrased, "extralinguistically" (Nos. 47, 48). —It is easy then for an opponent to refute whoever affirms the reality of a referent by enclosing him in a dilemma: either the shown referent is merely what is shown, and it is not necessarily real (it might be an appearance, etc.); or else, it is more than what is shown, and it is not necessarily real (how can one know that what is not there is real?). This dilemma is the one that assails all philosophies based on showing (Descombes, 1981a). They generally elude the dilemma through recourse to the testimony of some infallible third party, to whom what is hidden from the "current" addressee of the ostensive phrase is supposedly absolutely (constantly) revealed. There is little difference in this regard between the God of the Cartesians and the pre-predicative cogito of the phenomenologists. Both groups admit an entity who is in a state of "cosmic exile" (McDowell in Bouveresse, 1980: 896).

65. Real or not, the referent is presented in the universe of a phrase, and it is therefore situated in relation to some sense. For example, in *The door is open*, the sense in relation to which the referent is situated is under the regimen of descriptives. (It is important to note that sense is not always presented under this regimen, and that consequently the referent does not always occupy the place of subject of the utterance. A prescriptive, *Open the door*, presents a sense without the referent (something like: the door opened by you the next moment) becoming the object of a description. An exclamative, *What a door! always open!*, an interrogative, *Did he open the door?*, a narrative, *The door opened*, all present senses even though their referents are not signified according to the rules of description). Whatever the regimen of the previous phrase, the reality of the referent can be affirmed merely in response to a question bearing upon that phrase, such as, *Which door are you talking about?* The typical answer is the ostensive phrase, *This one here*. This phrase is not sufficient to validate the previous phrase. The location of the door must be made possible independent of the current phrase. Recourse is then made to the system of names: *The door in Albert's house which opens toward the west*. With names, stable and common space-times are introduced. Descriptive: *The Empire has a capital for its political center*. Nominative: *This capital is called Rome*. Ostensive: *Here is Rome (This city here is the case)*. Another example: *Hic Rhodus, hic salta*. *Salta* presents the sense under the regimen of prescription, *Rhodus* the name, *hic* marks the ostension. That

referent is real which is declared to be the same in these three situations: signified, named, shown. Thus, respectively: in an internment camp, there was mass extermination by chambers full of Zyklon B; that camp is called Auschwitz; here it is. A fourth phrase states that the signified referent, the named referent, and the shown referent are the same.

66. The identity of the referents of the three phrases is not established once and for all. It has to be affirmed "each time." In fact, it is subject to the deictics of the ostensive phrase, and these designate what they designate when the phrase "takes place," without anything more. *This is the case* at instant $t + 1$ does not necessarily show the same referent as *This is the case* at instant t. In order to be assured, we have recourse to a name: *Rome is the case*. However, the rigid designator that the name is refers undoubtedly to a stable referent, but the referent of the nomination is in itself independent of the showing (Caesar's portrait is Caesar; a meter is a meter, regardless of the metal ruler) (Kripke, 1980: 54–57). We then throw ourselves back on the identity of the descriptions applicable to what is named. We say that *Rome is the case* at instant t and *Rome is the case* at instant $t + 1$ if in both cases *Rome* admits the same properties. But, to stick only to the sense, the referent at t and the referent at $t + 1$ can be identified only by means of a tautological proposition: xt is $P = xt+ 1$ is P. How can you know if it is the same x when different properties are attributed to it as in the phrases x is the *city which is the capital of Europe* and x is the *city where the Senate is seated* [*siège*] (or, to get out of descriptives: *City x must be laid to siege* [*assiéger*])? It can be known only if you presuppose an essence of x in Aristotle's sense or a notion of x in Leibniz's sense, where the definition contains the two predicates. This essence or this notion of x is stated: x is (P,Q). It presupposes in its turn that x designates the same referent, whether one attributes P or Q to it. This presupposition is tied to the naming of x. It is therefore not sense which can supply the identity of two referents, but the empty "rigidity" of the name. If the name can act as a linchpin between an ostensive phrase with its deictics and any given phrase with its sense or senses, it is because it is independent of the current showing and deprived of sense even though it has the twin capacity of designating and of being signified. But that it actually acts as a linchpin and endows its referent with a reality, that at least remains contingent. That is why reality is never certain (its probability is never equal to 1).

67. The reality of *this* (of what is shown by an ostensive phrase) is necessary, for example, for the validation of a cognitive phrase whose referent bears the same name as *this*. That reality is not a property attributable to the referent answering to the name. The ontological argument is false, and that seems to suffice to forbid one from following the speculative way, which requires an equivalence between sense and reality (Result Section). But neither is the reality of *this* a position (*Setzung*) of the referent, what corresponds in Kant to the presentation (*Dar-*

stellung) of a "given" to the receptive faculty (sensibility) in the forms of intuition. This presentation is not a pure "reception" of a given by a "subject" (Kant Notice 1). It is the family name of ostensive phrases: *This one there, That one a while ago* (just as prescription is the family name for phrases of command, of prayer, etc). It resorts to deictic operators. Reality cannot be deduced from sense alone, no more than it can from ostension alone. It does not suffice to conclude that the two are required together. It must be shown how the ostensive, *This is it*, and the descriptive, *It is the city which is the capital of the Empire*, are articulated into: *This is the city which is the capital of the Empire*. The name holds the position of linchpin. Rome is substituted for the deictic (*This is Rome*) and takes the place of the referent in the descriptive (*Rome is the city which is the capital of the Empire*). It can occupy other instances in phrases of a different regimen (*Rome, sole object of my discontent!**, I (Rome) declare you a heretic, etc.), phrases which can be substituted for the descriptive in our example. The name fills the function of linchpin because it is an empty and constant designator. Its quasi-deictic import is independent of the phrase in which it currently figures, and it can accept many semantic values because it excludes only those that are incompatible with its place in the network of names (*Rome* is not a date, Rome is in Italy, or in the State of Georgia, or New York, or Oregon, or Tennessee, but not in California, etc.).

68. Isn't the function so granted the name what Kant grants the schema (*KRV*, Analytic of the Judgment)? It too serves to articulate the sensible with the concept. —But, first, the schema operates exclusively in the framework of the validation of a cognitive, but not the name. Second, in critical reflection, the schema requires its deduction as an a priori necessary for cognition (in the Kantian sense). Here, I am doubtlessly deducing the function of names from the assertion of reality, but I cannot deduce their singularity: *Rome, Auschwitz, Hitler* . . . That I can only learn. To learn names is to situate them in relation to other names by means of phrases. Auschwitz is a city in southern Poland in the vicinity of which the Nazi camp administration installed an extermination camp in 1940. This is not a schema like a number. A system of names presents a world. The universes presented by the phrases that group names are signified fragments of that world. The learning of a name is done through other names to which senses are already attached and about which it is known how to show their referents through ostensive phrases. For example, I learn *white* (if it is true that color names are like proper names) (No. 61; Gorgias Notice) through *snow*, through *sheet*, through *paper*, along with their associated senses (to slide over, to sleep in, to write on) and their possible ostensions (*That there, that's snow*, etc.) whose validation refers yet again to names (*You know, as at Chamonix*). The same goes for Aristotle.

---

*Pierre Corneille, *Horace* IV, v, 1301. –tr.

69. How is sense attached to the name when the name is not determined by the sense nor the sense by the name? Is it possible to understand the linkage of name and sense without resorting to the idea of an experience? An experience can be described only by means of a phenomenological dialectic, as, for example, in the perceptive experience: this thing seen from this angle is white, seen from this other angle it is gray. The event is that while it was white a little while ago, now it is gray. It is certainly not white and gray at the same time and in the same respect, but it is so in succession at least. White and gray must be related together to the same referent, one as its current shade, the other as its currently possible shade. To the constitution of the referent's spatial existence (tridimensionality), there answers on the side of the perceiving instance the temporal synthesis of successive impressions. Thus, the "object" and the "subject" are formed together at the two poles of the perceptive field. — The only element to retain from this description is that it includes the possible in the constitution of reality. The thing one sees has a backside which is no longer or not yet seen and which might be seen. The phenomenologist says: similarly, vision does not take place along a line which puts the viewer and the viewed in contact, but within a field of visibility full of half-glimpsed lateralities. In order to see, one oscillates between the current or actual and the possible by repeated pulsations. Reality is not expressed therefore by a phrase like: *x is such*, but by one like: *x is such and not such* (Nos. 81, 83). To the assertion of reality, there corresponds a description inconsistent with regard to negation. This inconsistency characterizes the modality of the possible.

70. The ostensive phrase, that is, the showing of the case, is simultaneously an allusion to what is not the case. A witness, that is, the addressor of an ostensive phrase validating a description, attests (or thinks he or she is attesting) through this phrase to the reality of a given aspect of a thing. But he or she should by that very score recognize that other aspects which he or she cannot show are possible. He or she has not seen everything. If he or she claims to have seen everything, he or she is not credible. If he or she is credible, it is insofar as he or she has not seen everything, but has only seen a certain aspect. He or she is thus not absolutely credible. Which is why he or she falls beneath the blows of the dilemma (No. 8): either you were not there, and you cannot bear witness; or else you were there, you could not therefore have seen everything, and you cannot bear witness about everything. It is also upon this inconsistency with regard to negation that dialectical logic relies in regulating the idea of experience.

71. The idea of an experience presupposes that of an I which forms itself (*Bildung*) by gathering in the properties of things that come up (events) and which constitutes reality by effectuating their temporal synthesis. It is in relation to this I that events are phenomena. Phenomenology derives its name from this. But the idea of the I and that of experience which is associated with it are not necessary for the description of reality. They come from the subordination of the question of truth

to the doctrine of evidence. This doctrine was built up by Augustine and Descartes upon the ontological retreat (Heidegger) — I would prefer to call it the logical re-treat — which feeds the nihilism of a Gorgias (Gorgias Notice). But the neutraliza-tion of reality (the "neither Being nor Not-Being") leads Gorgias to the principle that "demonstrations say everything," which opens the way for the philosophy of argumentation and for the analysis of phrases. On the contrary, the monotheistic and monopolitical principle allows for the neutralization of reality, or at least the limitation of ostension by the rule of the possible, to be attributed to the finitude which befalls a witness deprived of the enjoyment or usage [*jouissance*] of every-thing. This *jouissance* is reserved for an absolute witness (God, Caesar). The idea of experience combines the relative and the absolute. Dialectical logic maintains the experience and the subject of the experience within the relative. Speculative logic endows them with the property of accumulation (*Resultat, Erinnerung*) and places them in a continuity with the final absolute (Hegel Notice).

72. The modern Cogito (Augustine, Descartes) is a phrase which presents its current addressor by means of the mark of the first person, and which concludes upon the existence of that addressor. The pronominal mark works like a deictic. *I* offers the same properties as *that*, neither more nor less. — Now a deictic does not by itself guarantee the validity of what it designates. The referent that is real is there, even when "it is not there" (Nos. 47, 48). It must transcend the universe of the current phrase. The deictic has no import outside the phrase universe that it currently designates. Thus, the *I* of *I think* and the *I* of *I am* require a synthesis. Descartes writes in effect: "This proposition, 'I am,' 'I exist,' whenever I utter it or conceive it in my mind, is necessarily true" (*Meditations*: II: § 3). But, from one 'whenever' to the next, there is no guarantee that I am the same. The synthesis of current evidences (ostensions) in turn requires, according to the principle of this philosophy, a current evidence which needs to be synthesized with the others (Hume, 1739, II: 251–63). A subject is thus not the unity of "his" or "her" ex-perience. The assertion of reality cannot spare itself the use of at least a name. It is through the name, an empty link, that *I* at instant *t* and *I* at instant *t* + 1 can be linked to each other and to *Here I am* (ostension). The possibility of reality, includ-ing the reality of the subject, is fixed in networks of names "before" reality shows itself and signifies itself in an experience.

73. It follows that reality does not result from an experience. This does not at all prevent it from being described from the standpoint of an experience. The rules to respect in undertaking this description are those of speculative logic (Hegel No-tice) and also those of a novelistic poetics (observing certain rules that determine narrative person and mode) (Genette, 1972: 161–62; 243–45). This description, though, has no philosophical value because it does not question its presuppositions (the I or the self, the rules of speculative logic). Now, these presuppositions are not necessary for the assertion that a referent is real. What is necessary for this

assertion is that the referent profits, so to speak, from the permanence of the name that names it (the rigidity of the named is the shadow projected by the rigidity of the designator, the name). What is equally necessary for this assertion, however, is a property that appears to contradict the former: a named referent is real when it is also the possible case (the object of an ostensive phrase) of an unknown sense (presented by a not yet current phrase). In the assertion of reality, the persistence of the referent (*It's really x*, it is recognized) is combined with the event of a sense (*Well! x is also this*, it is discovered).

74. It cannot be determined *a priori* which senses are appropriate to a real referent. There is "the case" of senses presented by phrases which have not yet taken place. Senses are attributed to Aristotle by means of descriptions (bearing names): *The philosopher born in Stagira, Plato's disciple, Alexander's tutor*. In nominative phrases, they are always substitutable for *Aristotle*. *That's Alexander's tutor* can be substituted for *That's Aristotle* without modifying its referential value (rigidity of nominative networks). It is not known in advance, though, how many such descriptions are appropriate, nor which ones they are. Every time a phrase (of a historian, of a philosopher, of a philologist) occurs in which *Aristotle* or one of his accepted equivalents is signified, a new expression turns out to be by that very fact substitutable for *Aristotle* or his equivalents under the same logical conditions. For example: "The thinker whose metaphysics Pierre Aubenque explains as lacking the status of a science." Now *this* description (with the name it includes) was not foreseeable. Conversely, it happens that a name is, by means of argumentation, connected back to phrases which were independent of it, in order to illustrate their sense. (For example, it may happen that a painter's vocation and his or her relation to colors are illustrated by the name *Oedipus* [Kaufmann, 1967].)

75. Is it possible that the number of senses attached to a named referent and presented by phrases substitutable for its name increases without limit? Try to count, while respecting the principle of substitutability, the phrases which are substitutable for names like *Moses, Homer, Pericles, Caesar. . . .* It cannot be proven that everything has been signified about a name (that "everything has been said about *x*") not only because no such totality can be proven, but because the name not being by itself a designator of reality (for that to occur a sense and an ostensible referent need to be associated with it), the inflation of senses that can be attached to it is not bounded by the "real" properties of its referent.

76. Certainly, the inflation of senses attached to a name is tempered by applying the logical rules analyzed by Frege (1892: 75–76). For, example, the phrase, *The emperor who had liver problems committed his own Guard to the battle* is not substitutable for *Napoleon committed his own Guard to the battle*, at least *salvo sensu*, because it connotes a relation (causal, concessive, etc.) between a state of health and a strategy which the other phrase disregards. (This does not mean that the first

phrase is senseless.) The inflation of sense can also be curbed by applying the rules for validating cognitive phrases. This is the principal function of the genre of discourse called historical inquiry with regard to names. If one wants to substitute *The emperor who had liver problems* for *Napoleon* without breaking the rules of the historical genre, which is narrative and cognitive, it needs to be assured that Napoleon did suffer from liver problems, that is, the proof that the referent is real must be able to be adduced under the general conditions for adducing proofs in history. The attracting of senses by names (which gives rise to mythemes, etc.) thus turns out to be subject to the regimen of cognitives, at least of those cognitives that bear upon noncurrent referents. This is what is called historical criticism. – Nevertheless, this temperament is of little consequence for two reasons. First of all, names are not the realities to which they refer, but empty designators which can only fulfill their current ostensive function if they are assigned a sense whose referent will be shown to be the case by an ostensive phrase. One does not prove something, one proves that a thing presents the signified property. Thus, historical cognition itself arouses a throng of senses (hypotheses, interpretations) in order to sift them out through the sieve that is the adducing of the proof.

77. The second reason that the inflation of sense attached to names cannot be absolutely halted (No. 76) is that phrases under the cognitive regimen, which undergo the sifting by truth conditions, do not have a monopoly on sense. They are "well formed." But poorly formed phrases are not absurd. With Stendhal's generation, Bonaparte's name was assigned a prescriptive value: *Be a popular hero of* virtù *like Bonaparte*. This value is to be counted among its senses although the phrase that presents it is not cognitive nor even descriptive. A phrase which attaches a life-ideal to a man's name and which turns that name into a *watchword* is a potentiality of instructions, an ethics and a strategy. This name is an Ideal of practical or political reason in the Kantian sense. This phrase presents what ought to be done, and simultaneously it presents the addressee who ought to do it. It does not arise from the true/false criterion since it is not descriptive, but from the just/unjust criterion because it is prescriptive. One may wonder whether it is just or not. But even if it were unjust, it is endowed with sense, just as a phrase is endowed with sense even if it is false (Wittgenstein, *TLP*: 2. 21, 2. 22, 2. 222). However, the sense pertinent for the criterion of justice and the sense pertinent for the criterion of truth are heterogeneous. Applying the rules for validating cognitives to senses which are not pertinent for the criterion of truth does not therefore allow for the attracting of these senses by names to be tempered. In the case of the young Bonapartist, the stakes placed in *Bonaparte* are aesthetic, ethical, and political, not cognitive.

78. Phrases obeying different regimens are untranslatable into one another. Consider arbitrarily merely the sense due to the form (syntax) of a phrase while disregarding the sense that proceeds from the lexicon. A translation from one lan-

guage into another presupposes that the sense presented by a phrase in the language of departure can be recovered by a phrase in the language of arrival. Now, the sense tied to syntactical form depends upon the regimen of phrases which the phrase obeys, and upon the genre of discourse in which it is inserted. This regimen and this genre determine a set of rules for the formation, linking and validation of the phrases that obey it. A translation presupposes therefore that a regimen and a genre in one language have their analogue in the other, or at least that the difference between two regimens and/or two genres in one language has its analogue in the other. It ought to be possible, for example, to recover in Chinese the connotation tied to the opposition in French between descriptives and narratives (*Il ouvre la porte / Il ouvrit la porte [He opens the door / He opened the door]*), at least if one is claiming to translate French into Chinese. Translation thus requires pertinences that are "transversal" to languages. Now, the constancy of these pertinences is assured directly or indirectly by the differences between phrase regimens and between genres of discourse. How then can phrases belonging to different regimens and/or genres (whether within the same language or between two languages) be translated from one into the other (No. 79)?

79. Of course, they cannot be translated in the proper sense of the word. But can't they be transcribed from one into the other? *You must come out* is a valid transcription of *Come out*. *That's a beautiful image* is a valid transcription of *What a beautiful image!* Is not the sense of obligation or of appraisal in the departing phrase conserved in each case by the arriving phrase? — The philosopher of logic can believe this because he or she is contented by identities of sense (definitions) (Wittgenstein, *TLP*: 3. 343), and he or she deems it negligible that the obligation is presented in one place as an invitation or even as a bit of information and elsewhere as an imperative command, or that the appraisal is formulated first as a constative, then as an exclamative. But whether child, diplomat, subordinate, or superior, the author of the image does not link up the same way with the original phrase as with its "transcription." For them, the analogy of "sense" between the two phrases is not only the analogy between the abstract concepts to which they can be reduced, but it should also extend to the universes which are presented by the two phrases and within which they are themselves situated. These universes are constituted by the way the instances (not only the sense, but also the referent, the addressor, and the addressee) are situated as well as by their interrelations. The addressor of an exclamative is not situated with regard to the sense in the same way as the addressor of a descriptive. The addressee of a command is not situated with regard to the addressor and to the referent in the same way as the addressee of an invitation or of a bit of information is (Nos. 80–83).

80. Phrases belonging to heterogeneous families can affect the referent of a single proper name by situating it upon different instances in the universes they present. A couple is about to break up. A third party (a judge or a witness) describes

the circumstances by saying: *x and y are about to break up. X's* phrase is an evaluative declaration: *I think it's better that we break up. Y's* phrase is a question full of pathos: *Then what have we been doing together for ten years?* Let us admit that the phrases attached to *x*'s name in these circumstances are cited in all three. If it is necessary to define *x* in these circumstances, is any of the three a better definition than the others? "Is" *x* more the addressor of a declaration, the addressee of an interrogative, or the referent of a description? All that can be said is that in the space of three independent phrases, his or her name consecutively occupies each of the three instances. And that this is what appropriately describes him or her under the circumstances. In saying this, though, one has recourse to a fourth phrase, which refers to the prior three and which arises from still another regimen (metalanguage). In this last phrase, *x*'s name occupies other situations (the three previous ones, but "encased") and is assigned another sense (it supplies the example of a referent whose senses are heterogeneous).

81. The referent of a proper name, *Bonaparte, Auschwitz,* is both strongly determined in terms of its location among the networks of names and of relations between names (worlds) (No. 60) and feebly determined in terms of its sense by dint of the large number and of the heterogeneity of phrase universes in which it can take place as an instance. This must not, however, allow for confusion between the object of history, which is the referent of a proper name, and the object of perception (No. 69). The latter is presented by ostensive phrases entailing deictics (*I* and *you, here* and *there, now* and *a little while ago*). By analyzing the universes of these phrases, the phenomenologist of perception elaborates the ideas of field and experience. The referent of a proper name (the object of history) is designated by a name which is a quasi-deictic and not a deictic. The name localizes the object within nominative networks without having to situate it in relation either to an *I* or to any deictic. The object of perception arises from a field (which is a loose complex of ostensives with deictics); the object of history arises from a world (which is a fairly stable complex of nominatives). It is when the object of history is further submitted to a procedure for validating a cognitive phrase (when it becomes an object of historical inquiry) that it also becomes the referent of ostensive phrases and thereby finds itself situated in a field by means of deictics. (*Look there it is, the proof I was looking for!*)

82. Reality: a swarm of senses lights upon a field pinpointed by a world. It is able to be signified, to be shown, and to be named, all three. The emphasis is sometimes put on one of these, sometimes on another. On the showing: *Well! There it is, the knife Elisa gave you* (thus in the order: shown, signified, named). Emphasis on the naming: *This one over here, that's Hector, the husband of Madame the President* (shown, named, signified). Emphasis on the sense: *Something for recording the voice? That's a mike, like this one here, I bought it in Brussels* (signified, shown, named).

83. The referent of an ostensive (object of perception) and the referent of a nominative (object of history) are utterly different (No. 81). They, nevertheless, have one trait in common. Phrases which are not the current phrase and which are currently unknown refer to them by assigning them senses other than the current sense (No. 69). Just as *This page is white* (seen from here) *and is not white* (seen from there, it is gray), so *Napoleon is a strategist* (in one network of names) *and is not a strategist* (in another, he is an emperor). The (perceptive) field and the (historical) world are both "hollowed out" by the negation which is entailed respectively (and differently) by the shown and the named. A "swarm" of possible senses, of indeterminate quantity and quality, inhabit this "hollow."

84. What does it mean for these senses to be possible? Isn't being possible the essential property of sense? Limiting ourselves to the logical sense of sense, we find that it is presented by well-formed expressions, by propositions. These occupy places in "logical space" (Wittgenstein, *TLP*:3. 4). A proposition's place is defined by the possibility of its truth. This is calculated by means of truth tables, which define all the possible relations between two elementary propositions. Wittgenstein, in setting up the truth tables, traces out this "logical space" (*TLP*: 5. 101). Its borders are tautology, on the one hand, and contradiction, on the other. The first one's truth and the second one's falsehood are necessary. *If p, then p, and if q, then q*, on the one hand, *p and not-p, and q and not-q*, on the other hand, "are the limiting cases – indeed the disintegration (*Auflösung*) – of the combination of signs" (*TLP*: 4. 466). They are expressions devoid of sense (*sinnlos*); they teach nothing, precisely because they are necessary. The expression *It rains or it doesn't rain*, makes nothing known about the weather we're having (*TLP*: 4. 461). They are propositions, though, they are not absurd (*unsinnig*), and they accordingly still belong to "logical space" (*TLP*: 4. 462; *TB*: 12. 11. 1914).

85. The logical genre of discourse is not the cognitive genre. The question of knowing whether a real referent satisfies the sense of a proposition does not arise from the former. The cognitive question is that of knowing whether the combination of signs with which it is dealing (the expression, which is one of the cases to which the truth conditions apply) makes it possible or not that real referents correspond to that expression. "The truth-conditions of a proposition determine the range that it leaves open (*Spielraum*) to the facts" (*TLP*: 4. 463). But these facts can neither confirm nor refute the proposition insofar as it is logical (*TLP*: 6. 1222), for it holds its possible truth only from its place in "logical space." Thus, the possible is the logical modality of sense. If a proposition is necessary, it has no sense. Whether or not it is true for a reality is not a question of logic. Sense (*Sinn*) and reference (*Bedeutung*) must always be distinguished (*TB*: 112). This distinction is difficult because the logical possibility (the sense) is presupposed in order to establish the reality of the corresponding referent. All that follows is that the cognitive regimen presupposes the logical regimen, not that they merge.

86. Logically speaking, *possible* adds nothing to *sense* (No. 83). If it is a question, though, of the possible senses of a named and shown referent, this possibility ceases to arise solely from "logical space," it includes the relation of this space to the referent of a phrase, or rather of two phrases (the nominative and the ostensive) which are not propositions. Neither the phrase that shows nor the phrase that names conforms to "logical form." They are not well-formed expressions. Coordinated together, they place a referent, so to speak, under the "lens" of the proposition. The possibility of sense thus signifies the possibility for the logically established sense to be validated by cases, that is, by a named and shown referent. It is this possibility that Wittgenstein treats (without always distinguishing it clearly from the logical possibility) when he wonders about the "the range that [a proposition] leaves open (*Spielraum*) to the facts." Prisoner (at the time of the *Tractatus*) of a general model of the proposition as *Bild* (picture), he metaphorizes the encounter of possible sense with reality as the exercise of a representational (essentially optical) constraint over what can be grasped from a world of extralinguistic facts. Tautology and contradiction are like the borders of the representational apparatus [*dispositif représentatif*]: "Tautologies and contradictions are not pictures of reality. They do not represent any possible situations (*Sachlage*). For the former admit *all* posssible situations, and the latter *none*" (*TLP*: 4. 462, 4. 463). The limits at which point the combination of signs (sense) disintegrates are also those that restrict the presentation of reality: the "shutter" is opened too far with tautology and closed too much with contradiction. Overexposed, logical space registers white; underexposed, it registers black. If we leave aside (as Wittgenstein later does) the metaphor of a photographic device that supplies pictures of states of things in the form of propositions, the following remains: under the cognitive regimen, the validation of a logical phrase by "reality" requires that one show *this*, which is a case of a referent corresponding to the sense (*Sinn*) presented by the phrase, and that one name *this* (thereby transforming it into a this).

87. In order for this double operation to be possible, it is not necessary to resort to the hypothesis of "simple objects" designated by names as if by feelers that touched them (No. 55; *TLP*: 2. 1515). This is not a hypothesis, since it is not falsifiable. It depends, in effect, upon the principle of an isomorphism between names and objects, of a "common form" for the disposition of objects in the world and for that of names in language (*TLP*: 2. 17, 2. 18, 3. 21). Now, this principle cannot be validated, since it is the principle that authorizes validations: "Propositions can represent the whole of reality, but they cannot represent what they must have in common with reality in order to be able to represent it − logical form" (*TLP*: 4. 12). "Propositions cannot represent logical form: it is mirrored in them. What finds its reflection in language, language cannot represent. Propositions show the logical form of reality [. . .] . What *can* be shown, *cannot* be said" (*TLP*: 4. 121, 4. 1212). − If this is the case, then we shouldn't talk about a logical form common

to language and reality. Which changes nothing as far as what is necessary for cognitively validating an expression endowed with sense, namely, an ostensive and a nominative. It is not a question of constructing a theory, but of describing (*PhU*: § 109) what is indispensable for a logically significant phrase to find its cognitive validation, and thus to become cognitively true. It suffices that something be shown and named (and thus can be shown as often as desired because it is fixed within nominal networks, which are independent of deictics) and that this something be accepted as a proof until there is further information, that is, until the cognitive it illustrates is refuted by a new argument or until a counter-example is adduced. In this way "what today counts as an observed concomitant (*Begleiterscheinung*) of a phenomenon will tomorrow be used to define it": such is "the fluctuation of scientific definitions" (*PhU*: § 79). In this way, what has definitional value today will be shelved tomorrow as accessory. This is troubling only for a thought which wants not only that concepts not be "blurred" (*PhU*: § 70ff.), but also that realities be articulated as concepts. A metaphysical requirement.

88. Reality is not a matter of the absolute eyewitness, but a matter of the future. The logician, for whom "nothing is accidental" requires that possible senses be preinscribed (*präjudiziert*) in the object; otherwise, this object, which is what it is (the theory of simples) (No. 55), could be affected after the fact (*nachträglich*) by some new sense, as if by chance. Taken from "logical space" and applied to the world of named realities, this requirement implies, for instance, that the predicate *passes the Rubicon* is preinscribed in the notion of Caesar (Leibniz, 1686: § XIII). Such a notion is a phrase whose addressor would be an absolute eyewitness, God. This principle is only valid—even in logic—if simple objects are admitted and if tautology is the ideal of truth (*TB*: 20. 11. 1914). But "simples" are empty referents answering to names. They are only "filled" (with reality) by descriptive phrases (at least under the cognitive regimen) and by ostensive phrases, whose combination with nominative phrases is always problematical. Under these conditions, the fact that new senses can be "attributed" to named referents does not constitute an enigma. The referent of the name *Caesar* is not a completely describable essence, even with Caesar dead (No. 74). Essentialism conceives the referent of the name as if it were the referent of a definition. The referent of a definition is only possible as such (*TLP*: 2. 011, 2. 012, 2. 0121). For it to become real, it is necessary to be able to name and show referents that do not falsify the accepted definition. The "object" is thus subjected to the test of reality, which is merely negative and which consists in a series of contradictory attempts (No. 90) to designate cases accessible to the operators of the test through the use of names. In the course of this test, no "simple" can hold up. The simples will be changed, if necessary.

89. What is absolutely required, on the contrary, is the contingency of the future. By this, not only the contingency of "events" should be understood but also the contingency of sense. It was possible in 1932 that Karol Wojtila would one day

be elected pope and that Neil Armstrong would one day walk on the moon. The two "events" were logically possible, since neither of them was absurd, like the phrase *The sum of the angles of a triangle is Wojtila*. In 1932, however, the respective senses of these "events" were not equally possible according to the cognitive regimen, that is, according to reality. At that time, there were means to certify (through nominatives and ostensives) all phrases relative to the predicate, *to be pope*, but not those to certify any phrase relative to the predicate, *to walk on the moon*. The latter belonged to the genre of narrative fictions that mix what is validatable with what is not. In 1982, it could be validated or invalidated in conformity with the rules for cognitives. By "possible sense" of a named and shown referent, we can then at least understand the following, with *p* being the phrase that expresses this sense: *P is possible if and only if it is now true or if it will be true that p* (Rescher, 1967: 33ff.). We can free the definition of the possible from its bearings on the deictic *now* and specify what is meant by truth: *There is a moment t which is contemporaneous or posterior to the moment taken as origin o, and at that moment t the sense presented by p is validated.* The possible is thus introduced into the order of the cognitive by the validation of the sense and by the dating (nomination) of the moment taken as origin. Contrariwise to the logician's warning, we are then no longer considering the "event," a word that itself presupposes what it is about (something new happens), but the ostensive phrase that shows the named case (Gardies, 1975; 85).

90. Negation is at the heart of testimony. We do not show the sense, we show something. That something is named, and we say: that at least *does not prohibit* the admission of the sense in question. "Validation" consists in showing cases of provisional nonfalsification. Reality is the referent of an ostensive phrase (and of a nominative one). This referent is cited (invoked, for example, in scientific debate) 1: as what refutes the sense contrary to the sense in question; 2: as what does not prohibit maintaining the latter until there is further information. The example presented to the tribunal of cognition does not, properly speaking, have any conclusive authority, it is permissive: "sometimes (at least this time that I am showing to you) it is not prohibited from thinking that . . ." There is no evidence, only a reprieve granted to scepticism. Not *It is certain that . . .* , but *It is not excluded that . . . .* By naming and by showing, one eliminates. Proof is negative, in the sense of being refutable. It is adduced in debate, which is agonistic or dialogical if there is a consensus over the procedures for its being adduced. If the ostensive and the nominative suffice, however, to exclude, for instance, that Charlemagne was a philosopher, it follows only that he was a nonphilosopher. And this is not to say what he was. To refute phrase *p* allows *non-p* to be affirmed, but *non-p* is undetermined. *Nonphilosopher* is not *emperor*. The latter predicate is conserved only as a possibility. Reality is invoked by ostension and nomination as the prohibition to deny a sense. It allows for all the contrary senses to be placed in the position

of possibilities. Among these, the greater probability of one of them will be proved by refuting the others and this by means of new ostensions and nominations. Thus the "hollow" (the shadow Wittgenstein talks about) (*TB*: 9. 11. 1914, 15. 11. 1914) entailed by the named and shown referent is also the possibility of the senses entailed by reality. And as this possibility is a modality axed on the future, this "hollow" is also time considered as the condition of modalizations.

91. By imagining a proposition as a "body" that occupies a "place" in "logical space," and the negation of this proposition as the "shadow" projected by this "body" onto this "space" (*TB*: 9, 15, and 23. 11. 1914, 9. 6. 1915), Wittgenstein transfers into the logical order the "hollow," which, in the (sensible) field, envelops the referents of ostensives. He thus admits the analogy between logical negation and "perceptive" negation. And as he understands the latter on the model of the experience of the sensible by a subject (an eye) (*TLP*: 5. 6 ff.), he half-opens the door of logic onto phenomenology (Tsimbidaros). Now, phenomenology is what, uncontrolled, and with the pretext of the "description of experience," will command his later research. An I will be presumed to make "use" of language, to "play" it with "another" or "others." This is a success for anthropomorphism, a defeat for thought (No. 188). It is necessary, on the contrary, to transfer into ordinary language the principle clearly formulated by Wittgenstein himself for logical language: what is required to understand the latter is not the experience that something behaves like this or like that, but the presupposition that something *is*. "That, however, is not an experience." The logic of ordinary language, like logic, is "prior to every experience." It is "prior to the question 'How?', not prior to the question 'What?' " (*TLP*: 5. 552). A sensible field, a historical world must be described without recourse to experience. The uncertainty of the future must be understood as a "logician" would (and this is not to engage in a "logic of time"). The negation implied in the modality of the possible that reality entails must be understood without metaphorizing it into the experience of a subject, but rather as a linking of phrases. The addressor must be understood as a situated instance in a phrase universe, on a par with the referent, the addressee, and the sense. "We" do not employ language (*PhU*: § 569). Moreover, when it is a question of reality, it must be understood that reality is not only at play in cognitive phrases linked up with nominatives and ostensives. Reality plays itself out in the three families that have just been named, but also in all the other families of phrases (which are nonetheless untranslatable into the first three as well as into one other).

92. Reality entails the differend. *That's Stalin, here he is.* We acknowledge it. But as for what *Stalin* means? Phrases come to be attached to this name, which not only describe different senses for it (this can still be debated in dialogue), and not only place the name on different instances, but which also obey heterogeneous regimens and/or genres. This heterogeneity, for lack of a common idiom, makes

consensus impossible. The assignment of a definition to Stalin necessarily does wrong to the nondefinitional phrases relating to Stalin, which this definition, for a while at least, disregards or betrays. In and around names, vengeance is on the prowl. Forever?

93. "It's not for nothing that Auschwitz is called the 'extermination camp'."(Kremer in Vidal-Naquet, 1981: 85). Millions of human beings were exterminated there. Many of the means to prove the crime or its quantity were also exterminated. And even the authority of the tribunal that was supposed to establish the crime and its quantity was exterminated, because the constitution of the Nuremburg tribunal required an Allied victory in the Second World War, and since this war was a kind of civil war (Descombes, 1981b: 741; Declaration of 1789 Notice, § 5) resulting from a lack of consensus over legitimacy in international relations, the criminal was able to see in his judge merely a criminal more fortunate than he in the conflict of arms. The differend attached to Nazi names, to *Hitler*, to *Auschwitz*, to *Eichmann*, could not be transformed into a litigation and regulated by a verdict. The shades of those to whom had been refused not only life but also the expression of the wrong done them by the Final Solution continue to wander in their indeterminacy. By forming the State of Israel, the survivors transformed the wrong into damages and the differend into a litigation. By beginning to speak in the common idiom of public international law and of authorized politics, they put an end to the silence to which they had been condemned. But the reality of the wrong suffered at Auschwitz before the foundation of this state remained and remains to be established, and it cannot be established because it is in the nature of a wrong not to be established by consensus (Nos. 7, 9). What could be established by historical inquiry would be the quantity of the crime. But the documents necessary for the validation were themselves destroyed in quantity. That at least can be established. The result is that one cannot adduce the numerical proof of the massacre and that a historian pleading for the trial's revision will be able to object at great length that the crime has not been established in its quantity. — But the silence imposed on knowledge does not impose the silence of forgetting, it imposes a feeling (No. 22). Suppose that an earthquake destroys not only lives, buildings, and objects but also the instruments used to measure earthquakes directly and indirectly. The impossibility of quantitatively measuring it does not prohibit, but rather inspires in the minds of the survivors the idea of a very great seismic force. The scholar claims to know nothing about it, but the common person has a complex feeling, the one aroused by the negative presentation of the indeterminate. *Mutatis mutandis*, the silence that the crime of Auschwitz imposes upon the historian is a sign for the common person. Signs (Kant Notices 3 and 4) are not referents to which are attached significations validatable under the cognitive regimen, they indicate that something which should be able to be put into phrases cannot be phrased

in the accepted idioms (No. 23). That, in a phrase universe, the referent be situated as a sign has as a corollary that in this same universe the addressee is situated like someone who is affected, and that the sense is situated like an unresolved problem, an enigma perhaps, a mystery, or a paradox. — This feeling does not arise from an experience felt by a subject. It can, moreover, not be felt. In any case, how can it be established that it is or is not felt? One comes up against the difficulties raised by idiolects (Nos. 144, 145). The silence that surrounds the phrase, *Auschwitz was the extermination camp* is not a state of the mind [*état d'âme*], it is the sign that something remains to be phrased which is not, something which is not determined. This sign affects a linking of phrases. The indetermination of meanings left in abeyance [*en souffrance*], the extermination of what would allow them to be determined, the shadow of negation hollowing out reality to the point of making it dissipate, in a word, the wrong done to the victims that condemns them to silence — it is this, and not a state of mind, which calls upon unknown phrases to link onto the name of Auschwitz. — The "revisionist" historians understand as applicable to this name only the cognitive rules for the establishment of historical reality and for the validation of its sense. If justice consisted solely in respecting these rules, and if history gave rise only to historical inquiry, they could not be accused of a denial of justice. In fact, they administer a justice in conformity with the rules and exert a positively instituted right. Having placed themselves, moreover, in the position of plaintiffs, who need not establish anything (Nos. 10, 11), they plead for the negative, they reject proofs, and that is certainly their right as the defense. But that they are not worried by the scope of the very silence they use as an argument in their plea, by this does one recognize a wrong done to the sign that is this silence and to the phrases it invokes. They will say that history is not made of feelings, and that it is necessary to establish the facts. But, with Auschwitz, something new has happened in history (which can only be a sign and not a fact), which is that the facts, the testimonies which bore the traces of *here*'s and *now*'s, the documents which indicated the sense or senses of the facts, and the names, finally the possibility of various kinds of phrases whose conjunction makes reality, all this has been destroyed as much as possible. Is it up to the historian to take into account not only the damages, but also the wrong? Not only the reality, but also the meta-reality that is the destruction of reality? Not only the testimony, but also what is left of the testimony when it is destroyed (by dilemma), namely, the feeling? Not only the litigation, but also the differend? Yes, of course, if it is true that there would be no history without a differend, that a differend is born from a wrong and is signaled by a silence, that the silence indicates that phrases are in abeyance of their becoming event [*en souffrance de leur événement*], that the feeling is the suffering of this abeyance [*cette souffrance*]. But then, the historian must break with the monopoly over history granted to the cognitive regimen of phrases, and he or she must venture forth by lending his or her ear to what is not presentable under the rules of knowledge. Every reality entails this exigency insofar as it entails possible unknown senses. Auschwitz is the most real of realities in this respect. Its name marks the confines wherein historical knowledge sees its competence impugned. It does not follow from that that one falls into non-sense. The alternative is not: either the signification that learning [*science*] establishes, or absurdity, be it of the mystical kind (White, 1982; Fackenheim, 1970).

Presentation

94. It is not the thinking or the reflective I that withstands the test of universal doubt (Apel, 1981), it is time and the phrase. It does not result from the phrase, *I doubt*, that I am, merely that there has been a phrase. Another phrase (the one we just read: *There has been a phrase*) has linked onto the first one by presenting itself as what follows it. And a third one, the one we just read,/*There has been a phrase / follows / I doubt /*, has linked onto the first two by presenting their linkage in the form of a temporally ordered series (*There has been . . . , follows . . .*).

95. *I doubt* is not a first phrase, no more than *I think* or *Es denkt* or *Cogitatur* or *Phrazetai*. There are two reasons for this. First reason: *I doubt* presupposes *I* and *doubt* or *I* and *think*, and so on. And each of these "terms" presupposes in turn other phrases: definitions, examples of "usage." It presupposes language, which would be the totality of phrases possible in a language. Like all totalities, language is the referent of a descriptive phrase, a referent whose reality cannot be established for want of an ostensive phrase (the phrase descriptive of the whole is a phrase of the Idea, in the Kantian sense). One can, in fact, describe, *Language is this and that*, but not show, *And this is language*. The totality is not presentable. Second reason: to verify that *I doubt* or any other phrase presumed to be the first in position is in fact there, one must at least presuppose the ordinal series of events, from which the predicate *first* derives its sense. Now, this series itself results, as Wittgenstein explains about propositions, from a "general form of passage [*Uebergang*] from one proposition to another" (*TLP*: 6. 01). This form is

59

an operation by means of which the series of whole numbers takes place (*TLP*: 6. 02). This operation must always be able to be applied to its result. Now, with this always, which connotes the principle of the recursivity of the application of the operation to its result, it is succession itself which is already presupposed. Such is the operator of the series: *And so on* (*TLP*: 5. 2523). So, the affirmation that a phrase is first presupposes the temporal series of phrases of which this phrase presents itself as the first.

96. It should be added that the phrase *I doubt* presupposes not only language and the serial operator (succession) but also a prior phrase onto which it links by transforming the regimen according to which the prior phrase presented its universe. The "same" universe that had been asserted is now problematical. Apart from this presupposed prior phrase, there is understood [*on sous-entend*](Ducrot, 1977: 33–43) a question which is applied to it: *What is not doubtful?*

97. But the phrase that formulates the general form for operating the passage from one phrase to the next can be presupposed as an *a priori* for the formation of the series. It nonetheless still takes place after the phrase that formulates the passage. This at least is the case for No. 94, where the phrase which formulates the form of the passage from the first to the second phrase, which formulates the series under the circumstances, comes in third position. Shouldn't we distinguish between a logical or transcendental priority and a chronological priority? –One always can and undoubtedly always must if what is at stake is that the passage from one phrase to the other be effectuated under the logical or cognitive regimen (especially that of implication). One rule of this regimen is then to disregard the fact that *a priori* propositions or definitions and axioms are themselves presented by phrases in ordinary language which are chronologically prior to them. One rule is to disregard even the chronologism–be it a meta-chronologism–that remains unexamined in the idea of logical priority (for example, in the operator *if, then*). As opposed to the logician or the theoretical linguist, the philosopher has as his or her rule not to turn away from the fact that the phrase formulating the general form for operating the passage from one phrase to the next is itself subject to this form of operating the passage. In Kantian terms, the synthesis of the series is also an element belonging to the series (*KRV*, Critical Solution of the Cosmological Conflict: 444). In Protagorean terms, the debate over the series of debates is part of this series (Protagoras Notice). In Wittgensteinian terms, "the world is the totality of facts," "a picture is a fact," and "logical pictures can depict the world (*die Welt abbilden*)" (*TLP*: 1. 1, 2. 141, 2. 19). (But a phrase should not be called a "picture." Wittgenstein later renounces this) (No. 133).

98. Philosophical discourse has as its rule to discover its rule: its *a priori* is what it has at stake. It is a matter of formulating this rule, which can only be done at the end, if there is an end. Time can therefore not be excluded from this dis-

course without it ceasing to be philosophical. On the other hand, time is in principle excluded from logical discourse. Kant asks that the clause *at one and the same time* be excluded from the statement of the principle of contradiction. The validity of the principle of contradiction is not subordinate to a condition of the possibility of experience, since this principle extends to every possible (intelligible) object, whether given or not (*KRV*, Highest Principle of all Analytic Judgments: 191). Heidegger, on the contrary, observes that the clause should be maintained because, according to him, the issue is not that of an identity of an object (an existent) in time (its intratemporal identity), but of the very possibility of the identification of an object. Whatever the latter might be, its identification as an object requires a synthesis of pure recognition (Heidegger, 1929: §§ 33c, 34). This assures that it is one and the same object which was and will be in question. Heidegger thus situates the principle of contradiction in a transcendental, and not in a formal, logic. The problem for the former is the constitution of an object identical to itself across different views (he writes, "aspects") at different nows. That is why Heidegger identifies primordial time with the faculty of having ideas in general, the transcendental (productive) imagination or faculty of presentation (*Darstellung*). But is it possible to admit faculties, when the idea of faculties presupposes a subject whose organs they are?

Kant 1

Metaphysical illusion consists in treating a presentation like a situation (Nos. 115, 117). The philosophy of the subject lends itself to this.

The idea of a given (an immediate given) is a way of receiving and censuring the idea of a presentation. A presentation does not present a universe to someone; it is the event of its (inapprehensible) presence. A given is given to a subject, who receives it and deals with it. To deal with it is to situate it, to place it in a phrase universe. We can follow this operation at the beginning of the Transcendental Aesthetic (*KRV*, B: § 1).

Intuition is the immediate relation of cognition to objects. This relation only takes place when objects are given "to us." This immediate giving, in turn, only takes place "in so far as the mind is affected in a certain way" by the object. And this certain way is sensation. No object is given to the mind except through sensation. It is necessary then, in the logic of the philosophy of the subject, to presuppose in the latter a "capacity for receiving representations" (or receptivity), which is a capacity for being affected by objects by means of sensibility.

An addressee instance is thus put into place in the universe presented by the quasi-phrase that the sensible given is. Put into place in the heart of the subject of knowledge which, as understanding, judgment, and reason, is otherwise presented by the Kantian phrase as a categorial, schematic, and ideal activity. Through activity, the subject situates itself upon the addressor instance of sense.

But, activity is already exerted on the level of the Aesthetic in the forms of intuition. Sensation supplies only the matter of the phenomenon, which gives but the diverse or the singular because it is merely affection, the impression (*Wirkung*) of the object upon the representative faculty. There is no hope of universality by sensation alone. Never talk about tastes or colors. Sticking to this, we would never even have givens properly termed, but only momentary impressions, affects, unrelated to objects. Simple states of *Gemüth* [the heart], idiolects. A threatening empiricism, as is always the case with receptivity (femininity?).

In fact, to examine the Kantian text, the constitution of the given by sensibility requires not one phrase (or quasi-phrase) but two. There is also an active "subject" in sensibility, this time situated as addressor. The activity of this subject imprints the forms of space and time, which are not givens, upon the sensations. In submitting to spatio-temporal filtering, matter in turn receives a sense which it could not produce and which turns it into a phenomenon. Matter receives the forms of space and time from an addressing instance, the active subject of sensibility.

The first two pages of the Transcendental Aesthetic can thus be broken down into two moments, each of which is structured like a phrase universe. First moment: an unknown addressor speaks matter (as we say, to speak French) to an addressee receptive to this idiom, and who therefore understands it, at least in the sense by which he or she is affected by it. What does the matter-phrase talk about, what is its referent? It does not yet have one, it is a sentimental phrase, the referential function is minor in it. What is important is its conative function, as Jakobson would have said. The matter-phrase relates only to the addressee, the receptive subject.

Second Moment: this subject passes into the situation of addressing instance and addresses the phrase of space-time, the form phrase, to the unknown addressor of the first phrase, who thereby becomes an addressee. This phrase, as opposed to the matter phrase, is endowed with a referential function. Its referent is called the phenomenon. As Kant writes, sensible impressions are "related to objects" called phenomena. The referential function which then appears results from the capacity the subject has–which is an active capacity–to show the moment and the place of whatever it is that by its matter produces the effect (*Wirkung*) or sensible impression upon the addressee of the first phrase. This is what we call the ostensive capacity: *It's over there, It was a little while ago.* This second phrase, which applies deictic markers onto the impressions procured by sensation, is called in the Kantian lexicon, intuition.

The "immediacy" of the given, as we see, is not immediate. On the contrary, the constitution of the given requires an exchange of roles between addressor and addressee instances, and thus requires two phrases or quasi-phrases: respectively, the one where impression occurs and the one where the putting into (spatio-temporal) form occurs. This permutation involves two partners who alternate between addressor and addressee. Through this dialogical or dialectical linking, a referent is constituted, the phenomenon.

The "first" addressor, however, the one who affects the subject through sensation, remains unknown to the latter. This signifies that the matter idiom, if it is understood, is not comprehended by the subject in the sense that the subject does not–and according to Kant will never–know what the impression that it felt in the phrase of the first (or noumenal) addressor refers to. In order to endow the matter phrase with an "objective" referential value, a supplement needs to be brought in by means of a second quasi-phrase, the form phrase, which picks up the first phrase and returns it to its former addressor. This second phrase speaks the idiom of space-time. Does the first addressor, now an addressee, in turn understand the language of the forms of intuition which the subject speaks to it? Do space and time have a validity in themselves? The subject will never know anything about this either, which is why the object its quasi-phrase institutes on the referent instance is definitively a phenomenon, whose reality value will remain, if not forever suspect, at least forever suspended in operations of validation (*Analytic of Concepts and of Judgments*). If there were an "intellectual intuition," as Kant writes, there would be no need for the entire edifice of the *Critique*. The subject would know the language of the first addressor and would comprehend immediately (or at least through the mediation of a single phrase uttered in a language known to both interlocutors) the referential value of the first phrase.

Whence there follow several implications. First of all, there is a differend between the first addressor and the subject. The subject knows its idiom, space-time, and can only accord referential value to a phrase uttered in this idiom. But it knows, *qua* addressee affected by sensation, *qua* receptivity, that something, some sense, on the side of the other seeks to phrase itself and does not succeed in phrasing itself in the idiom of space-time. This is why sensation is a mode of feeling, that is, a phrase awaiting its expression, a silence touched with emotion. This expectant wait is never gratified, the phrase that does take place is uttered in the language of space-time forms, which the subject "speaks" without knowing if it is the language of the other. This differend is on the scale of the loss of the concept of nature. This concept is able to be accepted in the second part of the *Critique of Judgement*, but only as an Idea, without there being any example, any ostensible case, which can be shown in order to give a proof drawn from experience that the other (the in-itself [*l'en-soi*]) "phrases" the signs it makes to the subject in the (teleological) idiom of the subject. It is not forbidden to presume it, but it is not permitted to have knowledge about it, except by falling into a transcendental illusion.

Nevertheless, the differend with the *en-soi* does not go as far — so the analysis of the phrases from the Transcendental Aesthetic shows us — as to take its non-sense into account. What is taken into account is its silence, but its silence as a phrase that impresses and affects, thus already as a sign. The break with empiricism has not taken place to the extent that empiricism embraces the principle that the subject is primarily an addressee. The break does take place in the doubling of the phrase constitutive of the object: the putting of matter into spatio-temporal form, which gives forth phenomena, owes nothing in Kant (as opposed to Hume) to the first addressor. The associating of impressions by habit or contiguity presupposes rules of ordination which are not given, and therefore which do not belong to the idiom of the first addressor. By superimposing the form phrase, that of the active subject, the addressor, onto the matter phrase, in whose universe the subject is addressee, transcendental idealism comes to cover over empirical realism. It does not suppress it. There is a first phrase, and it does not come from the subject. That is why the covering over remains unstable.

In the third place, examining the apparatus of the Transcendental Aesthetic leads to, at least, a reconsideration of the notion of presentation in Kant, the *Darstellung*. In the theoretical realm, the presentation of an object (already constituted at the level of the Aesthetic) is required for the validation of a determinant judgment, that is, of a knowledge phrase. This presentation is what distinguishes the cognitive from the theoretical in general, which includes Ideas, whose presentation is impossible. Whether intuition is joined *a priori* to the concept (which is thereby declared to be *constructed*) or whether it is conjoined by means of experience as simply an *example* for the concept, "the act of adding intuition to the concept is called the *Darstellung* (*exhibitio*) of the object, without which (whether it happens mediately or immediately) there can be no knowledge" (1791: Supplements I, Second Section). Presentation is thus not a simple ostension, but the bridging of intuition with conception.

Despite the name it bears, the Kantian *Darstellung* is not at all the presentation of a phrase universe. It is the conjunction of two phrases from different regimens. The conjunction, for example, of an ostensive with a cognitive, a conjunction required by the regimen of knowledge: something is signified about a referent, and an example is shown which "verifies" this sense. It is the "business of the faculty of judgment" to effectuate the *exhibitio* "in setting a corresponding intuition beside the concept" (*KUK*, Introduction VIII). More generally, presentation supposes a capacity for finding the example or the case which fits a rule, and for finding it without a rule (1798a: § 44).

This capacity to judge in a nondeterminant fashion is exerted outside the realm of cognition: in morality, where just action needs to be determined with no instruction other than the moral law, which ought to leave that action undetermined; or in the aesthetic feeling, which declares an object to be beautiful or sublime on the basis of the pleasure that results from the harmonious or impossible relationship between the faculty of conceiving and the faculty of having objects. (Still, it would be necessary in this matter to account for a hesitation in the Kantian lexicon: the faculty of having objects, the imagination, is also called the "faculty of presentation") (*KUK*: § 17, 23).

Darstellung is, in general, an adjoining, a conjoining, a setting side by side, a comparison, between an established or an unknown rule and an intuition (or whatever takes the place of intuition) (Kant Notice 3). The subject presents an object before a rule, determined or not, with a view to validating this rule, or discovering it, or evaluating the object. The presentation does not come from anywhere other than the subject, it is the confrontation of the subject's works with other works by the subject, except that their joining together, whether regulated or not, takes place between heterogeneous faculties, that is, between phrases subject to different regimens or genres.

Now, this passage apparatus has already occurred in the Transcendental Aesthetic: the faculty of receiving sensible impressions is "bridged" with the faculty of coordinating and of objectifying them through the forms of space and time. In this regard, the redoubling or doubling that already affects sensibility indicates that the subject cannot have presentations, but only representations, not in the theatrical sense where a representation comes in the place of an absent object, but rather in the juridical sense where the "faculties" keep making representations, remonstrances, or grievances to each other, that is, to criticize each other through the confrontation of their respective objects. They thereby alternate relative to each other between the positions of addressor and addressee. Sensation would be no more than an intransmissible idiolect if it did not suffer the remonstrances of pure intuition. The latter would remain a punctual, ostensive phrase were it not subject to the exigencies of the imagination and of the concept, and these faculties in turn would be without any creative or cognitive import if they did not allow for the remonstrances of sensibility, and so forth.

The subject is therefore neither active nor passive, it is both; but it is only one or the other insofar as, caught in one regimen of phrases, it pits against itself a phrase from another regimen, and seeks, if not their reconciliation, then at least the rules for their conflict, namely, the subject's forever threatened unity. The only exception appears to be sensation, where through matter something seems to affect the "subject" that does not derive from it. We have also seen, however, that this something is situated right away as an instance in the dialectic of phrase universes, and treated as a first addressor and as a second addressee, so that its "giving" is transformed into a moment of exchange.

With Kant, a *Darstellung* is not a presentation, it is a situating (Nos. 114, 115, 116). The repression of presentation by representation (situation) is permitted and encouraged by the doctrine of the faculties, and finally by the metaphysics of the "subject." Cases are not events, but summons to appear. The question of the *There is*, momentarily evoked on the occasion of the sensible given, is quickly forgotten for the question of what there is.

99. What escapes doubt is that there is at least one phrase, no matter what it is. This cannot be denied without verifying it *ideo facto*. *There is no phrase* is a phrase, *I lie* is a phrase, even if it is not a well-formed expression (Koyré, 1947; Wittgenstein, *Zettel*: §§ 691, 692). *What do I know?* is a phrase. *The phrase currently phrased as a phrase does not exist* is a phrase (Burnyeat,1976; Salanskis, 1977). The phrase considered as occurrence escapes the logical paradoxes that self-referential propositions give rise to. These paradoxes reveal themselves when we apply to them the regimen to which well-formed expressions are subject, in particular the rule of consistency with regard to negation (or the principle of contradiction). This regimen forbids that a propositional function can be its own argument (*TLP*: 3. 332, 3. 333). But phrases are not propositions. Propositions are phrases under the logical regimen and the cognitive regimen. Their formation and linking are subject to the stakes of speaking true. The logically true proposition is devoid of sense (*sinnlos*) (*TLP*: 4. 461, 6. 1, 6. 11, 6. 113); the cognitively true proposition is endowed with sense (subjected to the rule of ostension by a *This is the case*). But the self-referentiality of a negative phrase prohibits a decision concerning its truth or falsehood (Russell, 1959: 74–85); and the self-referentiality of an affirmative phrase allows any statement to be demonstrated (Curry in Schneider). But phrases can obey regimens other than the logical and the cognitive. They can have stakes other than the true. What prohibits a phrase from being a proposition does not prohibit it from being a phrase. That there are propositions presupposes that there are phrases. When we are surprised that there is something rather than nothing, we are surprised that there is a phrase or that there are phrases rather than no phrases. And we are right. Logic "is prior to the question 'How?', not prior to the question 'What?' " (*TLP*: 5. 552). A phrase is a 'what'.

100. The phrase that expresses the passage operator employs the conjunction *and* (*and so forth, and so on*). This term signals a simple addition, the apposition of one term with the other, nothing more. Auerbach (1946: ch. 2 and 3) turns this into a characteristic of "modern" style, paratax, as opposed to classical syn-

tax. Conjoined by *and*, phrases or events follow each other, but their succession does not obey a categorial order (*because; if, then; in order to; although* . . .). Joined to the preceding one by *and*, a phrase arises out of nothingness to link up with it. Paratax thus connotes the abyss of Not-Being which opens between phrases, it stresses the surprise that something begins when what is said is said. *And* is the conjunction that most allows the constitutive discontinuity (or oblivion) of time to threaten, while defying it through its equally constitutive continuity (or retention). This is also what is signaled by the *At least one phrase* (No. 99). Instead of *and*, and assuring the same paratactic function, there can be a comma, or nothing.

101. "The phrase survives the test of universal doubt." But what in the phrase? Its reality, its sense? And is *the* phrase this "current" one or phrases in general? I note that *reality, sense, current, in general* are instances or quantities which are taken as referents in the phrase universes that constitute these questions. One phrase calls forth another, whichever it may be. It is this, the passage, time, and the phrase (the time in the phrase, the phrase in time) that survives the test of doubt. Neither the sense of a phrase nor its reality are indubitable. Its sense, because it is suspended to a link with another phrase which will explain it. Its reality, because its assertion is subject to the rules for establishing reality which entail the test of doubt (Referent Section). But for there to be no phrase, that is impossible.

102. For there to be no phrase is impossible, for there to be *And a phrase* is necessary. It is necessary to make linkage. This is not an obligation, a *Sollen* [an ought to], but a necessity, a *Müssen* [a must]. To link is necessary, but how to link is not (No. 135).

103. The necessity of there being *And a phrase* is not logical (the question '*How?*') but ontological (the question '*What?*'). It is nonetheless not founded upon any evidence (Apel). Evidence requires that a witness-subject independent of the linking of phrases be able to certify that this linking always takes place. The aporia is a triple one: 1° the object's evidence to a witness (namely, the ostensive phrase whose addressor he or she would be: *This is the case*) does not suffice to establish that object's reality (Nos. 61–64); 2° the idea of an "absolute witness for a reality" is inconsistent (No. 70); and 3° *And a phrase* is not an object for which one can bear witness, it is a presupposition for "objects," for their "witnesses" and so on.

104. By *A phrase*, I understand the phrase which is the case, *der Fall*, the phrase *token*, the phrase event. A phrase-type is the referent of a phrase-event. For a phrase to survive the test of universal doubt stems neither from its being real nor from its being true (No. 101), but from its being merely what happens, *what is occurring, ce qui arrive, das Fallende.* You cannot doubt that something

happens when you doubt: it happens that you doubt. If *It happens that you doubt* is a different phrase than *You doubt*, then another phrase is happening. And if it is found that it is not happening, but that it has happened, then it happens that this is found. It is always too late to doubt the 'what'. The question already has its answer: another question.

Gertrude Stein

"A sentence is not emotional a paragraph is" (Stein, 1931). (Because the feeling or the sentiment is the linkage, the passage. Does this happen to fall, or what? Or nothing, but nothing would be too much: A phrase, and *and*.) "If two sentences make a paragraph a little piece is alright because they are better apart." "A paragraph such as silly." "When it is there it is out there. This is a sentiment not a sentence. // Now that is something not to think but to link." "I am very miserable about sentences. I can cry about sentences but not about hair cloth." "It is very hard to save the sentence." "This is so light it is an emotion and so a paragraph. Yes so a paragraph." "Sentences make one sigh." "I would use a sentence if I could." "A sentence is saved not any sentence no not any sentence at all not yet." (When *A phrase* is saved, it will be *And a phrase* that is saved, and it might be that it is gained then.) "Never ask any one what a sentence is or what it has been." "We feel that if we say we we will go. // This is a simple meaning. A sentence that is simple in a cross with a meaning. // A sentence says you know what I mean." "You can see that a sentence has no mystery. A mystery would be a reception. They receive nothing." "Who knows how many have been careful. Sentences are made wonderfully one at a time. Who makes them. Nobody can make them because nobody can what ever they do see." "All this makes sentences so clear I know how I like them. // What is a sentence mostly what is a sentence. With them a sentence is with us about us all about us we will be willing with what a sentence is. A sentence is that they cannot be carefully there is a doubt about it." "The great question is can you think a sentence. What is a sentence. He thought a sentence. Who calls him to come when he did."

No comments. The selection done for the purposes of quoting is already outrageous. Another remark or two.

One. In French, the *paragraph* is a division (and/or its sign) within something written. It separates what it unites. The Greek word signifies what is written on the side. *Paragramma* is an extra clause in a law or a contract. *Paragraphè:* an objection made by the defense to the acceptability of a plea. *Paragraphein:* to add a clause, especially fraudulently (Liddell-Scott).

Two. To paragraph is to write *And, And moreover, And nevertheless* . . . The differend is reintroduced into the heart of what ought to regulate the litigation, in-between the law and the accused.

Three. "It is out there. This is a sentiment. That is something not to think but to link." The linking is subject to doubt, silly, not thought out, without a rule.

Four. A phrase is not mysterious, it is clear. It says what it means to say. No "subject" receives it, in order to interpret it. Just as no "subject" makes it (in order to say something). It calls forth its addressor and addressee, and they come take their places in its universe.

Five. "One at a time, wonderfully." The wonder is the time, the occurrence. Latin *vice*,

English *weak*, German *weichen*, *Wechsel* (?). A phrase is the event, something rather than nothing, and something that gives up its place: weakness. In "Saving the Sentence" (1931): "A sentence has wishes as an event." Its wishes: to give up its place to another, *invice*.

Six. To save the phrase: extract it from the discourses in which it is subjugated and restrained by rules for linking, enveloped in their gangue, seduced by their end. Let it be. The way Cage writes for sounds. In "Sentences and Paragraphs" (*Ibid.*): "Nothing is noisy." As in *Silence.*

Seven. The outrage of selecting phrases from Gertrude Stein's text: "I" utilize them, make them serve an argument, a discourse that subjugates phrases, that fills the abysses in "my" text, separates and unites them from afar. In Stein's text, a phrase is one time, an event, it happens. The anxiety that this will not start up again, that Being will come to a halt, distends the paragraphs.

Eight. "Feminine writing": inscribe that this cannot be filled in, from one sentence to the next? Would it be a genre?

Nine. These are ordinary phrases as well as phrases of metalanguage: "If it is very well done they make it with butter. I prefer it not with butter." And their paragraphism: "What is a sentence with tears. Is she using red in her tapestry red in her tapestry."

105. For *And a phrase* to be necessary signifies that the absence of a phrase (a silence, etc.) or the absence of a linkage (the beginning, the end, disorder, nothingness, etc.) are also phrases. What distinguishes these particular phrases from others? Equivocality, feeling, "wishes" (exclamation), etc. (Nos. 22, 23, and Gertrude Stein Notice).

106. Give a definition of what you understand by *phrase*. − By such a prescription, you are presupposing an object called a *phrase*, a phrase-type. You are also presupposing, are you not, that a complete description of it should be given in order for us to be able to debate and to arrive at an agreement on the nature of this object? Let me show you that $1°$ the substitution of a phrase-type (or of the object, *phrase*) for a phrase event is required by a phrase regimen, the definitional regimen (only terms taken as objects of a metalanguage and for which definite descriptions have been established are introduced into discourse), and by a genre of discourse, the dialogical genre. Your prescription is one of the rules of this regimen and this genre. Does this hold a preeminent authority (Plato Notice)? $2°$ It does not seem that the genre of discourse (if there is one) which is obeyed by the phrases that compose the present book privileges the definitional regimen. The question is: How to define definition? By an endless regression in the logical order, unless recourse is made to a decision or to a convention. Or an endless progression in the succession of phrase events, and here there is no exception, only time (Descombes, 1981a).

107. Give a definition of what you understand by *phrase*. − A definition is a phrase that obeys logical and cognitive rules. But your *Give a definition . . . ,* for instance, is a prescriptive that does not obey these rules. − Agreed. That does

not at all prohibit you from giving a definition of this prescriptive. There is no need for the definition and what is defined to arise from the same phrase regimen. —Indeed, but it is necessary that the value of a phrase that is the object of a definition (which is taken as the referent of a definitional phrase) be transformed on account of its being taken as the referent of another phrase, the definitional one, which is metalinguistic (Nos. 43, 45, 46). In order to validate the command *Give a definition of the phrase*, a definition of the phrase must be given. If we answer by observing that this command is a phrase that does not obey the regimen of logical and cognitive phrases, that command is situated as the referent of the "current" phrase, it is turned into a counter-example of a logical or a cognitive phrase. This command is not validated, it is used, in its capacity as the referent of an ostensive phrase (*Here is a case of a noncognitive phrase*), to validate another phrase, a descriptive one (*Certain phrases are under a noncognitive regimen*) (Kant Notice 2, § 1). Now you are carrying out the same metalinguistic operation with *A phrase*. You are taking the expression *A phrase* as if it were a phrase. You are depriving it of its "currentness" (I wouldn't say of its context, cf. No. 141), of its referential and "pragmatic" import as an event, which calls forth many kinds of possible phrases. You command me to link onto it with a metalinguistic definitional phrase. You have the right to do so. But know that you are making a command.

108. Lacking a definition of *phrase*, we will never know what we are talking about, or if we are talking about the same thing. And in talking about phrases, aren't you also using a metalanguage yourself? —It's not easy to know what one is phrasing about (Antisthenes Notice), but it is indubitable that "one is phrasing," be it only in order to know this. As for the metalanguage at play in "my" phrases here, it has no logical status, its function is not to fix the sense of a term. It calls upon the capacity of ordinary language to refer to itself: *I've had enough of your /maybe's /*; */Mary/ is a proper name*; *His /I love you/ was a lot of playacting* (Rey-Debove, 1978).

109. Here are some phrases (for once, we'll drop the italics which are supposed to signal their autonymical value): It's daybreak; Give me the lighter; Was she there?; They fought till their last round of ammunition; May he escape the heavy weather!; Is the phrase /There is a phrase / denotative?; $ax^2 + bx + c = 0$; Ouch!; But I just wanted to . . . ; Perhaps you thought that I . . . ?; There is a phrase; This is not a phrase; Here are some phrases.

110. The young Scythians had orders to beget children with those good warriors, the Amazons. One of them unexpectantly comes upon one of these combatants right when she is squatting to relieve her bowels. "She nothing loth, gave him what he wanted" and asked him to return on the following day: *Phônèsai mén ouk éikhé, tè dé khéiri éphrazé* (Herodotus IV, 113): "Unable to express her

meaning in words (as neither understood the other's language), she phrased this to him by hand." French *Aïe*, Italian *Eh*, American *Whoops* are phrases. A wink, a shrugging of the shoulder, a taping of the foot, a fleeting blush, or an attack of tachycardia can be phrases. – And the wagging of a dog's tail, the perked ears of a cat? – And a tiny speck to the West rising upon the horizon of the sea? – A silence (Nos. 24, 26)? – *Ei d'axunèmôn ousa mè dékhei logon / su d'anti phônès phrazé karbanôi khéri* (Aeschylus, *Agamemnon*: 1060–1061). Back from Troy, Agamemnon has just entered the palace of Atreus, leaving Cassandra, his captive, motionless in the chariot. Clytemnestra entreats her to come in too. Frozen by her vision of the impending crime, Cassandra neither hears nor answers: "She bears herself like a wild creature newly captured" (1063). The queen grows impatient: "But if failing to understand our language, you do not catch my meaning, then instead of speech, make sign [phrase] with thy barbarian hand." – Silence as a phrase. The expectant wait of the *Is it happening?* as silence. Feelings as a phrase for what cannot now be phrased. The immediate incommunicability of desire, or the immediate incommunicability of murder. The phrase of love, the phrase of death. "Femininity" or "bestiality" as a blank in the argument (*logos, phônè*). The suspense of the linking. Comic: the Amazon on the stool; as well as tragic: the queen about to kill.

111. A phrase presents at least one universe (Nos. 18, 25). No matter which regimen it obeys, it entails a *There is* [*Il y a*]. There is what is signified, what it is signified about, to whom and by whom it is signified: a universe. *At least one universe*, because the sense, the referent, the addressor, or the addressee can be equivocal (Nos. 137–40).

112. The expression *There is* is a mark of presentation in a phrase. Are there other marks of presentation?

113. Could the presentation entailed by a phrase be called *Being*? But it is *one* presentation, or what in a phrase-case is the case. Being would be a case, an occurrence, the "fact" that it happens to "fall," that it "comes running" (*Fall, occurrence*). Not Being, but one being, one time, [*un être, une fois*].

114. A presentation can be presented as an instance in the universe of a phrase. Thus Being can be presented, as an existent. But the phrase that presents the presentation itself entails a presentation, which it does not present. Can we even say that this presentation slips away or is deferred? That would be to presuppose that it is the same for several phrases, an identicalizing effect of the definite article, *the* presentation.

115. A presentation is that there is at least one universe. A situation is that at the heart of a universe presented by a phrase, relations indicated by the form of the phrases that link onto it (through the phrase's regimen, which calls forth cer-

tain linkings) place the instances in relation to each other. *I saw it* is a phrase that situates three of the instances (the addressee instance is not indicated by the phrase), and this situation consists in particular in the determination of a tense. *It's there that I saw it* determines in particular a space-time in which the same three instances are situated. *I tell you that it's there that I saw it* situates in particular the place of the addressor thanks to the "constative" *I tell you that . . .* (Habermas, 1971: 111ff.). The forms of phrases indicate the situations of the instances with regard to each other. The set of these situations forms the presented universe.

116. The presentation entailed by a phrase-case is not presented in the universe that this phrase presents (but it may be marked in the phrase, for example by *There is*). It is not situated. But another phrase-case can present it in another universe and thereby situate it.

117. The categories of Aristotle, Kant, and others are families or species of situations, that is, families or species of relations between the instances presented in a phrase universe. It would be a mistake to call them genres or modes of presentation (or of Being) (Aubenque, 1966 176–80). The presentation of a phrase allows itself to be determined by genres only if it is situated in the universe of another phrase, that is, as a presented presentation. That is why genres of presentation, if there are any, are presentable only as genres of situation.

118. Let's admit for the sake of convenience two phrases (1) and (2), linked in the following way: phrase (1) presents a universe, it entails a presentation; phrase (2) signifies something about the presentation of phrase (1); it presents a universe in which the presentation of phrase (1) is in the situation, shall we say, of referent. The presentation (1) that is presented is not entailed in (2); the presentation (2) that is entailed is not presented in (2). A presented presentation and an entailed presentation do not therefore make two presentations. A set of two presentations is formed by two presentations presented by a single phrase, which is some phrase (3). The presentation entailed by the latter is not part of the set of presentations (1) and (2) that it presents, or: the synthesis of the series of presentations presented by a phrase-case entails a presentation which does not enter into the series presented by this phrase-case. It is presentable, though, in another phrase-case. And so on.

119. The universe presented by a phrase is not presented to something or to someone like a "subject". The universe is there as long as the phrase is the case. A "subject" is situated in a universe presented by a phrase. Even when the subject is said not to belong to the world, qua addressee or addressor of the presentation – thinking I in Descartes, transcendental Ego in Husserl, source of the moral law in Kant, subject in Wittgenstein (*TLP*: 5. 632; *TB*: 7. 8. 1916ff.), –this subject is nevertheless situated in the heart of the universe presented by the philosophical

phrase that says it does not belong to the world. What is not in the "world," the subject, is presented in a phrase universe where it is situated under the relation of transcendence, but transcendence is a situation immanent to the universe presented by the phrase that states it.

Aristotle

1. Before and after.

The sophist or the eristic can refute an opponent by playing upon the surface lexicon of language, by amphibolies, homonyms, divisions, and so forth, but also by playing upon the very categories of the *logos*, and these are then paralogisms (*Soph. Ref.*: 166 b 20). Parachronologisms (not Aristotle's word) are paralogisms that bear upon the category of time (Protagoras Notice). Categories are regulators which, in dialectics, allow for a referent's manner of signifying to be circumscribed. For example, *white* may be taken as an attribute, a substance, or a quality: *The rose is white*, *Can white be transparent?*, *They heat it white*.

The postpredicaments (ch. 10 to 15 of the *Categories*) cite two operators that regulate time in argumentation: *to protéron* and *to hama*, the prior and the simultaneous. The *hama* is part of the formulation of the principle of contradiction. If one and the same "object," one and the same substance in the Aristotelian sense, can accept contrary attributes, then one phrase may say that an object taken as referent has a given property, and another phrase may say that it has the opposite property, although both are true. But not at the same time. For example, *Socrates is sitting* and *Socrates is standing*. You need to specify when (*Cat.*: 4 a 10ff.). Otherwise, paralogism in relation to time is possible: "The same man is both seated and standing, for it is he who stood up who is standing, but it is the seated man (*ho kathèménos*) who stood up" (*Soph. Ref.*: 165 b 38). The sophism of the seated man includes a parallel version with the couple sick/healthy. Aristotle refutes this sophism by recourse to the *protéron* operator: "The phrase according to which the seated man does so and so or has so and so done to him is not single in meaning, sometimes it means the man who is seated now (*nun*), sometimes it means the man who was seated formerly (*protéron*)" (*Ibid.*: 166 a 4). Similarly, the man who was recovering is not sick now, he really is the sick man, but the formerly sick man.

This refutation presupposes the ability to enumerate, according to the opposition (dyad) anterior/posterior, the positions of something moving along a directional axis. Such is one definition of time given in the *Physics*: "For time is just this — number of motion in respect of 'before' and 'after'. " (219 b 1–2). The referent of the phrase under consideration is something moving. The phrase has truth at stake, its regimen is logical or cognitive. The truth of the attribution of a predicate to this moving body cannot be decided unless the position it occupies when the attributive phrase takes place is specified.

This position must be "numbered" (*arithmouménon*). To this end, a comparative ordering of two positions by means of the dyad suffices to avoid parachronologism. The number of motion need not be a cipher, drawn for instance from some chronology or chronometry. It is sufficient to apply the operator to two places (before/after) along the continuum of motion in order for the contrary attributes to be distributed into distinct positions. Thanks to this operator, the continuum turns out to be ordered according to the set of positions for the moving body. One of the latter's positions, whichever one it is (and by the same stroke, the disputed attribute), is always situated before or after any other position. "The mind pronounces that the 'nows' are two, one before and one after, it is then that we say that there is time, and this that we say is time" (*Physics*: 219 a 28-29).

If it is asked, 'before or after what?', if an origin is sought for this pinpointing, the answer at this stage in the analysis is that the comparison is made in an immanent fashion: the anterior before the posterior, and conversely. The constitutive operator of the series of states of the referent operates in the heart of this series. It follows that the referent (the moving body) not only is what it is in its supposedly present punctual state, but also implies its relationship with other states, whether anterior or posterior. Furthermore, the very notion of a punctual state of the referent, the state in which it supposedly is now, already implies the possibility of other states in which it has been and will be. Not only do *the before* and *the after* imply each other in an immanent fashion, but *the before/after* and *the now* also imply each other, without ever leaving the universe presented by the phrase which refers to the moving body.

This is all a matter of situation (No. 115). The referent being a moving body, if the phrase whose referent it is presents it in terms of its mobility, that is, if it first presents it as a, then as b, then it enumerates (as has just been attested by distinguishing *first* from *then*) its positions or attributes, and this enumeration (or number) minimally requires the dyad *before/after*. This dyad is indeed the number of motion, the numbered motion of the referent in the universe presented by this phrase. Number, like quantity, is not in the supposedly real referent (outside the phrase universe), but in the phrase, in the form of adverbs of time which organize two by two the positions or contrary attributes of the moving body. Now does not seem endowed with any privilege in this serialization. Before is a not yet now, after is an already no longer now, now is a now between two nows, that is, passing from one to the next. Once again, it is a question of cross-referencings within the heart of the universe presented by the phrase, and thus a question of situation, not of presentation.

2. Now.

A difficulty is born from this immanence, which makes Aristotle hesitate over the status to be given to the *now*. Isn't *now* not also the origin of diachronic cross-referencing? "For what is bounded by the 'now' is thought to be time" (*Physics:* 219 a 29). The formula appears to grant the temporalizing function to the present instant. However, the "is thought to be" followed by a very reserved *hypokeisthô* ("we may assume this") marks a difficulty in granting this function to the now.

Another formulation aggravates the uncertainty: "If the 'now' measures time, it is in so far as time involves the 'before and after' " (*Ibid.*: 219 b 11-12). It can be understood that the now is the permanent point of origin for the ecstasis of time. This will be the "modern" version of temporalization, the one that prevails in Augustine and Husserl: a constituting time, the "living present," in the charge of a transcendental subject, and a constituted, diachronic time on the side of the object, the diegetic referent. In which time, though, shall the synthesis of transcendental and empirical time take place? This synthesis must nevertheless take place, if it is true that the now never escapes diachrony.

Aristotle, ignoring everything about a philosophy of the subject, does not at all orient himself in this phenomenological direction. This is how he designates the difficulty: "The 'now' which seems to bound the past and the future — does it always remain one and the same or is it always other and other? It is hard to say" (218 a 8). Let's return to the hypothesis of immanence. The distinguishing limit between before and after, or the zone of contact between the anterior and the posterior, is itself affected by the before/after: the now is not now, it is not yet or already no longer, one cannot say now *now*, it's too early (before) or too late (after). What was future is now past, the time of a phrase. The limit is not punctual or linear, the posterior incessantly encroaches upon the anterior. The now [*maintenant*] is precisely what is not maintained [*ce qui ne se maintient pas*]. We do not see how it can serve as the origin for distributing the positions of a moving body into before and after. These essentially "vulgar" observations suffice to disqualify a constitution of time derived from the present: for, either the present is immersed in diachrony; or else, it is transcendent to it. In either case, it cannot serve to number it.

Aristotle opens up another path. He was asking whether now remains one and the same, or whether it becomes always other and other? He answers: "The 'now' in one sense is the same, in another it is not the same" (219 b 12). Considered as "being what it is this time" (*ho poté on*: 219 b 17, 219 b 26; *ho poté ôn*: 219 a 20; *ho pot'èn*: 219 b 11, 223 a 27), or "what turns out to be each time" (Aubenque, 1966: 436), it is what it is. But considered *tô logô* (219 b 20, 220 a 8), "in a phrase," or, if one prefers (the two expressions being substitutable in the Aristotelian text), *to einai*, "as an entity," as an instance presented by this phrase (219 a 21, 219 b 11, 219 b 27), it is other than itself. "As being what it is this time," the now is taken as an occurrence, as an event. I would say, as a phrase event. This is confirmed by: "in so far then as the 'now' is a boundary, it is not time, but it happens [*il arrive*] (*sumbébèken*)" (220 a 21). There is *There is,* a phrase taken as occurrence, as *what*, which rightly said is not the now, but now. But, as soon as the occurrence is grasped in the universe of another phrase (*tô logô*) which refers to it as if to an entity (*to einai*), now becomes the now, and it cannot be grasped as *what*, as (at) the time it happened. It undergoes the inevitable alteration of diachrony, it is contingent upon the phrase regimen.

Aristotle thereby distinguishes time which, in universes presented by phrases, situates the instances constituting these universes in relation to each other (the before/after, the now), from the presentation-event (or occurrence) which as such is absolute (now). As soon as one phrases the latter, it is placed among the relations of phrase universes. The presentation is then presented. In order to grasp the presentation entailed by a phrase, another phrase is needed, in which this presentation is presented. The "present" presentation is not able to be phrased now; it is only able to be phrased as a situation (before/after) in the universe presented by another phrase: it is then the former presentation. Aristotle disconnects the diachronic operators at play in phrase universes from the occurrence of the phrase (or the phrase-occurence). The "current" or "actual" presentation is impossible, the event is forgotten as such insofar as it is conserved (the after), anticipated (the before), or "maintained" (the now) [*le maintenant*].

3. Some observations.

3. 1.–This "reading" is still metaphysical, still subordinate to the hegemony of thought, Derrida would say (1968b: 63). –Yes, indeed, if it is true that, as a question, time already belongs to metaphysics. I would nevertheless like to show the following. The occurrence, the phrase, as a *what* that happens, does not at all stem from the question of time, but from that of Being/non-Being. This question is called forth by a feeling: it is possible for nothing

to happen. Silence not as a phrase in abeyance, but as a nonphrase, a non *what*. This feeling is anxiety or surprise: there is something rather than nothing. Scarcely is this phrased, than the occurrence is chained, registered, and forgotten in the occurrence of this phrase, which, in stating the *There is*, binds the occurrence by comparing it with its absence. Time takes place with the before/after implied in phrase universes, as the putting of instances into an ordered series. This serialization is immanent to them. Time is indeed a category of the existent. Being is not time. Presentation is not an act of giving (and above all not one coming from some *Es*, or some *It* and addressed to some us, to us human beings). Nor by presentation (every term to designate this is illusory and illusionist, I have said why) do I understand the act of a *dunamis*, of a potency, or of a will of this potency, a desire of language to accomplish itself. But merely that something takes place. This something is a phrase, undoubtedly (no. 99). Since a phrase presents a universe, for a phrase to take place is what I call presentation.

3. 2. –Your "reading" seems akin to the meditation which, in *On Time and Being* and the works of that period, converges upon the notion of *Ereignis* (Heidegger, 1962: 10-23). –Except that Heidegger's meditation persists in making "man" the addressee of the giving which in the *Ereignis* gives, and gives itself while withholding itself, and it particularly persists in making the one who receives this giving into the man who fulfills his destiny as man by hearing the authenticity of time. Destiny, addressee, addressor, and man are instances or relations here in universes presented by phrases, they are situational, *tô logô*. The *There is* takes place, it is an occurrence (*Ereignis*), but it does not present anything to anyone, it does not present itself, and it is not the present, nor is it presence. Insofar as it is phrasable (thinkable), a presentation falls short as an occurrence.

3. 3 –The question of time is raised here within the problematics of the phrase. The *Geben* (?) does not give (?) existents, it gives (?) phrases, which are distributors of existents (instances in universes). Even phrases become existents for other phrases. But they "have happened," as Aristotle says with respect to *now*. The presentation is that a phrase happens. But "as such," as *what*, it is not within time. "Vulgar" time is within the universe presented by the phrase. There is no vulgar time, though, as Derrida is right to say (*Ibid.*: 59), or else, that's all there is, for the phrase is "vulgar" too.

3.4 –What allows you to phrase something as a presentation, if no one is its addressee and no one can refer to it without falling short of it? Are you, in your turn, making the hypothesis of a trace (*Ibid.*: 65ff.)? Of a silence or a blank that effaces the event? Is the *Ereignis* in effect (Heidegger, 1953-1954: 22) the lightning flash that makes something (a phrase universe) appear, but blinds as it blinds itself through what it illuminates? Is this withdrawal itself a phrase (Nos. 22, 110)? Which of the four kinds of silence is it (Nos. 24, 26)? Or is this some other kind of silence?–It is another kind of silence. One that does not bear upon an instance in a phrase universe, but which bears upon the occurrence of a phrase. There would be no more presentations. –But you wrote: "For there to be no phrase is impossible" (No. 102)! –That's just it: the feeling that the impossible is possible. That the necessary is contingent. That linkage must be made, but that there won't be anything upon which to link. The "and" with nothing to grab onto. Hence, not just the contingency of the how of linking, but the vertigo of the last phrase. Absurd, of course. But the lightning flash takes place–it flashes and bursts out in the nothingness of the night, o clouds, or of the clear blue sky.

120. There wouldn't be any space or time independent of a phrase.

121. If asked from where you hold this notion that space and time are like kinds of situations, it may be answered that it is held from phrases like *The marquise went out at five**, *It had happpened, He had arrived***, *Get out of here, Asleep! Already?*, etc. But above all from the phrase *From where do you hold . . .* ? which presupposes space and time. And it may be added that I do not hold it, phrases can so hold themselves, that is, they can situate their instances so and situate themselves so in relation to others. Space and time are headings that group the situational effects produced in phrase universes by expressions like *behind, much later, just below, was born, in the beginning*, etc. (and *etc.*). There are phrases whose regimen requires these marks (such as narratives), others which exclude them as an assumption (such as mathematics, or logic, even if there is a logic of time).

122. There are as many universes as there are phrases. And as many situations of instances as there are universes. –But you say that there are families of instantial situations such as space and time (No. 121)? Then, there are phrase universes that are at least analogous to each other?–A metalinguistic phrase has several of these different phrases as its referent, and it states their resemblance. This resemblance removes none of their heteogeneity (Bambrough, 1961: 198–99). Space or time or space-time are family names attributed to these situations. No element is common to all. –Are you a nominalist?–No, resemblance may be established by the procedure for establishing the reality of a referent (Nos. 63ff.), but not by "use," as Wittgenstein thinks, prey to anthropological empiricism. –But among the kinds of phrases required by this procedure, there is the ostensive, which makes use of spatio-temporal deictics, *over there, then*, etc.! –That only shows that metalanguage is part of ordinary language (Desclès and Guentcheva Desclès, 1977: 7).

123. Isn't your way of partitioning phrase universes anthropocentric and pragmatic? From where do you hold it that they entail four instances?–From the ways to link. Take the phrase *Ouch!* You link onto the addressor with *Are you in pain?*; onto the addressee with *I can't do anything about it*; onto the sense with *Does it hurt?*; onto the referent with *The gums are always very sensitive*. The instances are valences of linkage. —For human language perhaps, but what about a cat's

---

*La marquise sorit à cinq heures; since Paul Valéry, this sentence has served as *the* example of cliché in the French novel. Cf. English: *'Twas a dark and stormy night.*–tr.

**Il était arrivé: By itself, the French remains ambiguous and could mean either the impersonal "it had happened" or the personalized "he had arrived" depending on whether the pronoun il is understood to be impersonal or to refer to someone.–tr

tail?–You link onto the raised tail of a cat by, respectively: *What do you want?; You're bothering me; Hungry again?; They have very expressive tails*. I'm purposively choosing phrases where neither the instances nor their situation is marked. The partitioning is not pragmatic if the presupposition or prejudice of pragmatics is that a message goes from an addressor to an addressee each of whom would "exist" without it. Nor is it humanist: try to come up with nonhuman entities who could not occupy one or another of these instances! It is rare perhaps for all of the instances to be marked. (Many modern literary techniques are tied to the demarcating of instances: the addressor in *In Remembrance of Things Past*, the addressee in Butor's *La modification*, both addressor and addressee in Derrida's *La carte postale*, the referent in Claude Simon's *Les Géorgiques*, the sense in Robert Pinget's *L'apocryphe*, to mention recent French examples alone. And the presumed author (Puech, 1982). This de-marcating has the effect of making the phrases take place *sponte sua*: a critique of the prejudice that it is "man" who speaks. "Love of phrases, unlove of people." "His having always loved phrases is not, as far as I'm concerned, to his credit but I don't know my judgment to be infallible" (Pinget, 1980: 149, 57).)

124. The presentation entailed by a phrase is forgotten by it, plunged into the river Lethe (Detienne, 1967: 126–35). Another phrase pulls it back out and presents it, oblivious to the presentation that it itself entails. Memory is doubled by oblivion. Metaphysics struggles against oblivion, but what is whatever struggles for oblivion called?

125. Augustine's God or Husserl's Living Present is presented as the name borne by the instance that synthesizes the nows. It is presented, though, by means of the phrases in which it is presented, and the now of each of these phrases then remains to be synthesized with the others, in a new phrase. God is for later, "in a moment"; the Living Present is to come. These only come by not arriving. Which is what Beckett signifies. Time is not what is lacking to consciousness, time makes consciousness lack itself.

126. You qualify presentation, entailed by a phrase, as *absolute*. By qualifying it in this way, you are presenting it. Its quality as absolute is situated in the universe presented by your phrase, and is relative to it. This is why the absolute is not presentable. With the notion of the sublime (and on the condition that *Darstellung* be understood as we have here), Kant will always get the better of Hegel. The *Erhabene* persists, not over and beyond, but right in the heart of the *Aufgehobenen*.

127. What is not presented is not. The presentation entailed by a phrase is not presented, it is not. Or: Being is not. One could say that when an entailed presentation is presented, it is not an entailed but a situated presentation. Or: Being grasped as an existent is non-Being. This is how the first chapter of the *Wissen-*

schaft der Logik [*Science of Logic*] should be understood. What Hegel calls determination and which is the mainspring of the passage from Being to non-Being is the situation of Being (or of presentation) in a phrase universe, that is, the passage from the presentation entailed by the first phrase to the presentation (of the first phrase) presented by the second phrase. This "disintegration" (the passage from Being to existent or non-Being) only works, however, if the stakes of the second phrase are to present the presentation; that is, if the stakes of this second phrase are those of the genre of ontological discourse. One of the rules constitutive of the genre prescribes a linkage of this kind and the resulting passage or disintegration: the rule of the *Resultat* (Hegel Notice). There are many genres of discourse, though, whose stakes as prescribed by their rules do not involve presenting the presentation, and where "disintegration" is consequently not necessary.

128. This is why negation is needed to present the entailed presentation. It is only presentable as an existent, that is, as non-Being. This is what the word *Lethe* means.

129. The argument "that the unknown can be known, on the ground that it can be known to be unknown" (*Epistèton to agnôston, ésti gar épistèton to agnôston hoti agnôston*) is classed by Aristotle (*Rhetoric*: 1402 a) among the apparent enthymemes. He says it is a paralogism in which the absolute and the relative are confused (through a mistake or a ruse that he attributes to Antisthenes). The argument in effect resorts to insisting upon the presentation ("can be known," the absolute) all the way up to asserting what is unpresented (what is unsignified, "the unknown"), which is presented by the phrase *that the unknown* . . . , and which is therefore relative to it. To call this linkage a paralogism, though, is a decision constitutive of the genre of logical discourse, which is not concerned with the *quod* (No. 91).

130. The faculty of presenting for a single referent, its sense and the contrary (negation) of its sense (for the unknown, the sense of the unknown and the sense of the known; for Being, the sense of Being and the sense of non-Being) should not be called *die ungeheure Macht des Negativen*, the portentous power of the negative, as Hegel does (*PhG*, Preface: 93). If there is a power, where is it? In a phrase's ability to present a property as lacking in its referent? That's (only . . .) "the mystery of negation" (Wittgenstein, *TB*: 9, 15. 11. 1914) (No. 90). –In a phrase's ability to present a property as simultaneously present and absent? But such is not the case: one phrase presents it as present, another phrase presents it as absent. This is not "at one and the same time." –In the ability of two phrases relating to the same referent to say something and its contrary about it? But it needs to be established that this concerns the same referent (Nos. 68, 80). In this last case, what is portentous does not come from the negative, but from

the *Ereignis*. For it could be that there were no "second" phrase. The impossible, nothingness would be possible. What is portentous is that it is not so.

131. "Every phrase is." Is everything which is, a phrase? *Is* is not *which is*. Nor is *is*, for that matter, *is real*. It cannot be said that *Every phrase is real*. Even less so, that *Everything rational is real*. Reality is a property of a referent that remains to be established (Referent Section), it is not. This includes the reality of a phrase. That everything real is rational, yes, that can be said if *rational* signifies: in conformity with the procedure for establishing the reality of a referent. –In *Every phrase is, every phrase* signifies *everything which happens*; *is* signifies *there is, it happens*. But *It happens* is not what happens, in the sense that *quod* is not *quid* (in the sense that the presentation is not the situation). *Is* does not therefore signify *is there*, and even less so does it signify *is real*. *Is* doesn't signify anything, it would designate the occurrence "before" the signification (the content) of the occurrence. It would designate it, but it does not designate it, since by designating it it situates it ("before" signification), and thereby occults *nun* in *hustéron protéron* (Aristotle Notice). Rather *is* would be: *Is it happening?* (the *it* indicating an empty place to be occupied by a referent).

132. In sum, there are events: something happens which is not tautological with what has happened. Would you call what happens *the case*?–The case, *der Fall*, would be that something happens, *quod*, rather than what happens, *quid*. –Would you say that "the world is all that [which] is the case (*alles, was der Fall ist*)," as Wittgenstein does?–We could if we distinguished between *the case* and *that which is the case*. Wittgenstein also calls a fact (*Tatsache*) that which is the case (*TLP*: 2). He can then write that "the world is the totality (*die Gesamtheit*) of facts" (1. 1), or that "the sum-total of reality (*die gesamte Wirklichkeit*) is the world" (2. 063). *Totality* and *all* are not themselves cases. They are referents of Ideas in the Kantian sense. Or else logical quantifiers. One cannot proceed to test the reality of the whole. –But the case is not that which is the case. The case is: *There is, It happens*. That is to say (No. 131): *Is it happening?*

133. There is no "picture of the world" that "we" would "make" for ourselves (*TLP*: 2. 1). But the world as the whole of reality can be situated as an instance in a universe presented by a (cosmological) phrase. It gives rise to the antinomies described by Kant. These reveal that the referent *world* is not an object of cognition, it eludes the test of reality. The concept of a picture (*Bild, eikôn*) of facts condenses within itself the metaphysical illusion, the reversal or prejudice that phrases come after facts. In this sense, there is no representation. –By *world* (No. 60), I understand a network of proper names. No phrase can exhaust this network. No phrase can substitute a complete description for every name: "For it seems–at least so far as I can see at present–that the matter is not settled by getting rid of names by means of definitions" (*TB*: 13. 5. 15).

134. "You can't say everything" (Descombes, 1977). –Disappointed? Did you desire it? Or at least did something–"language"–want it? Wanted to unfurl its full powers? A will? A "life"? A desire, a lack? These are so many teleologies of fulfillment, or melancholias for the unfulfilled. –But you certainly accept (No. 23) that "something asks to be put into phrases"?–This does not imply that *everything* ought to or wants to be said. This implies the expectant waiting for an occurrence, for the "portentousness," that indeed everything has not been said (No. 130). The vigil. This waiting is in the phrase universe. It is the specific "tension" that every phrase regimen exerts upon the instances.

135. "What we cannot speak about we must pass over in silence" (*TLP*: 7). –Is the *must* (*Il faut, muss man*) addressed to man? To Spirit? It is not in their power to pass over in silence what they cannot speak about. Insofar as it is unable to be phrased in the common idioms, it is already phrased, as feeling. The avowal has been made. The vigil for an occurrence, the anxiety and the joy of an unknown idiom, has begun. To link is not a duty, which "we" can be relieved of or make good upon. "We" cannot do otherwise. Don't confuse necessity with obligation. If there is a *must* (*Il faut*), it is not a *You ought to* (*Vous devez*) (No. 102).

136. To link is necessary, but a particular linkage is not. This linkage can be declared pertinent, though, and the phrase that does the stating is a rule for linking. It is a constitutive part of a genre of discourse: after such and such a kind of phrase, here are those phrases that are permitted. The *Analytics* circumscribe in this way the genre of linkages for classical logic, the *Science of Logic* for modern dialectics, and the *Vorlesungen uber neuere Geometrie* [*Lectures in the New Geometry*] for modern axiomatics (Pasch in Blanché, 1955: 20–22). There are many genres of discourse whose rules for linking are not stated.

137. A phrase can be formulated in such a way that it co-presents several universes. It can be equivocal, not only with regard to the sense, but also with regard to the referent, the addressor, or the addressee. For example: *I can come by your place*. Equivocation can affect *I, come by*, or *your*. Restricting ourselves to the modal *can*, here are some co-presented universes:

1.1 I have the ability to do it.
1.2 I have the time to do it.
1.3 You have a place and I know the address.
2 It's possible that I'll do it.
3.1 I desire to do it.
3.2 I desire that you tell me to do it.
4 I have permission to do it.

Ability (1), eventuality (2), wish (3), right (4). Description (1, 2, 4); representation (3.1) (in the sense of Habermas' "representative" phrases (1971: 112): *I want,*

I fear, I desire that . . .); regulation (3. 2) (as in: *I order you, I beg you, I promise you to* . . .). Not only is the sense of *I can* equivocal, but its equivocalness is passed on to the other instances: *your* is not the same if it is part of the described referent or if it is the addressee of a prescription; the same goes for *I*.

138. A linkage may reveal an equivocalness in the previous phrase. *The door is closed* can give rise to *Of course, what do you think doors are for?*, or to *I know, they're trying to lock me in*, or to *All the better, I have to talk to you*, etc. In these linkages, the closed door ceases to be a state of things to be discussed or verified. It verifies the functionalist definition of doors given by an obsessive neurotic; it confirms the tale a paranoiac tells about them, etc. Are we dealing with the same door? With the same addressee, etc.? Let's suppose two interlocutors. They talk about the closed door. One says: *Of course*, etc.; the other: *I know*, etc. Here is a differend. The logician who would put order into their obscure contention by saying, *It's only a matter of a simple description*, would merely add to the differend. Some vignettes of these disorders along with their juridico-political impacts can be found in La Fontaine's *Fables*. Which is the pertinent linkage?

139. We suppose that the addressor of the subsequent phrase is "the same" as the addressee of the prior phrase. Couldn't it be said that the linkage is pertinent at least if the universe of the second phrase presents or co-presents anew, and therefore re-presents, one of the universes presented by the first phrase? For example, if you linked onto *I can come by your place* (No. 137) in version (1. 1) with *Can you walk?*, *Your car is fixed?*, or *You think so?* (= You really have the ability of movement to do so?). In version (1. 2) with *No, you won't have time*, *Yes, it's very close to your place*, *You think so?* (= You really have the availability of time to do so?). In version (1. 3) with *But I was thrown out*. In version (2) with *That would surprise me*, *You think so?* (= Is it even possible?). In version (3. 1) with *So you say* (= I don't believe in your desire to do so), *You think so?* (= Do you have the desire?). In version (3. 2) with *There's no need to* (= It's not my desire), *As you wish* (= I don't have any desires about this matter), *You think so?* (= Do you really want to know my desire?). In version (4) with *Oh good!*, *You think so?* (= Was this permission really given to you?). This makes for a lot of pertinences.

140. The addressee of the first phrase may link onto *I can come by your place* with *How is Chantal?* Would we say that this is not a pertinent linkage? Ducrot would say (1977) that it is not pertinent if we stick to the presuppositions just examined; but it may be pertinent if we also admitted something understood [*sous-entendu*]: *I can come by your place, Chantal isn't there*. Pertinence supposes a "good" rule for linking. There are a number of good rules for linking onto an equivocal phrase. It is here that the pragmatician (Engel, 1981) gets tangled up in the question of the speakers' intentions, in order to save communication from

its wreckage. The metaphysics of consciousness runs aground, though, upon the aporia of otherness: Husserl's fifth *Cartesian Meditation*. No matter what he or she says, the addressor of the linking phrase is situated in the universe presented by "his" or "her" phrase in a nonarbitrary way with relation to the phrase "of the other." Even *You think so?* is a way of linking without resolving the equivocalness: it is a question, and it suits every version of the first phrase. This way of linking is not entirely haphazard, it resorts to the interrogative at least.

141. But the context at least should allow us to decide what the addressor of the first phrase wanted to say and what the addressee, who is the addressor of the second phrase, would have had reason to understand . . . – The context needs to be presented, by means of phrases. This is what I have sketched out by presenting the co-presented universes. Or else, in invoking the context, your phrase situates you as the addressee in a cognitive universe in which the context is the addressor and informs you about itself. Why should you judge this addressor to be more credible than the addressor of the first phrase ?

142. For example, the phrase *The meeting is called to order* is not performative because its addressor is the chairperson of the meeting. The addressor is the chairperson of the meeting to the extent that the phrase in question is performative. The equation chairmanship-performativity is independent of the context. If the phrase is performative and the addressor is not the chairperson, he or she becomes the chairperson; if it is not performative and the addressor is the chairperson, he or she ceases to be the chairperson. –Doesn't this alternative, though, at least depend upon the context?–The context is itself made of phrases linked onto the phrase in question. Onto a phrase like *The meeting is called to order*, such phrases as the following can be linked: *Okay, you chair the meeting* in the first case, or *No way*, or *By what right?*, in the second. –But doesn't the occurrence of these phrases depend, in turn, upon the context?–What you are calling the context is itself but the referent of cognitive phrases, those of the sociologist for example. The context is not an addressor. Positivism, in particular the positivism of the human sciences in general, resides in this confusion between context and referent and between context and addressor. With the notion of context, the floor is turned over to the object of the "scientist" next door, as if this referent were an addressor.

143. Won't we know, though, anyway after the fact which universe was the one really presented by the initial phrase? Won't the subsequent series of phrases decide the regimen of the first phrase?–The subsequent series will decide nothing (no more than "history will tell if . . ."). If there is a decision, it comes from the genre of discourse wherein this series is "led." Imagine two opposite poles between which all the genres would be distributed. One of them, the discourse of cognition, stakes itself on leading the series toward clearing up the initial equivo-

cation. The other, the discourse of the unconscious, stakes itself on maintaining this equivocation to the greatest extent possible. This is not to say that one of them is more or less faithful than the other to the "essence" of language, nor that one is "originary" and the other secondary. In the order of discourses, they are like tautology and contradiction in the order of propositions: the rational phrase presents the universe that it presents, the phrase of the passions co-presents incompossible universes.

144. You call them incompossible (No. 143) because you are signifying them in relation to the discourse of cognition. Take Freud's analysis of the female fantasy which he entitles by the phrase "*Ein Kind wird geschlagen* [A child is being beaten]." The woman, that is to say, her name, is an addressee in the universe presented by this phrase (a troubled addressee: when the phrase takes place, there is masturbation). But she is also the referent: she is the beaten child. The instance of the referent, however, is also occupied by "another child" beaten by the father. As for the father, he is instantiated as a reference, but he is also not instantiated at all (he is effaced). And who is the addressor presented in these mixed universes? That addressor is never marked in the phrase or phrases. Would it be the big Other, according to Lacanian metaphysics? The incompossibles, as you see, coexist marvelously. –Yes, but they form a symptom. –They form an idiolect, to speak the language of Wittgenstein. –And the masturbating?–A mode of the simultaneous occurrence of the incompossibles, like a dream, a blush, a cramp, an oversight, an illness, a silence, a feeling, alcohol, or drugs. Agitation, in other words, a leaping from one version to another within a single instant: Pierre Guyotat's *Prostitution* (1975).

145. But isn't the body real?–The body "proper" is a name for the family of idiolects. It is, moreover, the referent of phrases obeying various regimens. *My teeth hurt*: this is a descriptive, paired with a co-presented request: *Relieve me of this*. The dentist turns your suffering into a case that verifies a cognitive phrase (by the three-phrase procedure: there it is; that there is called the neck of the tooth; chances are, it is a cavity in the neck of the tooth). In relation to this case, and by way of an answer to your request, the dentist prescribes certain actions proper to re-establishing your health (health being itself the object of an Idea). The same goes for other professionals of the "body" *mutatis mutandis*: for the sports coach, for the sex therapist, for the culinary artist, for the dance or singing teacher, for the military instructor, the body is a set of symptoms read and treated on the basis of an Idea of the good body. –But the toothache is painful, it's a lived experience, etc.! –How can you verify that it is lived experience? You are the exclusive addressee of this pain. It is like the voice of God: "You can't hear God speak to someone else, you can hear him only if you are being addressed" (*Zettel*: § 717). Wittgenstein adds: "That is a grammatical remark." It circumscribes what an idiolect is: "I" am alone in hearing it. The idiolect easily falls beneath the blows

of the dilemma (No. 8): if your lived experience is not communicable, you cannot testify that it exists; if it is communicable, you cannot say that you are the only one able to testify that it exists.

146. At least grant that while phrases from ordinary language are equivocal, it is a noble task to seek out univocality and to refuse to entertain equivocation. –That's Platonic, at the very least. You are preferring dialogue to differend. You are presupposing, first of all, that univocality is possible; and second, that it constitutes the healthiness of phrases. But what if the stakes of thought (?) concerned differend rather than consensus? In its noble as well as in its ordinary genre? In its best of "health," and at its most vigilant? This does not mean that equivocation is entertained. But, at the far end of univocality, something announces itself (through feeling) which that "unique voice" cannot phrase.

147. From one phrase regimen (descriptive, cognitive, prescriptive, evaluative, interrogative . . .) to another, a linkage cannot have pertinence. It is not pertinent to link onto *Open the door* with *You have formulated a prescription*, or with *What a beautiful door!* This impertinence may be opportune, though, within a genre of discourse. A genre of discourse determines what is at stake in linking phrases (Nos. 178ff.): to persuade, to convince, to vanquish, to make laugh, to make cry, etc. It may be opportune to link onto the chain in a nonpertinent way in order to achieve one or another of these effects. Teleology begins with genres of discourse, not with phrases. Insofar, though, as they are linked together, phrases are always caught up in one (or at least one) genre of discourse.

148. The stakes bound up with a genre of discourse determine the linkings between phrases. They determine them, however, only as an end may determine the means: by eliminating those that are not opportune. One will not link onto *To arms!* with *You have just formulated a prescription*, if the stakes are to make someone act with urgency. One will do it if the stakes are to make someone laugh. But there are many other means to achieve an end. The idea of seduction needs to be extended. A genre of discourse exerts a seduction upon a phrase universe. It inclines the instances presented by this phrase toward certain linkings, or at least it steers them away from other linkings which are not suitable with regard to the end pursued by this genre. It is not the addressee who is seduced by the addressor. The addressor, the referent, and the sense are no less subject than the addressee to the seduction exerted by what is at play in a genre of discourse.

149. An offense is not an impertinence, just as a wrong is not the damages (No. 41). An offense is the hegemony of one phrase regimen over another, the usurpation of its authority. *Open the door.* –You said to open the door, you have thus formulated a prescription. A discussion ensues in order to know if this is the case (the definition of a prescription, the conformity of the command with this definition, etc.). Suppose that it is the case. *You have formulated a prescription* is then

a validated phrase. It attributes a property to *Open the door*, that of being a prescription. Impertinence is to link onto the command by a commentary on the command, and not by its execution. An offense would be for the commentator of the command, who is also the addressee of the command, to say: "I have understood which phrase family *Open the door* belongs to, and I am by that fact therefore acquitted of this command." This is the speculative, and in general the metalinguistic, offense (No. 45).

150. The wrong implied in the last judgment: *After what I have just said, there is nothing else to say.* –But you are saying it! What are you adding to what has previously been said by declaring that there is nothing more to add? You are adding either that the preceding phrase was the last phrase, or else that the phrases to come after your "last" phrase will be tautologies of prior phrases. The first explanation is non-sense (the after-the-last); the second requires demonstrating that there is no new phrase to come. As for this demonstration, two things come down to one: either the demonstration is not made of tautologies of prior phrases, or else it is. In the first case, it refutes *de facto* what it establishes *de jure*; in the second, the demonstration has then already been done before it has been done. –And how do you know that it hasn't already been done?–I know only that what has not already been done is to demonstrate that it has already been done. And this demonstration will then refute *de facto* what it establishes *de jure*.

151. How can a phrase offend a phrase, or do it wrong? Do phrases have honor, or pride? An anthropomorphism; now, it's your turn?–In simple terms, you never know *what* the *Ereignis* is. A phrase, in which idiom? In which regimen? The wrong is still in anticipating it, that is, in prohibiting it.

Result

152. Model.
It's not that we discuss, he judges, but only that we think we discuss. Controversy belongs to a genre of discourse, the *dialéktikè*, the theses, arguments, objections, and refutations that the *Topics* and *Sophistical Refutations* analyze and seek to bring within norms. The "great" dialectics, speculative dialectics, dismisses this genre as frivolous: "Objections – if they really are connected to the thing against which they are directed – are one-sided determinations. . . . These one-sided determinations, insofar as they are connected to the thing, are *moments of its concept*; they are thus brought forth in their momentary place during the latter's exposition, and their negation within the dialectic immanent to the concept must be demonstrated." Consequently, in regard to a work which seeks to compile objections, such as the one undertaken by Göschel (the author of the *Aphorisms* commented upon here by Hegel),"Science could demand that such work be superfluous, since it would arise only through thought's lack of culture and through the impatience proper to the frivolity of defective thought" (Hegel, 1829: 380–81). Science, in the Hegelian sense, does not simply brush aside the *dialéktikè* as did Aristotelian didactics. It encloses the *dialéktikè* within its own genre, speculative discourse. In this genre, the two of *dialéktikè*, which is what provides material for paralogisms and aporias, is put into the service of the didactic end, the one. There are no true discussions.

But here is a phrase (the speculative rule) which is nonetheless up for discussion. The fact that this is so is "our" entire affair, an affair of linking phrases. Is oneness the goal of and hence the law for linking phrases? Does not man, the "we"

86

in "our" affair, owe his unique name solely to his linking together of events in the direction of the one?

A chain of phrases comes to be linked together on the basis of this rule. Here are some of its links:

"It lies in the definition of negative dialectics that it will not come to rest in itself, as if it were total. This is its form of hope."

"Dialectics is obliged to make a final move: being at once the impression and the critique of the universal delusive context, it must now turn even against itself."

"According to its own concept, metaphysics cannot be a deductive context of judgments about things in being, and neither can it be conceived after the model of an absolute otherness terribly defying thought."

"[Metaphysics] would be possible only as a legible constellation of things in being [*als lesbare Konstellation von Seiendem*]."

"[Metaphysics] would bring [things in being] into a configuration in which the elements unite to form a script."

"The smallest intramundane traits would be of relevance to the absolute [*Relevanz fürs Absolute*]."

"Metaphysics immigrates into micrology. Micrology is the place where metaphysics finds a haven from totality."

These phrases are taken from the end of *Negative Dialectics* (Adorno, 1966: 406–8). It is stated there that "the micrological view cracks the shells of what, measured by the subsuming cover concept [this is directed against Hegel and the Kant of the first Analytic], is hopelessly isolated and [this view] explodes [the] identity [of the case], the delusion that it is but a specimen" (p. 408).

This question of the specimen [*l'exemplaire*] is decisive. It is the question of the name. What conceptual sense is borne along by the so-called proper name? By what intelligible, dialectical phrase can the factual name be replaced? What does a proper name mean? According to Adorno, this is the speculative question. It presupposes the reversal of the singular into an example of the generic. That is why he writes, in the Preface to *Negative Dialectics*: "Part three elaborates models of negative dialectics. They are not examples; they do not simply elucidate general reflections. . . . —as opposed to the use of examples which Plato introduced and philosophy repeated ever since: as matters of indifference in themselves."

Now, in this third part, entitled "Models," the section "Meditations on Metaphysics" begins, shall we say, by several micrologies called "After Auschwitz." Here, and in adjacent passages, are to be found the following phrases:

"After Auschwitz there is no word tinged from on high [*vom Hohen getontes Wort*], not even a theological one, that has any right unless it underwent a transformation."

"If death were that absolute which philosophy tried in vain to conjure positively, everything is nothing; all that we think, too, is thought into the void."

"In the camps death has a novel horror; since Auschwitz, fearing death means fearing worse than death" (*Ibid.*: 367, 371).

If we discuss or dispute what is indisputable [*indiscutable*], speculative thought, is it only out of impatience, frivolity, and lack of culture? Is "Auschwitz" and "after Auschwitz," that is to say, Western thought and life today, something that disputes speculative discourse? If so, is it frivolous? If not, what happens to and what becomes of the speculative which would not be speculative? What then is the discourse named "Auschwitz" that disputes the speculative? Or that seeks, without success, to dispute it?

"After" implies a periodization. Adorno counts time (but which time?) from "Auschwitz." Is this name the name of a chronological origin? What era begins with this event? The question seems ingenuous when we remember the kind of disintegration the dialectic inflicts upon the idea of beginning in the first chapter of the *Science of Logic*, and already in Kant's *Second Antinomy*. Has Adorno forgotten this?

For him, "Auschwitz" is a model, not an example. From Plato through Hegelian dialectics, the example has the function in philosophy of illustrating an idea; it does not enter into a necessary relation with what it illustrates, but remains "indifferent" to it. The model, on other hand, "brings negative dialectics into the real." As a model, "Auschwitz" does not illustrate dialectics, be it negative. Negative dialectics blurs the figures of the concept, which proceed from the rule of the *Resultat*, and liberates the names that supposedly illustrate the stages of the concept in its movement. The idea of the model corresponds to this reversal in the destiny of dialectics: the model is the name for a kind of para-experience, where dialectics would encounter a non-negatable negative [*un négatif non niable*], and would abide in the impossibility of redoubling that negative into a "result." Where the mind's wound would not become scarred over. Where, writes Derrida, "the investment in death cannot be integrally amortized" (1968a: 107).

The "Auschwitz" model would designate an "experience" of language that brings speculative discourse to a halt. The latter can no longer be pursued "after Auschwitz." Here is a name "within" which speculative thought would not take place. It wouldn't therefore be a name in Hegel's sense, as that figure of memory which assures the permanence of the referent and of its senses when spirit has destroyed its signs. It would be a name without a speculative "name," not sublatable [*irrelevable*] into a concept.

153. Experience.

The word *experience* is *the* word of the *Phenomenology of Mind*, the "science of the experience of consciousness." Experience is the "dialectical process which consciousness executes on itself" (*PhG*: 144, 142). In the sphere that belongs to it, experience supposes the speculative element, the "life of the mind" as a life which "endures death and in death maintains its being" (*Ibid.*: 93). This abode liberates the *Zauberkraft* [magical force] of the mind, the power to convert the negative into Being, the "*göttliche Natur des Sprechens* [divine nature of speech]" (*Ibid.*: 160). Can one still speak of experience in the case of the "Auschwitz" model? Is that not to presuppose that the "magical force" is intact? Is the death named (or unnamed) "Auschwitz" thus an "abode" where the reversal, the old paradox of the affirmation of non-Being can take place? "Since Auschwitz fearing death means fearing worse than death." What makes death not yet the worst is its being not *the* end but only the end of the finite and the revelation of the infinite. Worse than this magical death would be a death without reversal, an end which is simply the end, including the end of the infinite [*la fin de l'infini*].

It could not therefore be said to be an experience, since it would have no result. Its not having a speculative name, however, does not preclude the need to talk about it. The question raised by "Auschwitz" is that of the genre of discourse that links onto "Auschwitz." If it is not the speculative genre, which one can it be? How does it authorize itself, if it is not thanks to the *Aufheben*? If it is not thanks to a movement which, by passing the *Selbst* [self] from the position of referent in the universe of an unmediated phrase to that of addressor and addressee in the universe of a phrase "linking onto" the preceding one, in effect authorizes the second phrase. For what is formulated in the latter about the referent of the former would be formulated by this referent itself, qua addressor, and addressed to itself, qua addressee. Apart from this movement, how can "Auschwitz," something thought from the outside, a referent placed only "near itself" (*an sich*) [*auprès-de-soi*] "for us" (*für uns*), be interiorized, suppressed as an unmediated position, and show itself to itself, know itself, in the identity (be it ephemeral) of a for-itself (*für sich*) [*pour-soi*]? Without this permutation, there is according to Hegel only empty, subjective, arbitrary chatter, at best a regression to "ratiocinative" thought, to the discourse of understanding, to the "modesty" of finitude. Now, this finitude, he writes, because it is subjective vanity set up as an absolute, is "wickedness" (1830: § 386). Nevertheless, in declaring that one must speak about "Auschwitz" but that one can only speak about it truly if the anonymous referent of the phrase becomes its addressee and addressor and thereupon "names" itself, the summons to express the result of "Auschwitz" is an intimidation (or notification [*intimation*]) that prejudges the nature of the object. If the name hidden by "Auschwitz" is the death of the magical, "beautiful death," how could the latter, which sustains the speculative movement, rise back up from its death in the camps? And, on the other hand, supposing that "after Auschwitz" speculative discourse had died, does it follow that it leaves place only to subjective chatter and the wickedness of modesty? It is within speculative logic that this alternative is formulated. To accept it would be to perpetuate that logic.

Is it possible that some kind of phrase, in accordance with some other logic, takes place "after" the anonym "Auschwitz" and which would not be its speculative result? We would need to imagine that the cleaving introduced into Western thought by "Auschwitz" does not pass outside of speculative discourse, that is (since the latter has no outside), that it does not determine its effect inside that discourse in the guise of an incomplete, invalid, or unexpressed way out, as a kind of neurotic fixation upon a figure (that of "Auschwitzian" death) which would only be, all things considered, but a moment. Rather this cleaving cracks speculative logic itself and not merely its effects, it jams the functioning of certain but not all of its operators, it condemns that logic to the disarrangement [dérèglement] of an infinity which would be neither the good one nor the bad one, or which would be both.

154. Scepticism.

In making the name "Auschwitz" a model for and within negative dialectics, Adorno suggests that what meets its end there is merely affirmative dialectics. In the *Philosophical Propaedeutics*, Hegel makes a distinction within logic between "the dialectical side or side of negative reason, and the speculative side or side of positive reason" (1809: 12). This distinction is made again in the *Encyclopaedia*: "In the dialectical stage these finite determinations suppress themselves and pass into their opposites [. . .]. The speculative stage, or stage of positive reason, apprehends the unity of determinations in their opposition – the *affirmative*, which is involved in their disintegration and in their transition" (1830: § 82).

This distinction is not respected everywhere in Hegel's opus. In fact, how could it possibly be respected in a discourse whose resource is found precisely in the negative as a magical affirmative force? What ought to be surprising, rather, is that the opposition should have been made at all and that it should be maintained apart from its own dialecticalization, like a concession made on the side, though on a major point, to the understanding. This opposition is a trace, the scar of a wound in speculative discourse, a wound for which that discourse is also the mending. The wound is that of nihilism. This wound is not an accidental one, it is absolutely philosophical. Scepticism (of the ancient kind, it should be understood) is not just one philosophy among others; it is, writes Hegel in 1802, "in an implicit form [. . .], the free aspect of every philosophy." Hegel continues: "when in a given proposition expressing reasoned knowledge, one has isolated its reflective aspect, that is, the concepts enclosed within it, and when one considers the way in which these concepts are connected, then it necessarily appears that these concepts are sublated [relevés, aufgehoben] at the same time, or that they are united in such a way that they contradict each other; otherwise, the proposition would not be one of the reason, but one of the understanding" (1802: 229). In § 39 of the 1830 *Encyclopaedia*, Hegel refers to the 1802 article as though he still approved of it.

In § 78, however, a stern corrective is placed upon the philosophical freedom to disintegrate determinations: "Scepticism, made a negative science and systematically applied to all forms of knowledge, might seem a suitable introduction, as pointing out the nullity [*Nichtigkeit*] of such assumptions. But a sceptical introduction would be not only an unpleasant but also a useless course; and that because Dialectic, as we shall soon make appear, is *itself an essential element of affirmative science.*" This corrective had already been given in the Introduction to the *Phenomenology of Mind*: "Scepticism always sees in the result only *pure nothingness*, and abstracts from the fact that this nothing is determinate, is the nothing of *that out of which it comes as a result*" (137).

In the *Phenomenology of Mind*, the animals are given as examples of wisdom with regard to the truth of sense-certainty: they despair of the latter's reality and they eat it up (*zehren sie auf*) (159). Scepticism is unpleasant because it is the animality of the mind, its stomach, which consumes determinations. Such is the wounding fascination exerted by nihilism, a consumption or consummation that leaves no remains. The balm and the exorcism are as follows: to make this distressing negativity work for the production of an affirmation. Is the anonym "Auschwitz" a model of negative dialectics? Then, it will have awakened the despair of nihilism and it will be necessary "after Auschwitz" for thought to consume its determinations like a cow its fodder or a tiger its prey, that is, with no result. In the sty or the lair that the West will have become, only that which follows upon this consumption will be found: waste matter, shit. So must be spoken the end of the infinite, as the endless repetition of *Nichtige*, as the "bad infinity." We wanted the progress of the mind, we got its shit.

What would a result of "Auschwitz" consist in? What is a *result*? In the same paragraph § 82 of the *Encyclopaedia*, Hegel goes on to write: "The result of Dialectic is *positive*, because it has a *determined content*, or because its result is not *empty and abstract nothing*, but the negation of *certain specific determinations* which are contained in the result—for the very reason that it is a resultant and not an *unmediated nothing*." There is *Resultat* because there is determination.

But this determination is only determined, in turn, by the rules of that genre of discourse which is the speculative.

Hegel

1. In the preface to the *Phenomenology of Mind*, Hegel describes predication: on the one hand, the *Selbst* (that which is in question, the subject of the proposition) constitutes the base, *Basis*, or inert support; on the other hand, the contents attached to it obey a to-and-fro movement, they do not belong to the *Selbst*, they can be applied to other "bases" and give rise to other utterances. These utterances take the form of attributive judgments, and the contents are their predicates. Such is the "ratiocinative" phrase, *das Räsonnieren*. The philosophy of the understanding, in the Aristotelian and Kantian sense, is blocked, says Hegel, by the question: how can the relation (synthesis) between the predicate and the subject of a judgment be arbitrary? Conceptual, "grasping" thinking, *das begriefende Denken*, does not take as its subject the subject of the phrase, the quiescent *Selbst*(*ein ruhendes Subjekt*) that would impassively sustain accidents (*das unbewegt die Akzidenzen*

trägt) (Hegel is no longer even talking about predicates). Its subject is rather "the very *elbst* of the object, manifesting itself as the development of the object," that is, "a self-determining active concept which takes up its determinations and makes them its own" (*PhG*: 118).

Three aspects are to be foregrounded in this change of "subject" from Kant to Hegel. First of all, the discourse of the understanding distinguishes within a phrase between the referent (the object, the *Selbst* or the substance in the Aristotelian sense) and its sense (the concept). Its "difficulties" stem from this distinction. The Hegelian "solution" consists in its suppression: the referent is none other than the concept, than its sense. That about which something is phrased is also that which is phrased (the real is rational). This identity is already the case for natural languages, but it remains in itself and is apparent in them only "for us," who are addressees external to the "current" phrase and already situated within speculative discourse. Within the latter, this exteriority is interiorized, the "for us" becomes "for itself," the *Selbst* comes to occupy the addressee instance of the speculative phrase, thus replacing the "we," which is either rejected or included within speculative discourse. The *Selbst* thus occupies three instances: referent, sense, and addressee. Two questions need to be pursued after this: 1) that of the speculative addressor; 2) the simple identity of instances as impossible (it is the Tibetans' "Om"); if the same occupies various instances, it does so contradictorily. The secret mechanism of what Hegel calls determination, which he sets to work in order to escape empty identity, consists in the arranging of phrase universes into several instances.

Second aspect: the change of "subject" which is translated into the speculative idiom by the passage from the "in itself" to the "for itself" corresponds to what the logician and the linguist (in different senses) call the formation of a metalanguage onto an object-language. It is not the door which has to be opened, it's the phrase *Open the door* which has to be averred (Nos. 45, 149).

Third aspect: the speculative apparatus needs the *Doppelsinnigkeit* [ambiguity] and the *Zweifelhaftigkeit* [doubtfulness] of the terms that form phrases (or of the phrases themselves: for Hegel, terms are undeveloped phrases). Duplicity and doubtfulness are signs that the *Selbst's* identity is contradictory. It is not merely a case of transitory properties, prior to the final univocality. In the *Aesthetics* (1835: I, 306), the symbol, for example, is characterized by its "essentially *zweideutig*" nature: the lion engraved on a medal is a "visible shape and existent." Is it a symbol? Perhaps. If it is, what does it symbolize? That remains to be decided. Whence two levels of uncertainty: sensible or symbolic? And in the second case: which signification? Once the answers are expressed, the equivocation is dissipated, the symbol is dislodged, a sense is attributed to a referent.

But equivocation and doubtfulness ought to be found once more in the language phrase that links onto the sensible phrase. It is an "advantage" for the mind (*WL*: 32; 1830: § 96) to find multiple senses for the words of a natural language. This advantage is at its height when the senses are opposed, *entgegensetzte*. The more frequently this is the case in a language, the more it is inhabited by the "speculative spirit." "It can delight a thinker [. . .] to find the union of opposites naïvely shown in the dictionary as one word with opposite meanings." This delight is at its height with the German *aufheben*: not only does it unite the affirmative *raise* with the negative *remove*, as does Latin *tollere*, but the affirmation already contains the negation: to raise is to preserve (*erhalten*), and "in order to preserve it, something is removed from its immediacy and so from an existence which is open to external influences" (*WL*: 107).

If thought's delight culminates in *aufheben*, it is because this term from ordinary language is also the name *par excellence* of the speculative operation. The *Selbst*, or subject of the ordinary phrase or phrase of the understanding, is *circulated* by speculative discourse among the various instances presented by that phrase. In this becoming, it is at once preserved and removed.

In doing this, speculative discourse only does what ordinary discourse does "naïvely." It is not the metalanguage of an object-language, but the object-language itself preserved and removed. (Dialectical) logic "is not something distinct (*nichts Unterschiedenes*) from its object and content; for it is the inwardness of the content, the dialectic which it possesses within itself, which is the mainspring of its advance" (*WL*: 54). The *Selbst* is removed from one instance to another, from the sense in itself (referent) to the sense for itself (addressee), but it is preserved and raised since it is reflected in the speculum of the phrase universe. Speculative discourse claims merely to liberate the *Selbst*'s infinite movement of alteration, which is potential in the universe of the slightest phrase on account of its being disposed in several instances. It allows the *Selbst* to wander through the relational situations that unite the instances in the phrase universe.

2. Speculative discourse is this wandering. Truth cannot be expressed in one phrase, since it is the unraveling of its equivocation, and so it requires several phrases linked together. The speculative linkage is not haphazard. The wandering follows rules: three indispensable ones, to stick to the dialectics of Being (*WL*: 82).

First, to say *being*, is to say nothing that is determined, it is to say nothing (*Nichts, néant, nothingness*): and, therefore, to say *nothing* is also to say *being*, since being is nothing. Thus, *being* vanishes into *nothingness*, and *nothingness* into *being*. Their identity is engendered from the reciprocal vanishing of one term into the other: it is the same whether one says *being* or *nothing*. This is an empty identity. To say *being* or *nothing* is to say nothing; or else, being and nothingness are the same thing. "Ratiocinative" thought stops here, upon this void.

A second rule frees up the situation: "Looking at the proposition more closely, we find that it has a movement which involves the spontaneous vanishing of the proposition itself. But in thus vanishing, there happens in it (*geschieht an ihm*) that which is to effectuate (*ausmachen*) its own proper content, namely, becoming" (*WL*: 90). If one says *Being and nothingness are the same thing*, this phrase, by dint of its form as an attributive proposition, blocks discourse within empty identity. It harbors something else, however, which is not a sense for itself, but an "effectuation" that traverses it: the movement of the vanishing of being into nothingness and of nothingness into being that reasoning has just effected (rule 1). This movement is the "proper content" of the phrase about being and nothingness. It is already becoming, but becoming does not yet appear to itself (it appears "to us").

Third rule: this "content" (the movement of the reciprocal vanishing of being and nothingness), so long as it is not expressed in the form of a phrase, does no more than "happen" to it: the phrase is only its effect. Nor does the phrase express it in itself. An unexpressed effect (*nicht ausgedrückt*) is not a speculative result. A term (another phrase) must express the content of the phrase *Being and nothingness are the same thing*. But how do we get to this expression? If, for example, we say that the phrase signifies the unity of being and nothingness, what are we doing? *Wir meinen*, we give our opinion, we opine. Now, according to Hegel, "the *Meinen* is a form of subjectivity, which does not belong to the presentation in this series (*das nicht in diese Reihe der Darstellung gehört*)" (92). It is necessary to eliminate every phrase introduced from the outside, subjectively, unless it is relevant to the presentation (here, in the sense of exposition, *dar-*), every heterogeneous third term. "The third in which being and nothingness reside (*Bestehen*) must also take place here, and it has done so; it is *becoming*" (92). The sought-for third "must" take place in the same "current" presentation as the two opposites and must make a series (*Reihe*) with them. Now, we have *already* found it, although unexpressed, in the movement through which their reciprocal vanishing was presented. It has already taken place in this presentation, but only as an effect. Its effectuation has preceded its expression. "What is the truth is neither being nor nothing, but that being — does not pass over (*übergehen*, transit) – but has passed over (*übergegangen*) into nothing, and nothing into being" (*WL*: 82–83). The past tense marks the delay of the expression for itself with regard to the effectuation in itself, but this delay attests that the third term (becoming, passage) can only be presented in the series after the two others, as their dialectical sum. The effect would be like 1 + 2; a result would be like 3 x 1.

I will try to formulate the argument another way. The concept of series implies that of passage (Nos. 94–97). But the passage from one term to the next can be marked only in a series, only as a term, and only after the fact (these three restrictions forming only one). The passage is only expressed with its terms past. —Objection: is this to say that every past was a passage? That would be to give the edge [*donner le pas*] to the continuous, to the before/after, over the *Ereignis* (Aristotle Notice). Such a privilege does not seem doubtful (or equivocal) in Hegel's thought. It bears the name of *Selbst, soi*, self.

We have thus disengaged three rules for the formation and linking of phrases which are necessary to speculative discourse. The rule of equivocation allows into this discourse only a term or a phrase capable of copresenting several universes. The rule is guaranteed by the fact that a simple phrase, which presents only one universe, nevertheless copresents within itself several instances.

The rule of immanent derivation or paradoxical rule bears upon the linking and prescribes that *If p, then not-p*, and *If not-p, then p*. *If you win, then you lose; if you lose, then you win* (Protagoras Notice). *If Being, then Not-Being; if Not-Being, then Being* (Gorgias Notice). This rule elaborates equivocation in the form of reciprocal implication. It leads to contradiction: *p and not-p* (in Wittgenstein's sense). It permits the dilemma (in Protagoras' sense) at the price of a supplementary "round" of implication (on the side of *not-p*), which yields a "result" *q* in the ordinary sense: *If p, then q; and, If not-p, then p, then q* (No. 8).

The third rule, that of expression or result (in the speculative sense), prescribes that the passage from *p* to *not-p* and the passage from *not-p* to *p* be expressed together by a third term (or phrase) *q: If p, then not-p, then q; and, If not-p, then p, then q*. As opposed to an ordinary "result," the *and* is included in the rule, and both "rounds" are required on each side. This arrangement eliminates dilemma.

3. So we think we have isolated speculative discourse as a genre: a set of possible phrases subject to a group of rules of formation and linkage. But the concept of rule stems from "ratiocinative" thought, from the understanding. It introduces the (formalist) distinc-

tion between phrase (here the phrase of speculative discourse) and operators for forming and linking these phrases, rules that is. The investigation into the rules that we have undertaken is situated at a metalinguistic level with regard to the examined language (speculative discourse). The latter is placed in the position of object-language. Speculative discourse and formalist discourse are therefore opposed.

But opposition is the very mainspring of speculative discourse. It is also at play between speculative discourse and the discourse that thinks itself foreign to it. What has the supposed metalanguage done? It has elaborated the presuppositions of speculation (taken as its referent). It has isolated a signification of this discourse (that it is ruled by nonderived rules) which is contrary to the signification speculation gives itself (I am the very engenderment of the true in the linkings of phrases). It has given a name to the result of this opposition (the speculative is one genre of discourse, there are others). The examination of speculation has thereby unknowingly, and thus only in itself, effectuated the principal operations that speculation not only effectuates but also expresses for itself. Phrase regimens and genres of discourse must then be considered as transitory results in the development of the *Selbst*. "Metalanguage" is the reflective moment of this development. You never get out of speculation.

It is not the we, but the self [*le soi*] that resists negativity. The we occupies a preeminent place in the *Phenomenology of Mind* because this work is elaborated in the field of the experience of consciousness where "the I is one side of the relationship and the whole relation" (1830: § 413). This privilege vanishes when logic, or objective mind, is involved, that is, when speculative discourse is extended to objects that are not part of consciousness. In these cases, the we is seen to occupy the necessary though subordinate place of the abstract moment, of the moment of exteriority, the place of the other of speculation (the understanding) within speculation. The we vanishes, however, in the supreme moment, that of the idea of philosophy, which is said to be "near and for itself [*an und für sich*]" (*Ibid.*: § 577). No we is needed at that time in order for this idea, which is God, to express its relation to itself.

In the *Encyclopaedia*, the expression *für uns*, for us, is generally combined with the expression *an sich*, near itself. Together, they mark the abstract moment in the development of the concept, wherein is maintained the exteriority between the object of thought, the self which is near itself, and the subject, the we that posits this self. The speculative moment, on the contrary, comes when this exteriority is dissolved, when the self comes "in the place of" the we (which is no longer there), when the object of thought becomes the thought that objectifies itself and the object that thinks itself, the *für sich*, the for itself.

Such is, for example, the difference between a cause and a goal: "It is only when near itself, or for us, that the cause is in the effect made for the first time a cause, and that it there returns *into itself*. The goal, on the other hand, is expressly stated as containing the determinations *in its own self* — the effect, namely, which in the purely causal relation is never free from otherness. [. . .] The goal then needs to be speculatively apprehended [. . .]" (*Ibid.*: § 204). Similarly, in the case of reciprocal action, (*die Wechselwirkung*), it is at first only "near themselves" and "in our reflection" that determinations of this form of effectivity are "nul and void" (*nichtige*); but the *Wechselwirkung* only attains its unity when the unity of the determinations "is also *for itself*," when reciprocal action itself suppresses each determination by inverting it into its opposite (origin and effect, action and reaction, etc.) (§ 155 and 156). The price paid for speculation is the suppression of the we as an identity that thinks or phrases from the outside.

The first *Realphilosophie* of Jena teaches that "the sign as *a real being* must thus directly vanish" and that "the name is in itself something *permanent*, without either the thing or the subject. In the name, the *self*-subsisting reality of the sign is nullified" (1804: 221–22). I, he, you, and we are signs, as are all pronouns; identity cannot take place within them. Identity takes place within names, and it takes place at the price of the designification of signs, of the destruction of pronouns. This is how "the thing works."

And are names, for that matter, needed for the thing not to work? The thing is even more omnivorous, it also devours names. For names again are merely what memory turns signs into (*Ibid.*: 221). Memory, though, is itself "the one-sided mode of thought's *existence*," its "mechanical" side, the kind of thinking that is "for us or near itself," as the *Encyclopaedia* recalls (§ 464 and Remark). On the contrary, then, if there were nothing but names, the thing would not work precisely because the name-machine, nominalism, would work in its place. Jacques Derrida "risks" the "proposition" according to which "what Hegel *could never think*, is a machine which would work" (1968a: 107). Machines function through a loss. Speculation is a machine that gains, and it is therefore a deranged machine. The "thing" only works by transmuting its wastes—including names and pronouns —into gains.

This discombobulation is a dialectical necessity which is itself its finality. "Reason," it is written in the Preface to the *Phenomenology*, "is *a doing in accordance with an end (das zweckmässige Tun)*." The model for this finality is taken from Aristotle. The speculative game appears monstrous only from the perspective of the understanding, but the understanding fails to recognize its presuppositions, accepting them as evidences, as axioms or as conditions of possibility. It admits first phrases. There are none. The first is also the last. Thus, you begin with philosophy's need for a figure in which mind is only "near itself," but every phrase is needed in order to express the object of this need and to suppress the need, in order for mind "to become for itself what it is near itself" (1830: 387 Remark.) To express oneself for oneself is the end [*fin*] that guides the rebounds of the self in the speculative phrase. This end is the "reconciliation of the self-conscious reason with the reason which *is* in the world—in other words, with actuality" (*Ibid.*: § 3). This goal is incessantly attained and accordingly never attained. If it is attained, it is not attained. When it is not attained, it is still attained. The rule of immanent derivation and of negative dialectics is here applied to the goal, that is to say, to the result itself. But a dialecticalized goal is still just as much of a goal. The teleology has merely been sophisticated. You never get out of speculation.

4. At least, it is necessary to have entered it. It is entered on one condition, the initial displacement of the subject into a polymorphous *Selbst*. This is the presupposition found at the "exit" which, according to the rule of the *Resultat*, is an entrance . There is one and only one X. It is the same under the various forms and throughout all the operations, and that is why it is totalized into a single *Resultat*, which is disintegrated in turn for new operations. It is also by supposing this same that the links from phrase to phrase are reputed to be necessary in terms of their mode and occurrence, and that dialectics is said to be a sublation [*relève*]. But this presupposition of the same is not falsifiable (No. 66). It is a rule that governs metaphysical discourse (as its closure). Philosophical examination never

reveals such a subject-substance. It reveals phrases, phrase universes, and occurrences, with, respectively, presentations, presenteds, and events.

Obviously, the presupposition of the *Selbst* cannot be objected to on the grounds that "in reality that's not the way it is." The objection can be raised, though, that it is a rule for a genre of discourse – the metaphysical genre – which seeks to engender its own rules, but precisely that this rule cannot engender itself from discourse.

That the engenderment of the rule be the stakes of the discourse (or, that one phrase in order to learn how one is able to phrase what one phrases) is the rule in the philosophical genre. One always "begins" by phrasing without knowing if what one phrases is legitimate. For, as long as the rule is what is at stake in the discourse, then the rule is not the rule of that discourse, and the discourse makes links any way it can, it tries itself out [*il s'essaie*]. And when the rule is "identified" as the rule of the genre one was trying out, what is at stake in that genre ceases to be its rule, and the genre ceases to be an essay or a critique. The third or "speculative" rule, the one about the *Resultat*, thereby remains necessarily presupposed. This is not the case for the first two rules: those of equivocacy and of immanent derivation. A prescription like *Equivocate* (or: *Dialecticalize*) *every phrase, including the present one* signifies that the operators of equivocacy and of dialectics must be applied to the prescription itself. To state it otherwise, in philosophical discourse, every phrase that presents itself as the rule of this discourse must be submitted to equivocation and dialecticalization and be put back into play. This self-mocking prescription corresponds to scepticism.

The speculative rule or rule of the *Resultat* is formulated, however, as *Engender every phrase as the expressed identity of the preceding ones, including the present phrase*. Now, considered by the understanding as a rule, this phrase is logically the first one, and has no predecessor. It cannot therefore be the expressed identity of the phrases that precede it. The objection can be made that, considered speculatively, this "beginning" has to be engendered and can come only at the end, as the result of the phrases which "follow" it from the beginning onward. But the beginning can appear as this final result only because the rule of the *Resultat* has been presupposed from the beginning. The first phrase was linked onto the following one and onto the others in conformity with this rule. But this rule is then merely presupposed and not engendered. If it is not applied from the beginning, there is no necessity in finding it at the end, and if it is not at the end, it wouldn't have been engendered, and it was therefore not the rule that was sought.

The stakes of philosophical discourse are in a rule (or rules) which remains to be sought, and to which the discourse cannot be made to conform before the rule has been found. The links from phrase to phrase are not ruled by a rule but by the quest for a rule.

155. We.

If, "after Auschwitz," the *Resultat* is lacking, it would be for want of determination. "Auschwitz" would have no speculative name because it would be the proper name of a para-experience or even of a destruction of experience. What determination would Auschwitz be lacking so as to turn it into an experience with a *Resultat*? Would it be that of the impossibility of a *we*? In the concentration camps, there would have been no subject in the first-person plural. In the absence of such a subject, there would remain "after Auschwitz" no subject, no *Selbst* which could prevail upon itself to name itself in naming "Auschwitz." No phrase inflected in this person would be possible: we did this, we felt that, they made us suffer this humiliation, we got along in this way, we hoped that, we didn't think about . . . , and even: each of us was reduced to solitude and silence. There would be no collective witness. From many former deportees, there is only silence. From many, there is only the shame felt before the testimony of former deportees. Shame and anger over the explanations and interpretations—as sophisticated as they may be—by thinkers who claim to have found some sense to this shit. (Especially over the argument that it is precisely because God failed that one should be faithful to Him). A kind of disauthorization (one at least of the four silences, perhaps more) (Nos. 26, 27). Would this be a case of a dispersion worse than the diaspora, the dispersion of phrases?

In a republic, the pronoun of the first-person plural is in effect the linchpin for the discourse of authorization. Substitutable for a proper name, *We, the French people* . . . , it is supposedly able to link prescriptions (such as articles in codes, court rulings, laws, decrees, ordinances, circulars, and commands) onto their legitimation "in a suitable way." Take an obligatory prescription: *It is an obligation for x to carry out act* α. The legitimation of this obligation can be written thus: *It is a norm for y that "it is obligatory for x to carry out act* α." (Kalinowski, 1972; Nos. 203–209). The republican regimen's principle of legitimacy is that the addressor of the norm, *y*, and the addressee of the obligation, *x*, are the same. The legislator ought not to be exempt from the obligation he or she norms. And the obligated one is able to promulgate the law that obligates him or her. In speaking the law, the former decrees that he or she must respect it. In respecting the law, the latter decrees it anew. Their names, *x* and *y*, are in principle perfectly commutable between at least the two instances of normative addressor and prescriptive addressee. They are thus united in a single we, the one designating itself by the collective name "French citizens." The authorization is then formulated thus: *We decree as a norm that it is an obligation for us to carry out act* α. This is the principle of autonomy.

This construction of a homogeneous we conceals, however, a double heterogeneity. First, there is the heterogeneity tied to the pronouns. The normative phrase is *We, the French people. decree as a norm that,* etc.; the prescriptive phrase is *We, the French people, ought to carry out act* α. But the two *we* 's do not occupy the same position among the instances in each of the two phrases. In the normative, the *we* is the addressor of the norm; in the prescriptive, it is the addressee of the obligation. On one side, *I declare*; on the other side, *You ought to.* The proper name masks this displacement, as does the *we* since it is able to unite *I* and *you*. It remains that, in the obligation, *I* is the instance that prescribes, and not the one addressed by the prescription. One may make the law and submit to it, but not "in the same place," that is, not in the same phrase. In effect, another phrase (the normative one) is needed to legitimate the prescriptive phrase. From this duality alone a suspicion is already born about the identity between the one who speaks the law and the one to whom the law applies (Kant Notice 2), as well as a certain scepticism.

The heterogeneity of the phrases aggravates this threat of dislodgement. The normative phrase resembles a performative (Nos. 204–9). It is sufficient that the norm be formulated for it to be the norm and for the obligation it norms to be legitimated. Instantly, its addressor is the legislator. Instantly, the addressee of the obligation is beholden to respect the prescription. The performative effectuates the legitimation of the obligation by formulating it. There is no need to link onto the norm in order for its legitimacy to be averred.

This is not the case for the prescriptive. It entails the requirement of a subsequent phrase, wherein it will be averred that the prescription has or has not been obeyed, that the new phrase universe it commands its addressee to present has or has not taken place. For, in the obligation, it is up to the addressee to link onto the chain (Kant Notice 2, § 6), and he or she can do so in many ways (Nos. 136–40). That is why it is customary to say that the obligation entails the freedom of the one who is obligated. This is a "grammatical remark," one that bears upon the mode of linking called forth by the ethical phrase.

Thus: on the side of the norm, a phrase universe imputed to an addressor and which is immediately everything that it is, without appeal (on the model of sublimity given by *Fiat lux et lux fuit*). On the side of the obligation, a phrase universe centered upon an addressee, with the expectation of the latter's responsibility to link in accordance with the command. A single proper name, whether singular or collective, designates an entity astride two heterogeneous situations. It is the property of proper names to receive such heterogeneities (Nos. 80, 81). But it is not legitimate, it is even illusory, in the Kantian sense of a transcendental illusion, to suppose a subject-substance that would be both a "subject of the uttering" (even though it is not the addressor in the prescriptive) and the permanence of a self (even though from one phrase to the next it leaps from one instance situation to another). Its proper name allows it to be pinpointed within a world of names, but not within a linking together of phrases coming from heterogeneous regimens and whose universes and the tensions exerted upon them are incommensurable with each other. The we would be the vehicle of this transcendental illusion, halfway between the rigid (constant) designator that the name is and the "current" designator that the singular pronoun is. It is not surprising that, in the "currentness" or "actuality" of obligation, the we that reputedly unites obligee and legislator is threatened with being split.

156. "Beautiful death."

This threat appears at its height when the obligation made to the addressee is that he or she die. Imagine for a moment that the canonical formula for "Auschwitz" is *It is a norm decreed by y that it is obligatory for x to die*. It may be concluded that the content of the order, the addressee's death, prohibits the formation of the we. It would be absurd for the *we* of the norm to decree its own vanishing. But this is not at all so. Public authority (family, state, military, partisan, denominational) can order its own addressees to die. Or, at least, to prefer to die. The *Die* needs to be modalized: *Die rather than escape* (Socrates in prison), *Die rather than be enslaved* (the Paris Commune), *Die rather than be defeated* (Thermopyles, Stalingrad). Death is prescribed as an alternative to another obligation (civic duty, freedom, military glory) if the latter is revealed to be impracticable. This is not the case for "Auschwitz." It is not a *Die rather than . . .* , but simply, a *Die*, that the SS authorities address to the deportee, with no alternative.

The "reason to die" always forms the bond of a we. The paradox of the order to die is that the name of its addressee, if he or she obeys the order, can never again figure upon the addressor instance of subsequent, direct phrases, and in particular of normative phrases like *I decree as a norm that . . .* He or she is condemned to the referent instance in direct phrases: he or she will be spoken about; and, if he or she is found situated upon the addressor instance, it will be in indirect phrases, which are themselves the referents of direct phrases: quotations, prosopopeias, recountings of all kinds.

By identifying oneself with the legislator who orders one's death, one nevertheless escapes the miserable fate of being the referent for every forthcoming phrase that may bear one's name: the scourge of the dead in Greek thought. One can only succeed in this by obeying the order, since by doing it, one decrees it anew as a norm. One thereby makes one's name enter into the collective name of the legislating authority, which is a constant addressor because it is a rigid designator. One escapes death by the only means known—the perpetuation of the proper name. This proper name must be proper not only to the interested party, but also to the collectivity (through patronym, eponym, or nationality), since the collective name is what assures the perenniality within itself of individual proper names. Such is the Athenian "beautiful death," the exchange of the finite for the infinite, of the *eschaton* for the *télos*: the *Die in order not to die.*

157. Exception.

"Auschwitz" is the forbiddance of the beautiful death. The content of the command, the death of its (supposed) addressee, is not sufficient to shatter the we. It would really be the converse, if death were at least prescribed to the addressee as an alternative to the effectuation of an Idea. But no alternative is permitted to the deportee. And, if he or she has no alternative, it is because he or she is not the addressee of an obligation. The canonical formula of "Auschwitz" cannot be *Die, I decree it*, a phrase that allows the equivocation of a possible substitution of I for you to hover. Rather, the formula would be, if we focus on the SS as "legislator": *That s/he die, I decree it*; or, if we focus on the deportee as the one "obligated": *That I die, s/he decrees it.* That which orders death is excepted from the obligation, and that which undergoes the obligation is excepted from the legitimation. The authority of the SS comes out of a we from which the deportee is excepted once and for all: the race, which grants not only the right to command, but also the right to live, that is, to place oneself at the various instances of phrase universes. The deportee, according to this authority, cannot be the addressee of an order to die, because one would have to be capable of giving one's life in order to carry out the order. But one cannot give a life that one doesn't have the right to have. Sacrifice is not available to the deportee, nor for that reason accession to an immortal, collective name. One's death is legitimate because one's life is illegitimate. The individual name must be killed (whence the use of serial numbers), and the collective name (Jew) must also be killed in such a way that no we bearing this name might remain which could take the deportee's death into itself and eternalize it. This death must therefore be killed, and that is what is worse than death. For, if death can be exterminated, it is because there is nothing to kill. Not even the name Jew.

The SS does not have to legitimate for the deportee's benefit the death sentence it apprises him or her of. The deportee does not have to feel obligated by this decree. The universes of the two phrases *That s/he die, I decree it* and, *That I die, s/he decrees it* have no possible common application. That is what is marked by the shattering of the prescriptive phrase and of its legitimation into two phrases issuing from that fissure. The addressee of the SS norm is the SS. The addressor of the prescription the deportee receives is unknown to him or her, and is not "recognizable" by the addressee, who cannot come to place him- or herself at the addressor instance in a legitimating linkage. Dispersion is at its height. My law kills them who have no relevance to it. My death is due to their law, to which I owe nothing. Delegitimation is complete, it confirms the suspicion cast upon the we that supposedly assures the linking of the prescription onto the norm, namely, that it is a fiction. Were this *we* called humanity (but then it wouldn't have been a collective proper name), then "Auschwitz" is indeed the name for the extinction of that name.

That is why the question "Auschwitz"? is also the question "after Auschwitz"? The unchaining of death, the utmost obligation, from what legitimates it is perpetuated "after" the crime; scepticism, and even nihilism, have every reason to feed off this endlessly. For it is not even true, as Hegel believes, that afterward it still remains for us to chew and digest, in our lair, the "nul and void" of the legitimating linkage, the extermination of a determined we. The dispersive, merely negative and nearly analytical dialectics at work under the name of "Auschwitz," deprived of its "positive-rational operator," the *Resultat*, cannot engender anything, not even the sceptical we that chomps on the shit of the mind. The name would remain empty, retained along with other names in the network of a world, put into mecanographical or electronic memory. But it would be nobody's memory, about nothing and for no one.

158. Third Party?

That genre of discourse which is speculative dialectics cannot accept this kind of an end. It does not consider itself beaten by nihilism. Consider again the two phrases: *That s/he die, that's my law* and *That I die, that's his/her law*. The preceding analysis emphasizes that a we has become impossible with each "partner's" passage into the third person (that is, into the situation of referent) in the other's phrase.

It has become impossible, though, only because it has been presupposed that the we must be formed by the conjunction of an I and a you. *We* has been confused with the subject of the autonomy that legitimates the obligation.

But *I* and *s/he* can also form a we. The we, for example, of a representative, a spokesperson, or an envoy. Only, this we is addressed to a third party: *My comrades and I, we declare to you* . . . This we takes place only when it is situated in a phrase universe in which a you is likewise situated. It is addressed. Now, "Auschwitz" is the name of a phrase or rather of two phrases which have no addressee marked in the universes they present. This is what the Nazis mean when they state that they make laws without having to refer to anyone other than themselves, and what the Jews mean when they suspect that God could not have wanted their lives to be sacrificed to Him in this way. The absence of an addressee is also the absence of a witness. The sublation of "Auschwitz" lacks an instance which could relay into a new phrase, for itself, what is presented on the Nazi side and on the deportee's side, as only near itself.

"Auschwitz" would be the coexistence of two secrets, the Nazi's secret and the deportee's secret. Each knows something "near oneself" about the other (one: *That s/he die* and the other: *That's his/her law*), but neither can state it to anybody. What is possible at the "peak" of communication would be a double agent. An agent is double, however, only for a third party who can bear witness to the fact that this agent knows about each partner what each of them knows about oneself and the other. Lacking this third party, a double agent is not a double agent but two plain agents with two pseudonyms. The agent is double only when unmasked, once the secret has been divulged and a single name assigned to him or her by a third (fourth) party.

But the third is there, objects speculation. The dispersion without witnesses that "we" have characterized as the extinction of the third needed to be expressed by a third. That *we* has vanished at Auschwitz, "we," at least, have said it. There is no passage from the deportee's phrase universe to the SS's phrase universe. In order to affirm this, however, we needed to affirm one universe and then the other as if "we" were first the SS and then the deportee. In doing this, "we" effectuated what "we" were looking for, a we. In looking for it, this we was looking for itself. It is expressed then at the end of the movement since it was effectuated from the beginning. For, without the presupposition of this permanence of a thinking "we," there would have been no movement in search of a whole. This we is certainly not the totalization of the I's, the you's, and the s/he's in play under the name of "Auschwitz," for it is true that this name designates the impossibility of such a totalization. Instead it is the reflective movement of this impossibility, that is, the dispersion which comes to self-consciousness and is sublated out of the annihilation and into the affirmation of nothingness: The we composed at least of *I* who write and *you* who read.

159. Without a result.

The contingent name for this merely effectuated movement is "Auschwitz." But its speculative name, its name as a concept, ought precisely to designate the conjunction of two unconjugateable phrases: a norm without an addressee, a death sentence without legitimacy. We think of terror. But the Jacobin Reign of Terror allows no exceptions: even I, Robespierre, fall under its universalizing logic. The legislator is obligated to the transparency of pure will by the same token as everyone else, he is thus suspect like them. This particular terror merely verifies the principle of autonomy. At "Auschwitz," on the other hand, exception is what rules. Its speculative name is not the rational terror that is extended infinitely because goodwill is to be required from every you. Nazism requires nothing from what is not "Aryan," except for the cessation of its appearing to exist. On the other hand, it requires from every "Aryan" (its sole addressee) to meet his or her obligation to the purity of his or her racial origin, in particular by suppressing all that is not "Aryan."

If there is terror in Nazism, it is exerted internally among the "pure," who are always suspected of not being pure enough. They cleanse themselves of suspicion by excepting themselves from all impurity through oaths, denunciations, pogroms, or final solutions. This terror does not contain within itself the principle of its infinite extension, since it cannot apply to what is incapable of being "pure." Jews (and others) are not suspect, they are already judged. Rational terror is inclusive and "progressive" in the sense that it is faced with an infinite amount of suspicion to be cast upon anything that can be presented: the tribunal will be permanent, goodwill is never good enough. Racist or exceptive "terror" is exclusive and regressive, suspicion is limited to the "good" race. Whatever presents itself that is not of this race is bad before it presents itself, it is bad in its origin. It was bad, and it is therefore null, since the will is of no avail: it "availed itself" in the beginning, once and for all. It is a "terror" without a tribunal, and without a pronounced punishment. Death is sufficient, since it proves that what ought not to live cannot live. The solution is final.

The particular exception that reaches its peak at "Auschwitz" rests upon the principle of an election: within the world of names from history, the vital force has chosen from among all others the name "Aryan" with which to manifest itself. As opposed, however, to another election, the one that prescribes that the Jewish people listen to the transcendence of its principle and testify at its own expense against all presumptions against the law (including those done by this people), election by the vital force prescribes only the elimination of what is not elected and which, through some inexplicable "smudge," is still living despite everything. Goodwill is hereditary and is proven by one's genealogical tree. Aristocracy (blood and soil, soldier and "laborer") recognizes no addressee other than itself for the legitimating phrase. It does not even kill the others, it offers its final solution to the problem of the vital force by helping them vanish.

This is in truth not a terror, but simply a police action of vitalism, a political or policing Darwinism. The confusion between genealogy and the good is assured by the myth or narrative of Northern peoples. Under this name and thanks to this narration, an entity forgets its contingency and is able to raise superstition to the delirium of its being a necessity and a virtue. The legitimation is heteronomous, and the prescription is limited to a "people," it cannot be shared with the outside, where only the dead are.

This is what speculative discourse ought to be naming conceptually and what would reside near itself within the empirical name of "Auschwitz." Has it named it? Has it named it by my pen, in what precedes? Speculative discourse cannot help but hesitate over the name to give it, and it will hesitate a long time: how can what spirit has gained at "Auschwitz" be discerned? Spirit is not in contradiction with itself there, it excepts itself from its own universal finality, from the future of its own effectuation and expression. It makes an exception there: two phrases are "together," in the place and time designated by the historian, but they are not together dialectically. In one, the legitimation of the murder does not call upon a universal law, but only upon a particular and nominative one; in the other, death does not call upon a legitimation and cannot be sublated into a sacrifice. As for "us," "afterward," we receive these two phrases as two silences. Far indeed from signifying these silences in the phrase of a *Resultat*, "we" deem it more dangerous to make them speak than to respect them. It is not a concept that results from "Auschwitz," but a feeling (No. 93), an impossible phrase, one that would link the SS phrase onto the deportee's phrase, or vice-versa.

160. Return.

In *Menexenus*, Plato lampooned the praise of the "beautiful death" (Plato Notice § 1). Like everyone, Socrates wishes to "die well," but he doesn't want the praise of "well-dead" citizens made before living citizens to persuade the latter of their own virtue. It is just for Athens to be the name of the normative authority and for those dead in its name to acquire the right to be named Athenians. What is not just is that epideictic discourse allows the living who listen to it to be assimilated with the dead heroes. The listeners, says Socrates, have not yet proven that they merit the name of Athenians by wanting the law of the city more than anything. The assumption is that they are not yet dead for the city, that many will not die for it, and that many will live their lives out without civic virtue. Confusion is produced, however, by means of the we that covers over the paralogism. They, the dead, are heroes; they are Athenians; we, the living, are Athenians; we, the Athenians (dead and alive), are heroes. The we is first extended to the living: I, the orator, and you, the assembly; then to the dead: they, you, and me. Through this slippage of the pronoun substituted for the name, the supreme virtue that one ought to "die well" becomes a privilege of exception: that of being well born. Exception turns the moment of virtue around: it has already taken place.

I, an Aryan, tell you, an Aryan, the narrative of our Aryan ancestors' acts. The single name *Aryan* occupies the three instances in the universes of the narrative phrase. The sense of this phrase is always, directly or indirectly, that of the "beautiful death." We tell ourselves that we have died well. It is an epic of exception. The *s/he*'s, the *you*'s, and the *I*'s are substitutable under a single name, thanks to the *we*. The closed narrative cell operates prescriptively. The imperative is hypothetical: if you are Aryan, tell, hear, and carry out the Aryan "beautiful death." But it is not the sense (the beautiful death) that contains the founding potency, it is the mode of linking. If you hear, tell or do. If you tell, hear or do. If you do, tell or hear. The implications are reciprocal. You don't therefore enter into the narrative cycle, you are always already there, or you are never there. Such is the genre of mythic narrative. It is not cyclical in its theme, but in its (if you will, pragmatic) transmission. That is why tradition obeys a ritual protocol: I, an Aryan, tell you this story that an Aryan told me, so tell it, carry it out, Aryans. The prescription that issues from the rules for the transmission of the narrative is independent of the time when the phrase takes place. Tell = has told = will tell; do = has done = will do. Moreover, the time of the narrations is not distinguished from the time of the diegeses: to tell or to hear is already "to die well," and "to die well" is still to hear and to tell. The people phrases itself by acting (by dying) and dies well by phrasing itself. Whoever is not of this people cannot hear, cannot tell, and cannot die well. This people alone is made up of "true men," that's the name one ethnic group calls itself by (D'Ans, 1978). It marks the founding exception.

That is why savages make war. They endlessly carry out, and thus endlessly hear and tell, the narrative of their we. They merit their name (Clastres, 1977). Who the adversaries are is of no importance. They are not adversaries. Nothing will happen through them that has not already happened.

Nazism restores this genre of discourse, which modernity has brought to ruin. It can do this only parodically, as if the great modern genres (scientific cognition, deliberative politics, interrogative philosophy, eschatological revelation) did not already propose wholly different stakes and modes of linking, and as if they did not oppose it with something worse than adversaries: cosmopolitan heroes. The parody consists in the deployment of the means to persuade the people of its exceptional nature. Nazi politics as directed toward the people is thus an aesthetics with an epideictic end: the funeral oration extended to all the trappings of the people's life. What is foreign to the people gives rise to a policing by extermination (Auschwitz) or to a sacrificial "beautiful death" (Stalingrad).

The linkage between the SS phrase and the deportee's phrase is undiscoverable because these phrases do not arise from a single genre of discourse. There are no stakes held in common by one and the other. In exterminating the Jews, Nazism eliminated a phrase regimen where the mark is on the addressee (*Listen, Israel*) and where identifying the addressor (the Lord) or the sense (what God wants to say) is a dishonorable and dangerous presumption. The genre of discourse called Cabbala (tradition) is, in terms of questioning and interpretation, at the furthest removes from the savage narrative tradition. The latter is placed under the regimen of the already there, the Jewish idiom placed under that of the *Is it happening?* Nazism assails the occurrence, the *Ereignis* (Aristotle Notice § 3; No. 131). It thereby attacks the time of all of modernity.

Between the SS and the Jew there is not even a differend, because there is not even a common idiom (that of a tribunal) in which even damages could be formulated, be they in place of a wrong (Nos. 7, 9). There is thus no need of a trial, not even a parodic one. (This is not the case with the communists). The Jewish phrase has not taken place. There is no *Is it happening?* It happened.

Speculative dialectics get stuck in the genre of mythic narrative. The latter yields no result, only identical repetition. What does not enter into this repetition, such as the Jewish idiom, is not sublated but disregarded, it is shoved into oblivion. Myth is not speculatively soluble. It must be (nonspeculatively) exterminated, and so it has been. But the destruction of Nazism also leaves a silence after it: one does not dare think out Nazism because it has been beaten down like a mad dog, by a police action, and not in conformity with the rules accepted by its adversaries' genres of discourse (argumentation for liberalism, contradiction for Marxism). It has not been refuted.

Silences, instead of a *Resultat*. These silences interrupt the chain that goes from them, the deported, and from them, the SS, to we who speak about them. It's not readily seen how those substances that they are for "us"—the "subjects" of the discourse referring to them—are "also" ("just as much," *ebenso sehr*) those subjects. Those silences signal the interruption of the *Selbst*, its splitting apart.

Obligation

161. The splitting of the self would, at least, have the finality of destroying its presumptuousness. Of recalling that the law is transcendent to all intellection. And this under the guise of an abhorrent buffoonery, as David Rousset calls it (1979). Certainly, someone who decides the law instead of being its addressee cannot be a judge but is necessarily a criminal. And someone who submits to a law decided in this way can only be a victim. Judge, he or she is not judged. Condemned or acquitted, he or she is not expiated. Still, the speculative non-sense of "Auschwitz" could conceal a paradox of faith (Kierkegaard, 1843).

162. Is the order Abraham receives to sacrifice his son any more intelligible than a memorandum directing round-ups, convoys, concentratings, and either slow or quick death? Isn't it a matter of idiolect (Nos. 144, 145)? Abraham hears: *That Isaac die, that is my law*, and he obeys. The Lord speaks at this moment only to Abraham, and Abraham is answerable only to the Lord. Since the reality, if not of the Lord, then at least of the phrase imputed to Him, cannot be established, how can it be known that Abraham isn't a paranoiac subject to homicidal (infanticidal) urges? Or a fake?

163. The question is not even that of obedience, but of obligation. The question is to know whether, when one hears something that might resemble a call, one is held to be held by it. One can resist it or answer it, but it will first have to be received as a call, rather than, for instance, as a fantasy. One must find oneself placed in the position of addressee for a prescription (the request being a modality of prescription).

164. — But the request that harries President Schreber, the one that overwhelms Abraham, and the one that galvanizes the SS are all different! — What do you mean to say? That one emanates from a fantasmatic figure, another from God, and a third from a political leader? You know that the addressor's identity is subject to differends: the phantom that, according to Flechsig, calls upon Schreber is called God in the Schreberian idiom, etc. — But these various authorities at least are not prescribing the same acts! They can be recognized by what they order done! — I am not saying that the content of the law is indifferent, but it does not allow one to distinguish the rightful authority from its imposture. Above all, the question, which is so to speak preliminary, is that the request emanating from this entity be received as though it were law. The only sign capable of guiding a third party in this is that the addressee is obligated. By the very assumption (of an idiolect), the third party has access neither to the addressor nor to the phrase. He is like Charcot faced with a hysteric, or like the friend you tell your dream to.

165. A phrase is obligatory if its addressee is obligated. Why he or she is obligated is something he or she can perhaps think to explain. In any case, the explanation requires further phrases, in which he or she is no longer situated as the addressee but as the addressor, and whose stakes are no longer those of obeying, but those of convincing a third party of the reasons one has for obeying. Phrases of commentary. The I's blindness may regain the upper hand on the occasion of such phrases.

166. — Why *blindness* (No. 165)? — Because it is impossible to deduce a prescription from a description. The fact that two million people are unemployed in a country does not explain that the unemployment must be remedied. For this to take place, a minor premise must be understood or presupposed, namely, the prescription that all those who can work ought to work. The blindness or transcendental illusion resides in the pretension to found the good or the just upon the true, or what ought to be upon what is. By found, I simply mean the seeking and articulating of implications which allow a prescriptive phrase to be concluded from cognitive phrases. The same goes for Abraham. God orders that Isaac be sacrificed to Him. Abraham obeys "because" God is the one giving the order. It is understood or presupposed that orders given by God are just. This commandment (from God) is just because God's commandments are all just and cannot be unjust. Now, nothing can be ascertained about a totality (which is never given), be it the totality of divine orders. Nor, therefore, can anything be affirmed about it cognitively. As for the ethos of God "Himself," it is accessible only through the totality of his commandments. But, as we have just said, this totality etc. (And finally, supposing that God and His orders are just, how can it be known that God is the one giving the orders?) (No. 162).

167. The angels themselves are prey to this blindness. "Driven out of Abraham's house," Levinas writes, "Hagar and Ishmael wandered in the desert. When their water supply was spent, God opened Hagar's eyes and she saw a well and gave drink to her dying son" (1976b: 260). So far, nothing abnormal, and we wouldn't expect anything less from a God who is The Good. Still, this generosity aroused some reproach from the divine counselors (or bad aeons) that are the angels: they see farther than the ends of their noses and are acquainted with the ruses of history: "The angels protested: Wilt Thou bring up a well for one who will one day make Israel suffer?" God undoes the Hegelian trap: "What does the end of history matter, says the Eternal. I judge each for what he is now and not for what he will become." Even God does not and should not know the totality of events. It would be unjust were He to take into consideration what will be done tomorrow in order to judge what is now. It is possible then that He would have given something to drink to Hitler when Hitler was thirsty.

168. To talk in terms of a holocaust is to signify that God commanded the hand of the Nazi butcher, with the Jewish people in the place of Isaac. It is admitted, though, that if the Lord of Abraham asked the father for the sacrifice of his son, it was in order to test Abraham's faithfulness to the Lord. Did God want to test the SS's faithfulness to Him? Was there an alliance between them? And did the SS love the Jew as a father does his son? If not, how could the crime have the value of a sacrifice in the eyes of its victim? And in those of its executioner? And in those of its beneficiary? Or else, was it God who offered up part of His people in sacrifice? But to what god could He offer them up? It is also said that Israel had to be punished for its faults, or fault: pride. Not one of these phrases, which describe the divinity's intention (testing, punishing) with a view to explaining the sacrifice, is falsifiable (Referent Section). Not one of them can stand as an explanation of the order to kill, that is, as its legitimation. The only way you can make a "beautiful death" out of "Auschwitz" death (Nos. 156, 160) is by means of a rhetoric.

169. The blindness is in putting yourself in the place of the other, in saying *I* in his or her place, in neutralizing his or her transcendence. If you were to lay bare the Lord's intentions, you would then know His idiolect, how it is spoken, the phrases whose addressor and addressee He is and which presumably engender the commandment, and the senses of those phrases. "Auschwitz" is deduced, for instance, from the Lord's anger against His people. But alone by itself, this implication is a crime against ethics: the people would be obligated by an order because they could understand its sense!

170. Instead, obligation should be described as a scandal for the one who is obligated: deprived of the "free" use of oneself, abandoned by one's narcissistic image, opposed in this, inhibited in that, worried over not being able to be oneself

without further ado. — But these are phenomenological or psychoanalytic descriptions of a dispossessed or cloven consciousness. Which are far too human, and humanist. They maintain the self even in the very acknowledgment of its dispersion. Could we begin with the dispersion, without any nostalgia for the self? And think therefore the splitting of the self apart from any finality, if it is true that finality is still the action of a self which is exerted upon an object beforehand and from a distance, even if this action momentarily cleaves that self? Of course, the idea of a splitting would also have to be abandoned then, since it presupposes a beautiful totality: the result.

Levinas

1. Condition for the scandal of obligation: "The interiority that ensures separation must produce a being absolutely closed over upon itself, not deriving its isolation dialectically from its opposition to the Other. And this closedness must not prevent egress from interiority, so that exteriority could speak to it, reveal itself to it, in an unforseeable movement" (1961: 148). As scandal for the ego, the ethical relation presupposes two kernel phrases: *The ego does not proceed from the other; the other befalls the ego.* If the ego was but the closed (abstract) moment of a dialectical alteration of the self, you could reveal nothing to me that I didn't already have in myself.

Levinas takes his departure from the impasse of Husserl's fifth *Cartesian Meditation*: the transcendental sameness cannot constitute others as other. The I [*je*] remains enclosed within its domain of constitution just as the ego [*moi*] is locked within its domain of experience, namely, the enjoyment of being and of having. The other is its other. This empirical and transcendental finitude is necessary, however, for the other to be other, to be "the marvel" (*Ibid.*: 292). There is an equivalency in the exclusive disjunction: if the ego proceeded from the other, the other would not be the marvel; if the other were not the marvel, the self would proceed from the other. It is thus either me, or the other. The other can only befall the ego, like a revelation, through a break-in. If sense belongs to the dialectic of the self, the event of the other turns it into non-sense. How can the other even befall it? The ego does not have in itself the sufficiency to understand this. The ego is tempted to explain it as a formation within its domain of constitution and experience. It is tempted to know it and is tempted by knowledge. But the other, as an exteriority whose reason does not lie within the ego, announces the insufficiency of knowledge. The other announces no sense, it is the announcement, the non-sense. "The messenger is the message" (1968a: 104-5).

Can we transcribe this? An addressor appears whose addressee I am, and about whom I know nothing, except that he or she situates me upon the addressee instance. The violence of the revelation is in the ego's expulsion from the addressor instance, from which it managed its work of enjoyment, power, and cognition. It is the scandal of an I displaced onto the you instance. The I turned you tries to repossess itself through the understanding of what dispossesses it. Another phrase is formed, in which the I returns in the addressor's situation, in order to legitimate or to reject — it doesn't matter which — the scandal of the other's phrase and of its own dispossession. This new phrase is always possible, like an inevitable temptation. But it cannot annul the event, it can only tame and master it, thereby disregarding the transcendence of the other.

By turning the I into its you [*toi*], the other makes him- or herself master, and turns the I into his or her hostage. The other is not master, however, because he or she dominates the I, but because he or she asks for the I. The I enclosed within the disposition of itself and of its world knows nothing about the other and can know nothing about him or her. The appearing of the other is not an event of cognition. But it is an event of feeling. The I, placed in the position of *you*, is someone to whom a prescription is addressed, the simple prescription that there be prescriptions (and not only descriptions, not only cognitions). The I in this situation learns nothing, since there is nothing to learn (a command is not a bit of information). The I does not even know if the other is also an I, nor does the I know what the other wants from the I nor even if the other wants something from the I, but the I is immediately obligated to the other. This is what the I's displacement onto the *you* instance marks: You ought to. Levinas comments upon the destituteness of the other: the other arises in my field of perception with the trappings of absolute poverty, without attributes, the other has no place, no time, no essense, the other is nothing but his or her request and my obligation.

Such is the universe of the ethical phrase: an I stripped of the illusion of being the addressor of phrases, grabbed hold of upon the addressee instance, incomprehensibly. The obligation is immediate, prior to any intellection, it resides in the "welcoming of the stranger," in the address to me, which does more than reverse a preexisting relation, which institutes a new universe. This upheaval precedes any commentary upon the nature of the other, of the request, of my freedom. Commenting on the *Shabbath* (88 a-b), especially the verse, "They did before they hearkened," Levinas writes: "The incomparable character of an event such as the giving of the Tora [is that] one accepts it before knowing it [. . .]. The doing in question is not simply the praxis opposed to the theory, but a *way of actualizing without beginning with the possible* [. . .]. They act before they hearken! [. . .] To hear a voice speaking to you is *ipso facto* to accept the obligation of the one who speaks" (1968a: 91, 95, 98, 104–5). This immediacy is to be compared with the immediacy of the performative phrase. I say, *The meeting is open*, or *War is declared*, and so they are. I hear: *Hail*, and I am the angel's obligee, the you of the other.

The emphasis is placed on the asymetricalness of the *I/you* relation (1961: 215). This relation is not reversible, it imposes and maintains the destabilization of a knowledge in which the I was *I* (the self itself, its identity). It cannot be repossessed by a phrase in which the I is *I*. In this phrase, the I no longer understands anything about ethics, it is able only to believe that it understands. The passage from the ethical phrase to the phrase of knowledge is done only at the price of forgetting the former. In the tension the cognitive phrase exerts upon the addressor and addressee instances, the you addressed by the I of the assertion is only a potential I. It will link by saying *I*, by agreeing or disagreeing about a referent, about an it, to be elaborated in common. *I* and *you* work toward the formation of a consensus.

To Buber's *Umfassung* [inclusion] (1976a: 40), Levinas opposes the forgetting of the "difference in stature" that separates the other and the ego in the request. Buber's description of the *dialogisches Leben* is ensnared by the return of the regimen of cognitive phrases in the description of the ethical relation. Ethics prohibits dialogue, since dialogue requires the permutation of names upon instances. Try as Buber might to emphasize the axis of address by freeing it of the referential relation, by going so far as to explain that the referent, the it, is the figure of a you *manqué*, out of reach, and to whom I do not speak but about whom it remains for me only to speak (Buber, 1938: 19, 27, 33), – it is precisely this alienation and this return of referential description which takes hold of Buber's phrase and makes him in turn objectify the *I/you* relation through the figure of dialogue (Levinas, 1976a: 46–47).

One implication of this objection: there is no true transcendence of the referent for Levinas. The object belongs to the dialectic of knowledge. What is "near itself" is called upon, according to the speculative rules, to be "for itself," to result. The speculative genre occupies the entire terrain of what is called reality. Ethical transcendence does not take place in this field. It does not take place at all, since the other is not localizable. If he or she were, I would be your master, and be presumed to know you. The ethical realm is not a realm, it is a mode of the *I/you* situation which happens unforeseeably as the scrambling of the phrase universe in which *I* is *I*.

2. In Levinas's thought, the obligation in question does not result from an authority previously legitimated by me or by us. If I am obligated by the other, it is not because the other has some right to obligate me which I would have directly or mediately granted him or her. My freedom is not the source of his or her authority: one is not obligated because one is free, and because your law is my law, but because your request is not my law, because we are liable for the other. Obligation through freedom or consent is secondary. It presupposes a liability, a fracture in the ego's fortress: "this closedness must not prevent egress from interiority." An aptitude for transcendence? We can transcribe this as: the addressor's capacity, after having been displaced onto the addressee instance, to remember that he or she wasn't supposed to be there. The scandal, or aptitude for this scandal, depends upon an entity's mobility among the instances of phrase universes, upon its resistance to this mobility, and upon its memory of the pre-encounter during the post-encounter (conversion). These conditions require the permanency of a proper name. On the contrary, the other in its destitution does not even have a name. He or she is not called, he or she is what calls.

This liability is nonetheless not a condition of possibility for ethics, it is not the *archè* of obligation. (These notions of condition of possibility, and of *archè*, crop up in *Totality and Infinity*, but are then rejected at the end of *Difficile liberté* and in "Humanisme et anarchie") (1968b). It is already the entirety of ethics, it contains together its two faces, freedom and persecution. The latter does not differ from the former as heteronomy differs from autonomy. Each requires the I's attachment to the other, its dependency, its being taken hostage. What gives rise to persecution is when the I is "passively" attached, against its will, and in its recurrent narcissism, which protests against this liability and does not accept exteriority. The return of the I in the *you* situation where he or she has been placed by the other turns the latter into a persecutor. I am accused because I betray you, because I exclude or except the you. "Atheistic creatures" endlessly accuse each other under the regimen of the "unlimited accusative" (1974: 132–33, 141–42, 150–51). Saying yes to the gift of the undecipherable message, to the election that the request is, the (impossible) alliance with the other who is nothing, signifies the assumption of the I's fracture. It is impossible to "slip away from the creature's imperious call," but "the assumption [of passivity] nowhere exceeds passivity" (1968a: 108).

How can something closed like the ego also be open and liable to the transcendence of an exteriority? Aren't we, in the final analysis, talking about a dialectic of the edge or the limit in an utterly Hegelian kind of movement: no interiority without exteriority, and the converse? No ego without other, no other without ego. Levinas attempts to break this reversible totality and to discombobulate speculative dialectics by reinforcing the dissymetry of the ethical instances. It can be admitted that there is no ego without the other, if the other is its other. The ego constitutes itself by losing itself and by sublating itself through its alienations in the narcissistic movement which pushes it to be for itself. But the other who without me would not be is nevertheless not my other, he or she is not a momentary alienation in my odyssey, but what discombobulates it. — How do you know? — By this discombobulation, by the dispossession, and the passion his or her request provokes. Far from enriching me, from giving me the opportunity to grow and to enlighten my experience, the arrival of the other suppresses me as the subject of an experience.

— But how can you say this, unless it is after you have "regained your spirits," and have reclaimed your situation qua I who phrases (or thinks one phrases), after you have overcome the ethical phrase in conserving it, and thus after you have included it as a moment in the becoming for itself of your experience? Doesn't writing — even your writing about liability — weave a mastery, an experience, a text together with what has no text, no experience, and no mastery? How can one write in the second person? The second person can only be described in the third person. One writes: *the you*. Isn't the reversion Levinas reproaches Buber for also at work in Levinas's text? Isn't that text a commentary on what every commentary must nonetheless fail to attain? Can that text not be phenomenological (No. 71)?

3. Perhaps writing ought to be understood, or rather presented, otherwise. Instead of being the description of an experience, conducted by an I in quest of self-knowledge, perhaps Levinas's writing is the testimony of the fracture, of the opening onto that other who in the reader sends a request to Levinas, of a responsibility before that messenger who is the reader. It is not a question of writing "in the second person," under the regimen of the *you*, but of writing to the other, under his or her law. Levinas's text would be the confiding of a hostage. It is in him that the liability would be assumed. He would say: Yes, you are my masters. Not you, of course, my readers who are named or nameable, but you toward whom I write, over and beyond the faces that can be seen poring over what I've written. For the one who reads is one who requests, one who calls. The one who writes is bound by this request, is upset, beside oneself, unsure whether one is binding or liberating oneself by writing. He or she puts him- or herself in our hands as readers. Are these the hands of good angels, or of bad ones? What messengers are we, what messages? The writer does not know, nor do the angels, for they are mistaken. Only one thing is sure, this ethical writing is saved from persecution only if it does not attach itself to "atheistic creatures," only if the ego of the writer does not claim, while the writing takes place, his or her rights over it, or rather over and against it. Writing would not be "the deliverance of a message." That is the presumptuousness of the I. He moans and groans, and sacrifices himself to his work, but he is deluding himself. Writing is not sacrificial, it is saintly (1977: 7-10). It is what is witness to the fracturing of the I, to its aptitude for hearing a call. In the reader,

the other does not request that the ego of the writer die, but that that ego assumes its liability.

As soon, however, as one begins to speak about what one reads, as soon as one compares what one has read with what one has requested or thought one requested, doesn't the reader, become commentator, inevitably turn into the persecutor of the work? From the sole fact that one thinks one knows what one requested and supposes the work's responsibility to be commensurable to the nature of one's request, is it not necessary that one then place oneself, while commenting, back under the regimen of descriptives, under the temptation of knowledge? How can a commentary not be a persecution of what is commented upon? Doesn't it bring forth the proof (from the sole fact that the reader speaks up) that in formulating his or her request, he or she supposes that he or she knows it or at least supposes it to be knowable, and that this request ceases to be a marvel to which writing makes itself accessible? Is the request then no more than a prescription provided with a content, a sense, to which the work is held, as a hostage is held for the observance of a promise?

Saintliness would disappear and the sacred would return with its sacrificial *Aufhebung*. It was thus the self who wanted the writer's writing, who drew its liability toward self-knowledge! The incommensurability of the request the self exerted upon writing with what writing gives in exchange would be no more than the negative moment, the moment of contradiction, the one which obeys the rule of immanent derivation (Hegel Notice) and whose result despite everything is still and always the for-itself. The for-the-other would be only the moment of an, imprudently and unduly isolated, splitting apart in the movement of the self toward itself. The writer and the reader would be two momentarily incommensurable figures of the same. Were one to aggravate the split, one would only make the speculative machine work better. It is in this way that the figure of Judaism was understood, from the beginnings of Hegelian thought, as an abstract moment, one meanly fixated upon its separation (the "alleged" transcendence of the request) in the movement of the beautiful totalization (Bourgeois, 1970: 118).

But doesn't the very commentary that has just been read already require what Levinas reproaches Buber for and what he detests in Hegel: namely, that writing and reading, the I and the you, be taken as referents in the universe of the phrase that comments upon them, and that this phrase signify each of the terms, as well as the terms taken together as a whole, which can certainly be asymmetrical without ceasing to be a whole? If this is the case, then speculation has already been enjoying its rights in this commentary, the rights of metadescription. Shouldn't Levinas recognize and observe these rights, he who strives to comment for his reader, in his or her place, through the mediation of a we that effaces the asymmetry of I and you, or what there is of that asymmetry?

That you are never me, that I am never you: can that be reflected upon, written reflexively? Written down, this is understood as follows: *that the you is never the I*, and *that the I is never the you*. In its wording, the ethical phrase is annihilated. Its secret, the asymmetry of the pronouns, is divulged and neutralized in their being autonymically grasped in the third person. The patience of the concept sets upon [*arraisonne*] the impatience of the request. It turns that impatience back against itself. "To do before hearkening" (1968a: ch. 4), but isn't this exactly what commentary does with ethics! It comments upon it as though it were a misunderstanding, and it thereby conserves in itself its own requirement that there be something ununderstood. The irony of the commentator easily goes as far as persecution: the less I understand you, he or she says to the Levinassian (or divine) text, the more I will obey you by that fact; for, if I want to understand you (in your turn) as a request, then I should not understand you as sense. Satan would be God's best servant, if it is true at least that he disobeys Him. For "the disobedient man obeys in some way" (Aristotle, *Soph. Ref.* : 180 b 1), he has been obligated, the command (or the request) has been heard as such, it is only its content that has not been understood. Satan is an ethical name.

But Hegel is not Satan, that name is a speculative name. The self does not obey – be it to disobey – it is in the process of being. God requests nothing and expects nothing from His creatures; the self goes forth to itself by way of God and His creatures.

What tribunal can know and rule on the differend between the ethical phrase (infinity) and the speculative phrase (totality)?

171. Levinas's "marvel" comes close to the "alienness" of the Gnostics, particularly in Marcion's case (Jonas, 1958: 49–51). Obligation alienates the ego: it becomes the you of an absolutely unknowable other. Jonas also uses the word *Unheimlichkeit*, which gathers within itself the contradictory relation between ego and other. In acceding to the request, I go out far away from my home, as a hostage, without ever taking up habitation with you, nor ever being your guest, since you have no residence, but I also thereby fulfill my calling, which is to be at home no longer. Freud, putting the id [*ça*] in the place of *you*, goes the wrong way when he assigns to the ego the call of evicting the id. He would be succumbing to the temptation of empty knowledge. But the analysis, supposing that it consists in this substitution, is still interminable. The true understood as appropriation of the other, even if it is done through some "graphism," is false.

172. – But doesn't the other or the stranger have all the traits of the *Is it happening?* (Nos, 131, 132) Should *Is it happening?* (*Arrive-t-il?*) be understood as *Are you coming?* (*Arrives-tu?*) If the Lord is not describable, how can you say that He is somebody, I mean an addressor? An unknown addressor is at least known as an addressor. – But, you're about to answer, since the call or the request turns my name into the name of an addressee, of a you, then an addressor – even if nothing more than an empty place for the instance of a hidden I – must indeed be presented at the same time in the same phrase universe! – Objection: when the universe in which you are the addressee entails an addressor instance that is left empty, and is perhaps "absolutely" not marked, not even by a silence, that is the ethical situation, or the disposition of the universe presented by a phrase of obligation. But that cannot be inscribed into your experience. For, in this universe, you are presented on the *you* instance, you are called, but experience and cognition take place in the first person, or at least as a self. What you judge to be the Lord's call is the situation of *you* when *I* is deprived of experience, "estranged," "alienated," disauthorized. You do not therefore have the experience of the Lord,

nor even of alienness. If you were to have that experience, it would not be the Lord, and it would not be ethics. You cannot therefore testify that whatever it is that calls upon you is somebody. And such is precisely the ethical universe.

173. Isn't the *Is it happening?* (Nos. 131, 132, 172) then a kind of call emanating from a phrase in abeyance? Doesn't it require an opening or availability to the occurrence in its strangeness? Didn't you name, however, the approach of what is not yet said as feeling (Nos. 22, 23)? The ego is certainly not what calls forth the event of the phrase that is untranslatable into common idioms. Isn't it the phrase, rather, that calls from afar upon Being, upon the occurrence? Now, in saying that the phrase calls, aren't you situating it on the instance of an addressor unknown in the universe of an interrogative phrase? Doesn't Heidegger say the same thing as Levinas, despite what the latter says? Isn't the I also divested here of its power qua addressor of sense to be no more than the ear of the unpresentable that calls out to it? – No, for this confusion to be possible, it would have to be supposed that the foreign phrase wants to phrase itself through you as its go-between, that it wants something from you because it would like to be itself. Or, that Being (or language) (*die Sage*) (Heidegger, 1953–54: 32) has need of man. But you are nothing but its advent (whether addressee or addressor or referent or sense even, or several of these instances together) in the universe presented by the phrase that happens. It wasn't waiting for you. You come when it arrives. The occurrence is not the Lord. The pagans know this and laugh over this edifying confusion.

174. Obligation should not be confused with *Redlichkeit*[uprightness], or probity in regard to *Rede* [speech] (Nancy, 1983: 63–86). The latter does not obligate: *It is necessary to link* is not *You ought to link*. It does not even suffice to say that there is no choice (Nos. 102, 103): one is not held by an occurrence the same way one is held to an obligation. Phrasing the occurrence, though, is a necessity of phrases. Obligation would take place only at the level of genres, which prescribe stakes: you ought to link on like this in order to get to that. For example, if your discourse ought to be philosophical, then you ought to link on with a view to finding the rule for the discourse (and then, you ought to pay attention to the *Is it happening?*). Obligation would take place only with its 'how', genres would fix this 'how' in accordance with their stakes. Obligation is hypothetical: if you want or desire or wish . . . , then you ought to . . . This is always on the condition of an end to be attained, which is whatever is prescribed by the stakes of the genre. – But the possibility (ability) of this 'ought' is not hypothetical, it is presupposed by the genres, by the *if* . . . , *then*'s. These give rise, but do no more than give rise, to obligation. It is thus that Kant questions the capacity of the 'ought' itself, without conditions.

175. The rules that form phrase regimens are not prescriptive and do not of themselves create obligations. The genres of discourse are what bring forth obli-

gations. For example, it is because the stakes of logical discourse, namely, to arrive at a tautology for the entire set of phrases and at a conviction procured through the principle of identity, already bear upon the examination of this tautology and this conviction that rules are established for their correct formation. These rules should be respected if one wants to speak "logically." It ought to be asked whether, in all genres of discourse, the formation and linking of phrases is not submitted to hypothetical prescriptions, to strategies aiming to pull off a success. If this is so, and if it is true that ethical prescription is not subordinated to a hypothesis, then wouldn't ethics therefore be a genre? Or, is the ethical genre the one whose rule is to admit no rule but that of obligation without conditions? It would thereby be akin to the philosophical genre. (How can you know that a prescription is unconditional?).

176. The tribunal whose idiom is that genre of discourse which is cognition, which therefore admits only descriptive phrases with cognitive value as acceptable, asks of the one who claims an obligation: which is the authority that obligates you (or will obligate you)? The obligated one is caught in a dilemma: either he or she names the addressor of the law and exposes the authority and sense of the law, and then he or she ceases to be obligated solely by the mere fact that the law, thus rendered intelligible to cognition, becomes an object of discussion and loses its obligatory value. Or else, he or she recognizes that this value cannot be exposited, that he or she cannot phrase in the place of the law, and then this tribunal cannot admit that the law obligates him or her since the law is without reason and is therefore arbitrary. In the idiom of cognition, either the law is reasonable, and it does not obligate, since it convinces; or else, it is not reasonable, and it does not obligate, since it constrains. This tribunal requires that the obligatory be only that which the obligated one can reasonably account for in argumentation. It therefore supposes that I can occupy the place of the addressor of prescriptions, that I can "assume" them. They are obligatory because I can understand their sense and explain it to the tribunal. The value of the explanation is its truth value, which is universal. Through this dilemma, the family of cognitive phrases annexes the family of prescriptive phrases, the I effaces the you.

177. Aristotle dissociates prescriptive from denotative phrases: "Every discourse is *sémantikos* [signifies something] (not as a natural tool (*organon*) but, as we have said, by convention [*kata sunthékè*]), but not every discourse is *apophantikos* [denotative], but only those in which there is truth or falsity. There is not truth or falsity in all cases: a request [a prayer, *euchè*] is discourse, but is neither true or false. The present investigation [*théoria*] deals with apophantic discourse: the others we can dismiss, since consideration of them belongs rather to the study of rhetoric or of poetry" [*De Interpretatione*: 17 a]. A logic of denotatives (apophantics) aims to determine the rules for forming simple phrases (the logic of predicates) or for linking them (the logic of propositions) which allow

for their truth to be calculated. A lexicon and a syntax need to be elaborated thanks to which these rules are formulated. They constitute the logician's metalanguage. Does Aristotle's dismissal of deontics have the effect of subtracting them from this metalanguage? Not necessarily, say some; obviously, say others. The former imagine the propositional kernels of deontic logic to be of the same form as those of propositional logic (Von Wright, 1967). Others, following Wittgenstein's indications (*PhU:* §§ 433, 458, 461, 505, 506, 519), represent them rather as obeying a paradigm: *It is obligatory for x to carry out act* α (Hottois, 1981). All agree, though, that if you want to speak about prescriptives, specific operators or functions have to be made use of, whether or not they are in addition to those of propositional logic. For example, the functions of obligation and of permission seem indispensable. — Nevertheless, this apparent unanimity shelters a new discord. For one can consider the obligatory, the permitted, and their derivative operators (the nonobligatory or the tolerated, and the nonpermitted or the prohibited) as entirely analogous to the operators of propositional logic: respectively, the necessary and the possible with their respective contradictories, the contingent and the impossible. The so-called square of Aristotle, the armature of the metalanguage that bears upon descriptions, thus remains the computational table thanks to which the value of prescriptives is calculated. One important consequence is that, under these conditions, commentary on prescriptive phrases is able to be of a nature not other than commentary on denotative phrases. If it is admitted that it is indispensable to elaborate, to discuss and to lay down prescriptions in order to turn them into norms, it is because it is presupposed that, between the language of the commentary on the commands and the language of the commands, the consequence drawn is a good one.

Kant 2

1. The law is not deduced.

To legitimate the law would be to deduce it. Kant understands deduction in the same sense as "jurists." There is a litigation (and perhaps a differend) over an affair "of rights and claims." Before deciding upon the facts, it is necessary to decide upon the legitimacy of the claims of each of the two parties: does one party have the right, for instance, to claim (or to refuse to the other) the profit from an inheritance? The party must bring forth the proof that it has this right, otherwise the plea cannot be received by the tribunal. Deduction is the adducing of the proof that the party has this right—it is authorization, in the strong sense of the word (*KRV,* B § 13: 120).

Kant transfers this question onto obligation. How does a prescription in general (of which a plea put before a tribunal by a party is a case) have the authority to obligate its addressee? To answer this question would be to deduce prescription. But how can the prescriptive phrase be deduced without making it lose its specificity? This is the difficulty exposited by the Deduction of the Principles of Pure Practical Reason in the Second *Critique* (*KPV,* Deduction: 43–51). For the phrases of theoretical reason, which are descriptive or cognitive, the deduction of principles that rule their formation, if it cannot be brought about speculatively from "sources of knowledge *a priori*" (as dogmatism believes), can at least have recourse to that *Surrogat* (*Ibid.*: 48), or expedient, which is experience. Deduction proceeds, in sum, everything else being equal, in the manner of the logician of science who extracts from the denotative utterances given in the corpus that serves as his or her reference, the axioms (in the modern sense) that these utterances presuppose. We know that, for the reader of Hume that Kant is, the principal of these axioms is causality.

The relation between the principles in the critical metalanguage of the Deduction and the object-language which is the discourse of science is isomorphous to the relation that unites the language of science with the "givens" of experience. This isomorphism between the two relations is in noway contradictory to the fact that the former is drawn from the level of the transcendental and the latter from the level of the empirical. Each of them relates descriptive phrases together. This isomorphism is even what allows Kant to declare that the deduction of principles, unable to be brought about directly "from sources," uses experience as a *Surrogat*. The metalanguage, which is the critical discourse effectuating the deduction of the principles of science, in particular the deduction of the principle of causality, remains isomorphous, on its level, to the object-language of science which is its referent. This isomorphism makes the deduction possible. Without it, and in the absence of the abovementioned "sources," we don't see how it would be possible to deduce the principles of theoretical reason, and, in particular, the principle of causality.

This isomorphic situation between the critical language of deduction and the object-language (cognitives), from which it must extract its principles, is lacking when the object-language is that of prescriptives. The Kantian argument is that prescriptive phrases, far from being regulated by principles like causality, on the same order as descriptive phrases, are themselves the cause of the acts they engender. This pure causality, or spontaneity, of prescription is not a fact of experience, since everything 'given' in experience is regulated by infinite sequences of causes and effects: whatever is the cause of this is also thought of as the effect of that. Here, therefore, there is an allomorphism or heterogeneity between the descriptive metalanguage of deduction and its supposed object-language which is the prescriptive phrase. This is why in regard to the deduction which is supposed to legitimate prescriptives through the practical principle, "one cannot hope to have everything as easy as it was with the principles of pure theoretical understanding" (*Ibid.*: 47). Kant exposits this failure of the practical deduction with a kind of satisfaction: "Thus the objective reality of the moral law can be proved through no deduction, through no exertion of the theoretical, speculative, or empirically supported reason; and, even if one were willing to renounce its apodictic certainty, it could not be confirmed by any experience and thus proved a posteriori." "Nevertheless," he adds just as quickly, "it [the reality of the moral law] is firmly established of itself" (48).

Is it necessary then to abandon all attempts to legitimate the prescriptive phrase? That would be to turn authority over to arbitrariness. The Kantian analysis takes a peculiar twist here: the functioning of the deduction can be maintained, but only on the condition that the direction be reversed: "Instead of this vainly sought deduction of the moral principle, however, something entirely different and unexpected [*ganz Widersinniges*] appears" (48). A deduction is found which works in a way opposite to the one which was sought. The critical metalanguage was supposed to draw out of an object-language the principle authorizing the prescriptive phrases found within it. Had it succeeded, this would have been at the price of suppressing the problem: the prescriptives situated on the referent instance in the universe of the critical phrase (the deduction) would have been by that very act turned into autonyms (Nos. 45, 46). They would have ceased to be prescriptives, that is, spontaneous causes, to become in effect "objects," that is to say, effects of the principle which would have been concluded by the deduction.

This failure does not, however, suppress the possibility of metalanguage; it reverses the direction it takes, but at the price of modifying its object. What can be deduced in the absence of the law is freedom. This new deduction is carried out starting from the law. But the law is then placed, within the justificatory argument, not as a conclusion, as the phrase that authorizes prescriptions, as the phrase which the metalanguage would have extracted from the object-language, but rather as a premise, as a phrase of that object-language, which the metalanguage comes to infer as what that object-language presupposes in order to authorize a phrase which asserts freedom. This would be the reversal of the deduction: "the moral principle [the law] itself serves as a principle of the deduction of an inscrutable [unerforschlichen] faculty [. . .], the faculty of freedom [. . .]" (Ibid.: 48–49).

Freedom does not express itself in the object-language, it can be phrased only in the critical commentary. But then it is necessary that the law, in its turn, be an expression belonging to an object-language . . . And in effect Kant proposes to call the consciousness of the moral law "a fact [Faktum] of reason" (48). In this fact, "pure reason shows itself actually to be practical" (43). Only, this "absolutely inexplicable" (44) fact is really only sort of a fact, a quasi-fact: the reality of pure will, which as Kant explains, "is given in the moral law a priori, as it were by a fact [Faktum]" (Ibid.). As it were by a fact, and not by a fact. This factum is only a quasi-fact because, as we have seen, the immediate determination of the will, which the law is, can never be established as a true and simple fact by means of a procedure (here a critical one) whose exclusive model remains that of the deduction of the principles for the cognition of facts (theoretical reason).

This "fact" of prescription or of obligation is so little a fact in the empirical and cognitive sense of the word, so little capable of being subsumed under a concept which would have been "deduced" from it and which would in turn allow its place to be legitimated through a cognizable experience, that Kant opposes it to such experience by relating it (we'll see how) to an Idea: "the moral law ideally [der Idee nach] transfers us into a nature in which reason would bring forth the highest good were it accompanied by sufficient physical capacities" (45). The realm circumscribed by the quasi-experience of the You ought to and in which the latter is inscribed is not the world nor even nature, but a "supersensuous nature," whose "idea really stands as a model for the determination of our will" (Ibid.). The moral "experience" is not an experience, the You ought to cannot be established as such in reality. The obligation is received, though, and that is why it can be called sort of a fact. But it is received in an ideal nature by the faculty of desire, and not in the real world by sensibility.

2. I am able to.

The pure prescriptive phrase is not legitimated and it is not able to be legitimated unless it vanishes as an obligation, that is, unless it loses its specificity. Conversely, though, the prescriptive phrase taken as a quasi-fact may serve as the point of departure for one deduction, the deduction of freedom. If you ought to, it is because you are able to. By formulating the canonical phrase of freedom in the second person, Kant favors a frequent error: you are obligated to carry out an act (it being understood: instead of being constrained to carry it out) only because you have the possibility (in the sense of contingency) not to carry it out. The freedom of choice concerning the content of the command would be empirical, and the manner of linking onto the command would be contingent.

We do not see how this freedom to refuse to obey the law would be, even indirectly, its legitimation. The freedom deduced from the law is not the contingency of linkages. On the contrary, "where the moral law speaks there is no longer, objectively, a free choice [*keine freie Wahl*] as regards what is to be done" (*KUK* § 5: 45). Even if you violate it, you still recognize the law. Obedience is one thing, the feeling of obligation or respect is something else. This is what the you in *You ought to* indicates. The addressee may indeed link on with a *I won't do it*, but he or she was still first a you grabbed hold of by the obligation. Obligation is analogous to a constraint insofar as it is the displacement of an I onto the addressee instance, its being taken hostage.

What is invoked in the phrase of freedom is not a power in the sense of an eventuality, but one in the sense of an ability to act, that is, an ability to be a first cause from the cosmological point of view. Such a cause cannot be validated through experience. No fact can be presented which might serve as an example of this first causality or spontaneity. If it is possible, however, to deduce the spontaneity of the situation of obligation, which is apparently its contrary, it is because the latter necessarily implies the former. How is this possible?

In "hearing" *You ought to*, the addressee would at the same time "hear" a phrase which he or she cannot attest, but which is, as it were, awaiting its formulation under his or her responsibility and which would be *You are able to*. As always (Nos. 22, 23), this imminent phrase, unable to be formulated in a description, is marked or announced as a partial silence, as a feeling, as respect. The question put to critical metalanguage is knowing whether the you in *You ought to* and the you in *You are able to* are the same you, whether the entity that is obligated and the entity that is a first cause are the same entity.

If they were the same, we would be brought back to the interpretation on the basis of free will, which has just been discarded. *You ought to* implies an addressor who is undoubtedly a mystery, who is "incomprehensible" and "inscrutable" (*KPV*: 5, 49), whom Kant calls freedom in the second *Critique*, but also God in the *Opus postumum*. How this addressor is possible cannot be explained (47), for him there is no phrase of cognition properly called. The quasi-fact of obligation, though, is like a sign marked upon the addressed entity in the form of a feeling. The obligated one sentimentally infers that there is some authority which obligates him or her by addressing itself to him or her. This sign signals that, in a regimen of phrases which is precisely not the regimen of descriptives, a causality which is not an explanatory principle of experience acts upon the obligated one. The entity harboring this spontaneous causality cannot be the addressee. The latter receives the announcement of spontaneity in the form of 'dependence,' 'constraint,' or 'coercion' (32). The addressee is not the one who is able to. The addressor is the one who is able to, who is the power. And if the addressor, in the universe of the phrase of obligation, were to speak about him- or herself, he or she would say *I*, as he or she would say *you* in obligating the addressee (*you ought to*).

To the *You ought to* then there corresponds, on the order only of an Idea, an *I am able to* and not a *You are able to*. This *I am able to* is not a phrase that links onto the *You ought to* by way of an entity which would be selfsame, I over here and you over there (as in free will), but the phrase *I am able to* ought to be the same phrase as *You ought to*. Along with the universe of the obligation, instantiated upon the addressee, *you ought to* copresents a universe of freedom, which is instantiated upon the addressor. As for knowing who says I, or even if this I says itself, that cannot be done. Under the general rubric of independence from "mechanical" causality, Kant multiplies solely negative descriptions. *I am able to* is to be understood as follows: I am not constrained by the linkages that regulate cognizable objects, especially not by empirical interests and motives, I transcend them. In this way, in the phrase of obligation, dependence upon the law is presented as a feeling, at the same time as independence from the regimen of cognition is presented as a mysterious presupposition.

The law remains undeduced. Freedom is deduced from inside the phrase of obligation itself as the immediate implication of an addressor from the effect of the addressee's feeling of dispossession. It is not known for whom freedom is freedom. All that is known is that freedom does no more than announce itself to the addressee of the law, through the feeling of obligation. The deduction of freedom is not comparable to the deduction of the principles of knowledge in the first *Critique*. The latter concludes upon concepts which make possible the cognition of the empirical facts that served as the premises for the deduction. It cannot be said *stricto sensu* that freedom makes possible the experience of morality, obligation. Obligation is not a fact that can be attested, but only a feeling, a fact of reason, a sign. Freedom is deduced negatively: there needs to be a potentiality of effect, which is not causality as the explanation of experience, in order for the feeling of obligation to take place, since experience does not obligate. The practical deduction of freedom is negative because it cannot start out from facts, but precisely from the opposite direction, from the *Widersinnige* [contrary to sense], which is the failure of facts and of cognitives before the quasi-fact of obligation. Facts are referents of cognitive phrases. Between the you of obligation and the supposed I of freedom, there is no question of referents, except insofar as they are to be "constituted" (70).

But, adds Kant, considered in and of itself, and no longer by comparison with the cognitive phrase, the ethical phrase brings forth a "sufficient" proof (49) for the "objective reality" of free causality. "Its *transcendent* use is changed into an *immanent* use, whereby reason becomes, in the field of experience, an efficient cause through ideas" (*Ibid.*). The power of the *I am able to* is not merely the power not to be determined by the series that form the world of experience, it is also in a positive way the power to obligate, it is in an immediate way the power of the law. The "immanence" of practical reason (pure will) can thus be understood as the situation of the addressor in the phrase of obligation. The I is ideal, but it is presented (as absent) in the universe of this phrase as what makes it immediately effective: at the same time (the time of obligation) as the you ought to, the I is able to. And as a specific regimen of phrases (without example among cognitives), obligation is by itself the proof of a causality which is not serial, but performative. —The difficulty of the phrase quoted above lies in that the efficiency of this power is stated to exert itself "in the field of experience." Two things come down to one: either this field is the referent for all *if . . .* , *then* linkings, and then performativity has no place there; or else, the performativity of freedom finds its place there, and then its form obeys the *if . . .* , *then* type, and the imperative is not categorical.

3. The abyss.

Thus, in the limitation placed upon the practical deduction (in the form of a reversal of its direction), the heterogeneity between ethical phrase and cognitive phrase is marked. This limitation is not due to some finitude of human beings. It results from the absence of a homogeneous language. An "abyss" (*KUK*, Introduction) separates every descriptive phrase, including the critical metalanguage of the deduction, from the prescriptive phrase. The latter, when taken as the referent of the former, must elude its grasp.

The objection is not long in coming. If the abyss between obligation and the world determined by cognition is impassible, then Kantian morals remain an abstraction. You indeed hear *Close the door*, but the door will never be closed. (Or, conversely, next to the world of morality, is the world of knowledge an abstraction?) — What is truly abstract is to raise the question of the abyss in an alternative way, such that it would have to be either filled in or hollowed out. Now, there is no abyss, as in general no limit, except because each party — to dip back into forensic or warrior symbolism — grants itself a right of inspection over the other's argumentation, and so extends its pretensions beyond its borders. It is at this price that each party discovers its borders.

In our own idiom, this signifies that a family of phrases not only encroaches upon another but also that it cannot avoid resorting to another in order to establish its own legitimacy (Nos. 40, 41). In fact, this is the reason why they each appear as adversaries before the judge or critical watchman. How would the latter know that ethics is not cognition unless he tried to elaborate the legitimacy of ethics upon the mold used for cognition, by attempting to deduce the "moral principle" as if it were a principle of cognition, at the price then of conceiving free causality as if it were a causality within the series of causes and effects (*KRV*: 410–11)? It is because he attempts this passage that he discovers its impossibility, that he ascertains that the moral law is not arrived at by deduction, and that he concludes that freedom is that cognitive monster, an originary causality. It is then that he comes to use a mode of passage which is no longer simply the extension of a legitimation from one realm to another, but the establishment of a differential for the respective legitimations. The "as if" is the generic name of this differential. It neither hollows out nor fills in the abyss, it passes or comes to pass over it, and takes it therefore into consideration. It is an *Uebergang* which is the model for all *Uebergänge* (Kant Notice 3).

The analogy resulting from the *als ob* is an illusion when the differences are forgotten and the differend smothered. It succeeds in being critical, on the contrary, if the modes of forming and of validating phrases are distinguished and if the fully disclosed differend can thereafter, following Kant's hope, be transformed into a litigation. The as-if depends upon the transcendental imagination for the invention of the comparison, but it depends upon the faculty of judgment for its regulation.

4. The type.

Just because the ethical phrase is untranslatable into the cognitive phrase, it does not result that the moral law has no effect in the world, but, to the contrary, in order to have an effect—and it must have an effect, otherwise it could not be said to be a "cause of events"—it must borrow its form from the functioning of theoretical reason, a form which is precisely that of conformity to the law (*Gesetzmässigkeit*). In the moral act, the maxim of the will must "stand the test of being made the form of a natural law in general, [otherwise] it is morally impossible" (*KPV*: 72). Why is this? Kant writes: "Even the most common understanding judges in this way, for its most ordinary judgments, even those of experience, are always based on natural law." When an act that is done or is about to be done needs to be evaluated, the understanding, pursues Kant, "always has the law at hand, but [. . .] this natural law serves only as the *type* of a law of freedom." It does not transfer intuitions into the ethical realm, nor the possibility of presenting schemata or examples which are tied to them, but simply "the form of the *Gesetzmässigkeit* [of what is "on the scale of the law"] in general." This "passage" is therefore a habitual one. Why then is it required? Without it, writes Kant, "the maxim of action is not so constituted as to stand the test of its application" (*Ibid.*). When the law is theoretical, the schema is what is charged with its application to the intuitive given, and what guides the judgment in determining that "it is indeed the case." In the practical realm, though, the judgment must regulate itself upon the Idea of the good, and there is no more of a schema for this Idea than there is for any other. "But to the law of freedom (which is a causality not sensuously conditioned), and consequently to the concept of the absolutely good, no intuition and hence no schema can be supplied for the purpose of applying it *in concreto*" (*Ibid.*: 71).

Thus, the passage is not made by the form of the intuition or the schema, but by the form of the law or rather of the *Gesetzmässigkeit*. Ethical judgment borrows this form from the theoretical in order to guide itself when a case needs to be established: "Ask yourself whether, if the action which you propose should take place by a law of nature of which you yourself were a part, you could regard it as possible through your will" (72). The *type* of legality is what formally guides the maxim of the will in the formulation of the categorical imperative, as well as in the evaluation of a just action. The *so dass* of the imperative *Handelt so dass* should be understood then as an "as if" rather than as a "so that": for universality cannot be effectively concluded from the maxim, but only indirectly presented to the evaluation made of it.

This type introduces the Idea of a suprasensible nature into the entire problematics of the will. If the qualification that "the natural whole is looked at as if it were a machine" were not there to transfer conformity to the law from the realm of cognition over into that of obligation, not only would the Idea of a "whole of practical, reasonable beings" have no pertinence in the ethical realm, but, furthermore, the Idea of a cosmopolitan society and of progress would have no pertinence either in the historical-political realm (Sign of History Section). The type is a complex bridging between two regimens, the regimen of cognition, how I know, and the regimen of the will, how you ought to. The form of legality is not introduced from one into the other without modification, because causality does not operate the same way in both. In the realm of the sensible world, causality is a concept that determines *a priori* the liaison between phenomena and constitutes the cognition of experience. In the realm of ethics, it is an Idea of the immediate efficacy of pure practical reason or freedom upon the maxim of action. This idea is signaled by the feeling of respect and constitutes the situation of morality, or obligation. In the first case, phenomena are bound together as causes and effects forming a series, the world in the Kantian sense (as opposed to nature, although Kant often employs this word when the occasion presents itself). In the second case, a feeling of obligation—respect—which does not belong to the series of phenomena (or whose cause is not found in the series), is reflexively tied back to an unknowable cause, such as pure practical reason, pure will or freedom, as the effect of that cause.

5. Commutability.

Here, though, it is necessary to forestall the recurring threat of a transcendental appearance which the analogy of legality introduces through the type. If the maxim of your will ought to be able to be set up as "a universal law of nature," to constitute "a universal legislation" (1785: 39, 58), it is apparently because the dissymmetry between *I* and *you* ought to be disregarded for the benefit of some universal, "humanity," the we of exchangeable I's and you's: "Act so that you treat humanity, whether in your person or in that of another, always as an end [. . .]," "as if [you] were at all times a legislative member in the universal realm of ends" (*Ibid.* : 47, 57). They are thus exchangeable not only upon the instance of the obligated one, the you of the *You ought to*, in order to form a community of hostages, but also upon the instance of the legislator, the I of the *I am able to*, in order to form a community of constituents.

Isn't an abyss filled in there, from the fact of this perfect symmetry? And isn't the regimen of obligation annexed right down to the form of its phrases by the regimen of cognition? If they are substitutable, the I's and the you's are only so in the eyes of a third party who conceives the whole they form on the model of a nature. Haven't they become referents for this third party? This third party may even bear one or both of their names and thus immanently reside within the supranatural world they form, albeit insofar as he or she conceives of this supranatural world of the obligated legislator, he or she ceases to be placed in the ethical situation of being obligated. Moreover, doesn't Kant implicitly avow this when, counter to everything that has been analyzed concerning the feeling of obligation, he asks that everyone treat him- or herself as the legislator, that is, that everyone put oneself into the situation of the I in the universe of the phrase *I am able to*? Isn't this the practical transcendental appearance, par excellence? Hasn't the commentary on the ethical phrase, here critical, but nevertheless still descriptive, once again obtained the inevitable result (as it is said that the transcendental illusion is inevitable) of reducing ethical legitimation to cognitive legitimation, in particular by imposing onto the former the rule of the latter, namely the rule of consensus and of exchangeability between partners, the rule of dialogue (Plato Notice)? And isn't Levinas's exigency the only safeguard against this illusion, namely, that one can only phrase ethics ethically, that is, as someone obligated, and not as a scholar, be he or she a critical one (Levinas Notice)?

The question of a suprasensible nature comes down at least to this: how is a community of ethical phrases possible? Kant introduces the term humanity in order to answer this question. Humanity is a concept which does not belong to the genre of critical discourse (especially not the 'deductive' kind), but to the genre of anthropology (in the Kantian sense of the word). The community of practical, reasonable beings (obligees and legislators, since that is the hypothesis) includes just as well entities that would not be human. This community cannot be empirically attested.

Concession: we can't really say if and how the object or referent intended by the Idea of this community is possible, but it is at least possible to conceptualize this community, it is not a "being of reason," or an empty concept: it is a community of persons. — But it may be asked whether the term person is not by itself inconsistent. It in fact signifies that the same entity occupies the legislating instance, that of the I in the *I am able to*, and the obligated instance, that of the you in the *You ought to*. On the scale of a single entity, it signifies autonomy. The community of practical, reasonable beings merely extends this principle of autonomy onto the scale of all possible entities, on the condition that they satisfy the definition of a practical, reasonable being, that is, of a person. By confusing and condensing the two instances — nonetheless recognized by Kant as completely dissymmetrical — into a sole "person," isn't their differend gainfully effaced? Why should the obligated entity also be the one that obligates? And why would this self be "humanity"?

6. Ethical time.

The time or tense [*temps*] peculiar to prescriptives puts up an invincible resistance to the formation of a nature, be it a suprasensible one. The type of conformity to the law is powerless to overcome this resistance. The regimen of prescriptives forbids any recursive linkings on the model of if . . . , then (No. 95), which Kant calls mechanical causality, and which are constitutive of series of phenomena (*KRV*, Antinomy of Pure Reason, Sections 7, 8, and 9, I and II: 443–64). Obligation is not conditional, but categorical; nor does it condition. Even when taken as an "effect" of pure will, it cannot in turn be the "cause" of an effect, of an act for example which would result from it. Causality through freedom is immediate, that is, without mediation, but also without recurrence. Its efficiency is instantaneous, pure will obligates and that's all. It is but "beginning." Contemporaneous with the ethical phrase, pure will in no way regulates the linking of this phrase with subsequent phrases: come what may. (The command will or will not be obeyed; its execution is awaited, but whether it is obeyed or not, it is still a command) (Nos. 45–56; 147–49; Kant Notice 2, § 2).

There is no moral diachrony. Pure ethical time is the now of the phrase which, with one stroke, presents the obligation and the obligated one (and perhaps the obligating one, the *I am able to*), each in their own way. The ethical phrase is unique, it is the first and last sign of an Idea, and it is possible at any time, in the manner of the world (*KRV*, Section 9, III: 469, 472–78). Like the *Is it happening?* but differently, the *You ought to* is a phrase whose occurrence is preserved from its occultation by a rule of linkage. (How it's different from *Is it happening?* is examined in Nos. 172–74).

It will be said that *You ought to* awaits a sequel, whether it is obedience or not, and thus sketches out something possible to come, or a future. But this is also the case for many phrases of other regimens, perhaps for all phrases, to the extent that none can be the last phrase (No. 17). This is the case, for instance, for cognitive phrases subjected to the procedure for establishing reality. This procedure calls upon the possibility of other senses and of other ostensions (Nos. 86–90). The mode of linking may be not necessary, but it is necessarily possible.

According to Kant, the action that follows upon a prescription must be "possible" (*Ibid.*: 473). This possibility is understood, though, as a compossibility: not only is the prescription executory, but it must also be executable, compatible with "natural conditions." This sense of what is possible calls upon the synthesis of the heterogeneity between nature and freedom. The universe presented by the phrase that linked onto the prescription must be able to give rise to a cognitive as well as to an ethical linking.

But what is an ethical linking? As an example of a phrase, Kants gives that of a "malicious lie" (*Ibid.*: 477–78). We link onto it by explicating it (sociology, psychology, etc.). But "we none the less blame the agent [. . .] as if the agent in and by himself began in this action [the lie] an entirely new series of consequences." Now, this "imputation" presupposes only that the liar is the addressee of an unconditional obligation – not to lie – which he has not respected. It does not at all imply that he is the author of an original series of consequences. For that cannot be a source of blame; and, if there is a series, it belongs to the world. Consequences, by definition, cannot be ethical. Obligation is not transitive. On the other hand, a phenomenon, here the lie, can give rise to an ethical phrase, the judgment of imputation. This judgment is what discontinuously, not necessarily, turns the lie not into a cause, but into a (negative) sign of the moral law. The same equivocation between the cognitive and the ethical can, in turn, befall this judgment. It may be taken as a consequence or as a sign (a sign of the absolute). But signs are not consequences.

Causality through freedom gives signs, never ascertainable effects, nor chains of effects. No "nature," not even a suprasensible one, not even as an Idea, can result from obligation. The imperative does not command one to act so as to produce a community of practical, reasonable beings, but as if the maxim of action were supposed to be a law of this community. As a sign, the ethical phrase is without sequel, and thus final. But as there is no final phrase, another phrase must link onto it. And, as this linkage cannot be the linkage of an ethical implication – which is an impossibility – this implication, if it is still an implication (a series of consequences), then is not ethical, but cognitive. The "possibility" required by Kant that pure obligation give rise to a phenomenon ascertainable in reality and explicable according to the rules of cognition, in other words, that it give rise to a referent, signifies that the you of the obligation should always be able to be taken as the referent of a subsequent cognitive phrase. We don't really see what would prohibit a linkage of this sort. We do see, however, that this linkage prohibits the making of a world (in the Kantian sense) with ethical phrases. Either implication, or obligation. There is no ethical community. " 'But [this community] will never come to that point!,' cried the Rabbi" (Buber, 1953: 93).

Genre, Norm

178. We see no reason to grant a "mystical" profundity to the abyss that separates cognitives and prescriptives. (Kant is sometimes drawn into this, as is Wittgenstein. Pascal, because he is the closest to the sophists, is in the last analysis more "reasonable," even with his tears of joy.) Incommensurability, in the sense of the heterogeneity of phrase regimens and of the impossibility of subjecting them to a single law (except by neutralizing them), also marks the relation between either cognitives or prescriptives and interrogatives, performatives, exclamatives . . . For each of these regimens, there corresponds a mode of presenting a universe, and one mode is not translatable into another.

179. — You aren't being clear. Does incommensurability affect the relationship between phrase regimens or the relationship between genres of discourse? — For every phrase regimen, there corresponds a mode of presenting a universe. A genre of discourse inspires a mode of linking phrases together, and these phrases can be from different regimens. The universe presented by a cognitive and the universe presented by an exclamative are heterogeneous. The stakes implied in the tragical genre, its intended success (shall we say, the feelings of fear and pity on the part of its addressees), and the stakes implied in the technical genre, its own success (shall we say, the availability of the referent for the addressor's wants) are, for their part, incommensurable, and they induce heterogeneous linkings, be they on the basis of the same phrase. A technician may link onto the

tragic, "How these vain ornaments, these veils weigh down on me!,"* which inspires pity, by seeking out light fabrics and a sober attire (and by laughing at the customer, or with her).

180. — You say that a genre of discourse imprints a unique finality onto a multiplicity of heterogeneous phrases by linkings that aim to procure the success proper to that genre. If this is the case, it follows that the heterogeneity of phrase regimens is not of such a kind that it would prohibit their common subordination to a single end. The abyss that separates them would then be, if not filled in, at least covered over or spanned by the teleology of genres of discourse. Let's go further. This would only be the case if the concatenation of phrases had nothing to do with any finality tied to a genre, and took place without genres, if their heterogeneity completely disjoined them and left their linkage unforeseeable and inexplicable, as it pleases you to describe them. Now, this is not possible. By your own avowal, the phrases that happen are "awaited," not by conscious or unconscious "subjects" who would anticipate them, but because, to speak as linguists do, they carry their own "set of directions" [*modes d'emploi*] along with them (Paolo Fabbri in a conversation), that is, they carry instructions as to the end pursued through them. And to insist, as you do, on the indetermination of the linkings is still to function in terms of certain stakes, those of persuading your reader of the heterogeneity of regimens and of the preeminence of the occurrence. This is done, therefore, in accordance with the finality prescribed by a genre or at least by a style (as Cage does with the musical phrase or Gertrude Stein with the literary phrase). — You really are reading a book of philosophy, the phrases in it are concatenated in such a way as to show that that concatenation is not just a matter of course and that the rule for their concatenation remains to be found (Hegel Notice §4; no. 174).

181. — Another implication of the same observation (No. 180). You say that genres of discourse impose onto phrases the finality of a concatenation able to procure a success proper to each genre. You would admit then that, as heterogeneous as they may be among themselves, genres of discourse are all subject to a single, universal principle, shall we say that of "winning" or "gaining" [*gagner*]. Certainly, the gain that is hoped for by pedagogical discourse, by dialogue, by tragedy, by folksongs, by technology, or by obligation is not the same. When Jaacob Yitzchak of Lublin conceded to Yeshaya that "when we seek to effect nothing, then and then only we may not be wholly without power" (Buber, 1953: 101), he circumscribed the stakes of the genre of ethics: its success (justice) would be the perfect disinterestedness of the ego, the relinquishing of its will. And even if children's games (such as playing mom and dad, or soldier and nurse

---

*Jean Racine, *Phèdre* I, iii, 158. –tr.

in the back of an apartment) do not have the stakes of beating an opponent, as in basketball or bridge, they assuredly still aim for a gain whose securement orients their every sequence, or "phrase." The securement of this gain is a pleasure shared then by spectators who are themselves the actors. — Okay, but by this reckoning, you've come back to the "language games" of the *Philosophische Untersuchungen*, and to their anthropology. But if that's not what you want, then you'll have to give credence to some metaphysical will, or else to a phenomenology of intentions like the Anglo-American philosophers of meaning.

Kant 3

1. The archipelago.

The Critique of Political Reason was never written. Within certain limits that remain to be determined, it is legitimate to see in the dispersion of Kant's historical-political texts the sign of a heterogeneity peculiar to the "object" of politics. This heterogeneity already affects the third *Critique*. There, the faculty of judgment is seen to be provided not with one object proper to it, but with at least two: art and nature. I say "at least" because there is some question about knowing whether this faculty of judgment is a faculty. Kant has earlier given a precise sense to the word *faculty*, that of a potential of phrases subject to a group of rules of formation and presentation (in the Kantian sense), when it was a matter of sensibility, understanding, and reason with respect to theory and of reason with respect to practice. In point of fact, though, the judgment already and necessarily intervenes each time that it is a question of saying "this is the case" in order to validate a phrase, or in order therefore to present an object permitting this validation. This takes place in cognitives under the regimen of the schema, in dialectical argumentatives under that of the symbol, and in prescriptives when it is a matter of evaluating responsibility and morality, under the regimen of the type (Kant Notice 2: § 4).

In the Introduction to the third *Critique*, the dispersion of the genres of discourse is not just recognized, it is dramatized to the point that the problem posed is that of finding "passages" (*Uebergänge*) between these heterogeneous genres. The "faculty" of judgment, by very reason of its ubiquity, that is, on account of the fact that it is called upon each time a phrase has to be validated by a presentation, appears as a force of "passages" between the faculties, to the point that it is accorded a major privilege in the area of unifying capacity. At the same time, a major flaw is recognized in the area of its ability to know an object that would be proper to it; in other words, it has no determined object. Which is why it may be asked whether it is indeed a cognitive faculty in the Kantian sense. Among all the genres of discourse, however heterogeneous they may be with respect to each other, what Kant obstinately (although perhaps it is his problematics of the subject that is obstinate in his place) calls the faculty of judgment is the determination of the mode of presenting the object that suits each respective genre.

What object could correspond to the Idea of this gearing of the faculties, which are understood as capacities for cognition in the broad sense, that is, as capacities to have objects (sometimes as realms, sometimes as territories, sometimes as fields) (*KUK*: 10)? This object could only be a symbol. Let's say, an archipelago. Each genre of discourse would be like an island; the faculty of judgment would be, at least in part, like an admiral or like a provisioner of ships who would launch expeditions from one island to the next, intended to present to one island what was found (or invented, in the archaic sense of the word) in the other, and which might serve the former as an "as-if intuition" with which to validate it. Whether war or commerce, this interventionist force has no object, and does not have its own island, but it requires a milieu – this would be the sea – the *Archepelagos* or primary sea as the Aegean was once called.

This milieu bears another name in the Introduction to the third *Critique*, that of field, *Feld*: "Concepts, so far as they are referred to objects, independently of the possibility or impossibility of the cognition of these objects, have their field, which is determined merely according to the relation that their object has to our cognitive faculty in general" (*Ibid.*). This cognitive faculty in general includes the understanding, the faculty of judgment, and reason. In accordance with the "serial arrangement" of representations drawn up by Kant at the end of the section on "Ideas in General" in the Dialectic of the first *Critique* (314), sensibility would also have to be included. All of these faculties find their object in this field, some delimiting a territory there, others a realm, but the faculty of judgment finds neither one nor the other, it ensures the passages between the others. Instead, it is the faculty of the milieu, within which every circumscription of legitimacy is caught fast. Furthermore, this is the faculty which has enabled the territories and realms to be delimited, which has established the authority of each genre on its island. And this, it was only able to do thanks to the commerce or to the war it fosters between genres.

2. Passages.

It is possible to specify some of the passages that constitute the archipelago. The transcendental illusion is one of its cases, an unhappy one. How do we know that dialectical phrases, which have the form of cognitive phrases, are not cases of this? And that the territory of the validity of reasoning does not thereby coincide with the realm of the understanding's legislation? Because, with respect to argumentative phrases, we cannot present an intuitable object, one given that is in space and time. Reason is impelled by its need (*Bedürfnis*) to maximize the concept and obeys "a merely logical prescription (*eine bloss logische Vorschrift*)" (*KRV*: 307) to advance toward the unconditioned. What is presentable to the phrase of reason as an object proper for its legitimation cannot be a phenomenon. Once the rule for forming the phrase has been identified (namely, that to reason is to conclude by means of a universal), the critique consists in playing out the rule for presenting it, after which the dialectical phrase will have been "isolated" (insulated) from the phrase of understanding. Transcendental illusion is not for that matter dispelled, but it is located. The "as if" which is the source of this illusion is set aright. The dialectical phrase acts as if it referred to phenomena. The critique requires that it refer to "as if phenomena." To symbols, that is.

Another case, eminent and legitimate, of the operation of "passages" is indicated in § 59 of the third *Critique*, where it is a question of showing that "the beautiful is the symbol of the morally good." The symbolizing operation in general is twofold, and is called analogy. It consists in "first applying the concept to the object of a sensible intuition, and then applying the mere rule of the reflection made upon that intuition to a quite different object of which the first is only the symbol" (*KUK*: 197–98). Kant gives two examples of this: a mere machine, the hand mill, may symbolize a monarchical State "governed by an individual absolute will"; a living body may symbolize a monarchical State "governed by national laws." In both cases, there is no resemblance between the symbolized object and the symbolizing object, which is "utterly different." There is an identity, though, between the reflective rule applied to the latter and the one applied to the former.

The same goes for the relation between the beautiful and the good. Reflection is brought to bear on the feelings (pleasure, respect) occasioned by objects respective to the two realms, and it discovers the same formal traits in them: immediacy, disinterestedness, freedom, universality. These are then (according to the genre of transcendental discourse) the conditions *a priori* for the possibility of those objects. Each trait, though, is applied differently in each realm. Immediacy of feeling is required in the case of the beautiful by the sensible, and in the case of the good, it is required by the concept. In the judgment of taste, freedom is the freedom of the imagination coming into harmony with the concept; in the moral judgment, it is the freedom of the will coming into harmony with itself, etc.

The analogy at work here is not identical, however, to the analogy presented by the hand mill or living body as symbols of political regimes. It is impossible, in effect, to consider the object of taste as a phenomenon on the same level as a hand mill or a living body. The latter can be given through a *Versinnlichung* [sensible illustration], an operation of sensibility in harmony merely with the laws of the understanding, but *Sinnlichkeit* [sensibility] and the understanding are not sufficient to grasp (and therefore to constitute) the object of taste. With the question of beauty, we are dealing with "the intelligible to which [. . .] taste looks [. . .]. In this faculty, the judgment does not see itself [. . .] subjected to a heteronomy of empirical laws [. . .]. It finds itself to be referred to something [. . .] which is neither nature nor freedom, [. . .] the supersensible" (*KUK*: 199). If there is "sensation" in the experience of the beautiful, it is in a sense utterly different from what is established in the Transcendental Aesthetic of the first *Critique*: "If a determination of the feeling of pleasure or pain is called sensation, this expression signifies something quite different from what I mean when I call the representation of a thing (by sense, as a receptivity belonging to the cognitive faculty) sensation" (*KUK*: 40).

If the beautiful symbolizes the good, then it is not because the aesthetic object is a phenomenon susceptible of a direct intuition which can be substituted, by analogy, for the ethical object (moral act), for which no intuition is possible. Nor is the aesthetic object any more of an object of experience, nor is there any intuition, at least insofar as it is aesthetic. Its form is perceptible, but the beauty of its form is not. Its aesthetic properties are not in itself, as givens, but in the feeling of taste, which obeys the four *a prioris* enumerated above. These are like the constitutive rules of the phrase (of feeling) which appraises beauty. The same rules are found in the *You ought to*, in the ethical phrase, in the feeling of respect. But they are not applied to the same instances as in the aesthetic appraisal. What is felt immediately in the ethical phrase is not the object, but the law (the concept of practical reason): the addressee is not affected by the referent but by the sense. The addressor of the ethical phrase is not the imagination but the will, etc.

Symbolization, then, does not occur here through a substitution of objects, but through permutations of instances in the respective phrase universes, and without recourse to a direct presentation. The expeditions to neighboring islands undertaken by the faculty of judgment do not just bring back empirical data, but they even bring back rules of formation (phrase families) and of linkage (genres of discourse), such as the four *a prioris.* What allows the critical judge to say, *This is the case*—or the convicting exhibit—is not necessarily a fact.

I will not go back over that case of analogy which the type is for practical reason (Kant Notice 2, § 4).

There are other cases, of less repute but no less strange, such as that "passage" which Kant ventures to present, in the first *Critique*, as an "Ideal of sensibility" and which he calls the "monogram" (*KRV*: 487). This is, he writes, "a blurred sketch drawn from diverse experiences," "an incommunicable shadowy image" in the judgments of painters (and physiognomists), a "model (not indeed realizable) of possible empirical intuitions," which "furnishes no rules that allow of being explained and examined." Kant turns this evanescent something or other into a creation of the imagination. This imaginary is not, however, an Idea of the imagination; it is an Ideal, and an Ideal of sensibility, because it is a kind of schema—an "as-if schema"—of the Idea of the imagination in the realm (or field?) of sensible experience. Here again, it is not a rule, but an "as-if rule," a regulative transport from the imagination to sensibility. And then, there is still and even more simply the Idea of the imagination itself, constituted by a passage in reverse going from reason to the imagination: intuition without a concept takes the place of the concept without intuition (*KUK*: 165–66, 189). As for this particular "passage," there is no need to underscore its importance in setting up a line of communication between subjective teleology and objective teleology.

3. Arrangement.

It would be tedious to pursue an inventory of "passages," others can be found in the field of the historical-political. One last observation on the archipelago. In the Concluding Note on the Solution of the Mathematical-transcendental Ideas, and Preliminary Observation on the Solution of the Dynamical-transcendental Ideas (*KRV*, Antinomy), Kant shows that, when it's a matter of deciding between the mathematical-transcendental Ideas, the judge is obliged to send both parties packing because all they can present by way of objects permitting the legitimation of their respective phrases (thesis and antithesis) are "conditions *within the field of appearances*": "in the two mathematical-transcendental ideas the only object we have had in mind is object as appearance." Now, neither one nor the other of these two parties can present such an object since theirs is a phrase of an Idea and not a phrase of a concept of the understanding. The dynamical antinomies (those of freedom and of the supreme being), though, "open up to us an entirely new view": "The suit in which reason is implicated [. . .], in our previous trial of it, has been *dismissed* as resting, on both sides, on false presuppositions. But since in the dynamical antinomy a presupposition compatible with the pretensions of reason (*der Rechtsgründe*) may perhaps be found, and since the judge may perhaps make good what is lacking (*ergänzt den Mangel*) in the pleas which both sides have been guilty of misstating [in the first two antinomies], the suit may be regulated by an arrangement [a compromise, *une transaction, vergleichen*] to the satisfaction (*Genugtuung*) of both parties" (*KRV*: 462).

This is nothing more than the exposition of the conditions for the synthesis of the heterogeneous. It is done in such a way, though, that the synthesis is clearly not *de jure*, and that the judge clearly effects the compromise without a rule which would authorize him to do so, except for the principle that heterogeneity ought to be respected in an affirmative manner. The same case will hold for the resolution of the antinomy of taste, and preeminently so for the resolution of the antinomy of the faculty of judgment in § 69–71 of the third *Critique*. Preeminently so, because, in a prolongation of "what is lacking in the pretensions of reason" in the Note from the first *Critique*, it is stated that "the judgment must serve as its own principle" (*KUK*: 233). And, in a prolongation of the "arrangement" made between the two parties in that same Note, it is stated that a similar arrangement is possible between teleological thesis and mechanical antithesis, between the thesis of nature and that of the world, since the former, which is the thesis of the properly reflective faculty of judgment which is "autonomous," takes nothing from the "heteronomous" usage of the determinant faculty defended by the opposing party. The name borne by this compromise is that of "guiding thread (*Leitfaden, fil conducteur*)" (*Ibid.*). The guiding thread is the way in which the reflective judgment, attentive to the singularities disregarded by the cognitive phrase, and "on the lookout" for these singularities to find an order in them, freely presupposes that order; that is, it judges as if there were one. If the thread guides, it is because there is an end. This end, though, cannot be directly presented as an object can: "the concept of that causality [through ends] is a mere Idea, to which we by no means undertake to concede reality" (*KUK*: 236).

The judge supplements for the absence of a universal tribunal or last judgment, before which the regimen of cognition and the regimen of freedom could be, if not reconciled (that they will never be), then at least put into perspective, organized, finalized in terms of their difference. This supplementarity is nonetheless authorized by the Idea of nature, in the Kantian sense. Nature is the name borne by the object of the Idea of objective finality, and this Idea is itself required by the reflective judgment when it seeks to account for the singular existences that the legality of the "mechanically" determined world does not explain (*KRV*: 379). Conversely though, if the activity of discerning, the *Genauigkeit* [exactness] or attention paid to differends at work in the critique, can take on this supplementarity by invoking the objective finality of nature, it is because it (critical activity) is itself a means set to work by nature in order to prepare its final end. (*KUK*: § 84).

In the *Verkündigung des Nahen Abschlusses eines Traktats zum ewigen Frieden in der Philosophie* [*Announcement of the Upcoming Conclusion of a Treatise of Perpetual Peace in Philosophy*] (1796), Kant writes that philosophy "is a state forever armed (*ein immer bewaffneter Zustand*) against those who erroneously misconstrue phenomena for things-in-themselves." This armed state "ceaselessly accompanies reason's activity." And if, in and around the Idea of freedom, it indeed opens up "the perspective of a perpetual peace among philosophers," it is not because they can come to a consensus concerning this Idea, but because this Idea can be neither proved nor refuted, even though there are the greatest practical reasons to admit the principle of freedom. That is why this "peace" to boot (*überdem*) presents still another advantage (*noch ein Vorzug*), that of "forever keeping alert (*rege*), or in a state of agitation, the forces of the subject, put into apparent danger from attacks [by the opponents of philosophy]." This agitated peace is a way of "furthering through philosophy the purpose of nature, which is to enliven this subject continuously and to ward off the sleep of death" (1796: 416–17). In nature's purpose, combative, critical, alert philosophy is a "proper means to enliven (*Belebungsmittel*) humanity in view of its ultimate end." If a victim of the positivist illusion such as Schlosser, for instance, comes to require that philosophy put an end to debate, he puts philosophy into alarm, into a state of alertness, and thus helps it fulfill its natural end. Without wanting to (since he wants the opposite), he helps reinforce this "combative disposition (or constitution) (*die streit-bare Verfassung*) which is not war (which can and should instead prevent war)," but which launches "pacific" expeditions across the archipelago.

It remains that if the critical watchman thinks he can supplement for the absence of a legal provision and go ahead and pass sentence over the differend concerning freedom, it is because he believes himself to be authorized by the Idea that nature pursues its ends by means of this supplementarity. But now, what authorizes him to resort to this Idea of a natural end capable, according to him, of authorizing him to judge without laws? Since it's an Idea (that of nature and thus of ends), he cannot present an ostensible this to validate the authorization. He can present an "as-if this," an analogon, a sign. That sign is his feeling, the feeling that one ought to and is able to judge even in the absence of laws. This feeling, however, is in turn only a proof (*Beweisen*) certifying that there is a right and a duty to judge outside the law if some nature pursues its ends by means of this feeling. No exit is made from the circle.

Even if we grant that the value signs have for the critical lookout man is what leaves the play of the judgment free with regard to them (finding the case for the rule and the rule for the case), that value nonetheless presupposes a kind of intention (a finality) on the side of what makes sign. By means of the feeling the philosopher has, an as-if subject would signal to him that, under the guise of this sign, a quasi-phrase has taken place whose sense cannot be validated by procedures applicable to cognition, but which still ought to be taken into consideration. Can one pass judgment on signs without presupposing such an intention, be it problematically? That is, without prejudging that an unknown addressor not only delivers but also addresses them to us to be decoded?

Concomitantly, though, if no guiding thread leads the way for the judgment's expeditions, how can the judgment find its way amid the labyrinth of passages? Would the *analoga* be pure fictions? For what needs would they be forged? This itself is impossible: the passages are what circumscribe the realms of legitimacy, and not the latter which would pre-exist the passages and tolerate them. What are we doing here other than navigating between islands in order paradoxically to declare that their regimens or genres are incommensurable?

Whatever acceptation is given to the Idea of nature, one's right of access to it is only through signs, but the right of access to signs is given by nature. Not even a denaturalized nature and signs of nothing, not even a postmodern nonteleology, can escape this *circulus* (No. 182).

182. Is this the sense in which we are not modern? Incommensurability, heterogeneity, the differend, the persistence of proper names, the absence of a supreme tribunal? Or, on the other hand, is this the continuation of romanticism, the nostalgia that accompanies the retreat of . . . , etc. ? Nihilism? A well-executed work of mourning for Being? And the hope that is born with it? Which is still the hope of redemption? With all of this still remaining inscribed within the thought of a redemptive future? Could it be that "we" are no longer telling ourselves anything? Are "we" not telling, whether bitterly or gladly, the great narrative of the end of great narratives? For thought to remain modern, doesn't it suffice that it

think in terms of the end of some history? Or, is postmodernity the pastime of an old man who scrounges in the garbage-heap of finality looking for leftovers, who brandishes unconsciousnesses, lapses, limits, confines, goulags, parataxes, non-senses, or paradoxes, and who turns this into the glory of his novelty, into his promise of change? But this too is a goal for a certain humanity. A genre. (A bad parody of Nietzsche. Why?)

183. Do ends show up right along with genres (Nos. 174, 179)? – They certainly do, and they take hold of phrases and the instances they present, especially 'us.' 'We' do not intend them. Our 'intentions' are tensions (to link in a certain way) exerted by genres upon the addressors and addressees of phrases, upon their referents, and upon their senses. We believe that we want to persuade, to seduce, to convince, to be upright, to cause to believe, or to cause to question, but this is because a genre of discourse, whether dialectical, erotic, didactic, ethical, rhetorical, or "ironic," imposes its mode of linking onto "our" phrase and onto "us." There is no reason to call these tensions intentions or wills, except for the vanity of ascribing to our account what is due to occurrence and to the differend it arouses between ways of linking onto it. – But how can one explain, or even describe, this reversal which gives currency to anthropocentrism, this transcendental appearance affecting the we, the illusion of enunciation?

184. Let's recapitulate (Nos. 180, 181): a phrase comes along. What will be its fate, to what end will it be subordinated, within what genre of discourse will it take its place? No phrase is the first. This does not only mean that others precede it, but also that the modes of linking implied in the preceding phrases – possible modes of linking therefore – are ready to take the phrase into account and to inscribe it into the pursuit of certain stakes, to actualize themselves by means of it. In this sense, a phrase that comes along is put into play within a conflict between genres of discourse. This conflict is a differend, since the success (or the validation) proper to one genre is not the one proper to others. *I can come by your place* (Nos. 137ff.) allows many diverse linkings, and if not all of them, then at least some of them, stem from different genres of discourse. The multiplicity of stakes, on a par with the multiplicity of genres, turns every linkage into a kind of "victory" of one of them over the others. These others remain neglected, forgotten, or repressed possibilities. There is no need to adduce some will or some intention to describe that. It suffices to pay attention to this: there is only one phrase "at a time" [*à la fois*] (No. 113). There are many possible linkings (or genres), but only one actual or current "time" [*une seule "fois" actuelle*].

185. The rules of formation and linkage that determine the regimen of a phrase have to be distinguished, as we have been doing, from the modes of linking that stem from genres of discourse. As Wittgenstein observes, the set of rules constituting the game of tennis or chess is one thing, the set of recommendations

which form a strategy for winning is something else. By ignoring the latter, you are considered to play "badly." But it's okay to play "badly": "I know, I'm playing badly but I don't want to play any better." In that case, all my interlocutor can say is: "Ah then that's all right" (Wittgenstein 1929–1930: 5). Not to mention that playing "badly" might be a good strategy, an unprecedented one, which will subsequently be said to be "well played!" Genres of discourse are stategies—of no-one.

186. There are as many different ways of winning as there are genres. The stakes of a genre are often set by a phrase of canonical value. This phrase may be formulated in the interrogative regimen. What about this? What should I do? Have you understood? Shall we judge that to be beautiful? It this is so, what can we do? Do you agree? Do you want to? Is it legitimate to . . . ? What happened? What will happen? What follows from this? How much is this worth? Success comes from giving an "answer" to the key-phrase. The "answer" is a phrase that suspends the question contained in the key-phrase. It is then asked whether this suspension is legitimate, and the answer to this last question becomes the object of new differends, whose various parties question the said answer on the basis of key-questions which set the stakes for their respective genres.

187. Phrase regimens coincide neither with "faculties of the soul" nor with "cognitive faculties." Genres of discourse don't coincide with them either. Now and then, certain overlappings are possible: certain descriptives might belong to the faculty of cognition, certain prescriptives to the faculty of desire. There is an affinity between the cognitive genre and the understanding, between the dialectical genre and speculative reason. But is there one between the narrative genre and all of its sub-genres? Is there a phrase regimen covering the realm of the "faculty of judgment"? What about interrogative phrases? And exclamative phrases? Are they particularly tied to feelings, to the "faculty of pleasure and pain"? A table of correspondences cannot be established. You might as well try to superimpose the tripartite metaphysical psychology of Platonist origin (which still governs, though from afar, the Kantian critical trilogy) onto the Aristotelian nomenclature for the genres of *logos*.

188. You don't play around with language (Nos. 91, 181). And in this sense, there are no language games. There are stakes tied to genres of discourse. When these stakes are attained, we talk about success. There is conflict, therefore. The conflict, though, is not between humans or between any other entities; rather, these result from phrases. At bottom, one in general presupposes *a* language, a language naturally at peace with itself, "communicational," and perturbed for instance only by the wills, passions, and intentions of humans. Anthropocentrism. In the matter of language, the revolution of relativity and of quantum theory remains to be made. No matter what its regimen, every phrase is in principle what

is at stake in a differend between genres of discourse. This differend proceeds from the question, which accompanies any phrase, of how to link onto it. And this question proceeds from the nothingness that "separates" one phrase from the "following." There are differends because, or like, there is *Ereignis*. But that's forgotten as much as possible: genres of discourse are modes of forgetting the nothingness or of forgetting the occurrence, they fill the void between phrases. This "nothingness" is, nevertheless, what opens up the possibility of finalities proper to the genres. If the manner of linking were necessary (filled in), there would not be several possible modes, no void would leave room for that causality exerted from afar, namely, "final causality."

189. The idea that a supreme genre encompassing everything that's at stake could supply a supreme answer to the key-questions of the various genres founders upon Russell's aporia. Either this genre is part of the set of genres, and what is at stake in it is but one among others, and therefore its answer is not supreme. Or else, it is not part of the set of genres, and it does not therefore encompass all that is at stake, since it excepts what is at stake in itself. The speculative genre had this pretension (Result Section; Hegel Notice). The principle of an absolute victory of one genre over the others has no sense.

190. Were politics a genre and were that genre to pretend to that supreme status, its vanity would be quickly revealed. Politics, however, is the threat of the differend. It is not a genre, it is the multiplicity of genres, the diversity of ends, and par excellence the question of linkage. It plunges into the emptiness where "it happens that . . . " It is, if you will, the state of language, but it is not *a* language. Politics consists in the fact that language is not a language, but phrases, or that Being is not Being, but *There is*'s. It is tantamount to Being [*à même l'être*] which is not. It is one of its names.

191. If capital were shown to be a genre of discourse, if its stakes were laid out along with the strategies it has for winning out over the other genres, by that alone could it be shown that its hegemony is not only unjust but vain. In its pretensions to total success, however, capital's superiority over the speculative genre resides at least in its not seeking to have the last word, to totalize after the fact all the phrases that have taken place in all the genres of discourse (whatever their finality might be), but rather in seeking to have the next word. (Marx accordingly puts *Das Capital* in opposition to the *Phenomenology of Mind*. In capital, there is a future, but there is none in the speculative genre.) The check exerted upon occurring phrases by the finality of capital is certainly not nothing, it is that of profitability. They are thus subordinated to stakes which seem to be what is at stake in all stakes, namely "winning" or "gaining" [*gagner*] (No. 181), even though that set of stakes is only one among others, that of gaining time (Nos 249, 250) as measured by interest calculated in terms of money. Within this genre,

though, under the conditions of this end, the most unheard of occurrences are greeted and even "encouraged" (—as if capital could "encourage" the *Is it happening?!*).

192. When Cézanne picks up his paint-brush, what is at stake in painting is put into question; when Schönberg sits down at his piano, what is at stake in music; when Joyce grabs hold of his pen, what is at stake in literature. Not only are new strategies for "gaining" tried out, but the nature of the "success" is questioned. Is it still a matter of "pleasing" through the beautiful, or of "pleasing/displeasing" through the sublime? Aren't the stakes analogous, rather, to those that orient the "philosophical" genre? A painting will be good (will have realized its ends, have come near them) if it obliges the addressee to ask about what it consists in. Everything is political if politics is the possibility of the differend on the occasion of the slightest linkage. Politics is not everything, though, if by that one believes it to be the genre that contains all the genres. It is not *a* genre.

193. The universe presented by a phrase is immediately "social," if by "social" it is understood that an addressor, an addressee, a referent, and a sense are situated together within it. By "immediately," I understand that none of these instances can be deduced from any of the others as if from an origin. "There is" a phrase universe, and, depending upon its regimen, "there are" situations between the presented instances, situations that shape that universe. A "deduction" of the social presupposes the social. The discourse, for instance, of the social "contract" is a narrative comparable to a myth. It recounts the birth of the social, but to the extent that it is recounting it, the social is already there as narrator, narratee, narrated, question, and answer to the question. The social is always presupposed because it is presented or copresented within the slightest phrase. Even *The sum of the angles of a triangle is equal to two right angles* implies an addressor, an addressee, and their nonfortuitous (didactic) relation.

194. It is also easy to understand that the "social" is immediately complex. In the universe presented or co-presented by a phrase, several instances are situated: an *I* or a *we* instance, a *you* instance, a *he*, a *she* or a *they* instance. None of them comprise the whole of the social. Even when the social is explicitly taken as a referent in the sociologist's phrase, it is also presupposed in the situating of all the instances presented by that phrase. The social is the universe which is formed by their situation insofar as that situation is related to human names, and which is signified by the phrase. The sense thereby presented obeys the regimen which the phrase obeys. This regimen can modulate the universe according to several modes of instanciation (for example, we and you facing them, we and them facing you, you and them facing us) and several modes of presenting sense (cognizing, prescribing, questioning, admiring, etc.). In addition, genres finalize these universe situations in accordance with certain stakes: convincing, persuading, affect-

ing, etc. The tension, or rather the discord, of the social is thereby immediately given with its phrase universe, and the political question is given along with the mode of linking onto it, that is, along with its finalization around a set of stakes.

195. It is just as easy to understand why the nature of the social—for example, its identification—by a definitional phrase, is immediately deferred. For, since it is given along with the universe of a phrase, since the finality (the direction of its sense, if you will) of this universe depends upon the phrase by which one links onto the preceding one, and since this linking is a matter for differends between genres of discourse, the nature of the social always remains to be judged. In this way, the social is the referent (the universe of a prior phrase taken as the referent of a subsequent phrase) of a judgment to be always done over again. It is a "case" pled contradictorily before a tribunal. And in this "case," the nature of the tribunal that must pronounce upon the case is itself the object of a differend.

196. A differend, I say, and not a litigation. It is not that humans are mean, or that their interests or passions are antagonistic. On the same score as what is not human (animals, plants, gods, God and the angels, extraterrestrials, seasons, tides, rain and fair weather, plague and fire), they are situated in heterogeneous phrase regimens and are taken hold of by stakes tied to heterogeneous genres of discourse. The judgment which is passed over the nature of their social being can come into being only in accordance with one of these regimens, or at least in accordance with one of these genres of discourse. The tribunal thereby makes this regimen and/or this genre prevail over the others. By transcribing the heterogeneity of phrases, which is at play in the social and in the commentary on the social, the tribunal also necessarily wrongs the other regimens and/or genres.

197. It cannot even be said that (necessarily, civil) war, class struggle, or revolutionary violence are more just than the tribunal because they would expose the differend instead of masking it under litigation. Vengeance is not an authorization (No. 44). It shows that another tribunal and other criteria of judgment (should there be any) are possible and seem to be preferable. But, supposing the change took place, it is impossible that the judgments of the new tribunal would not create new wrongs, since they would regulate (or think they were regulating) differends as though they were litigations. This is why politicians cannot have the good at stake, but they ought to have the lesser evil. Or, if you prefer, the lesser evil ought to be the political good. By evil, I understand, and one can only understand, the incessant interdiction of possible phrases, a defiance of the occurrence, the contempt for Being.

198. It could be said that the social is given immediately with a phrase universe (be it the one presented by the tail of a cat), and that it is given as immediately determined by, in principle, the regimen of that phrase, even though its determination is straightaway the object of another phrase, whose linking on cannot help

but be the occasion for differends between genres of discourse. It could be said for that very reason that politics is immediately given with a phrase as a differend to be regulated concerning the matter of the means of linking onto it. It is just as pointless to ask questions about the "origin" of the political as it is about the social. The social is implicated in the universe of a phrase and the political in its mode of linking. There is just as much of a Cashinahua politics as there is an Athenian or a Jacobin politics, even if in the former the prevalence of narrative wards off the threat entailed by the occurrence (Cashinahua Notice). The civil war of "language" with itself is what is always at play in one as in the other. The only difference lies in the manner of instituting the litigations to regulate the differends.

199. Politics always gives rise to misunderstandings because it takes place as a genre. This genre varies according to the nature of the authorization inscribed in the normative prefix. The names invoked (the *y*'s) (Nos. 155, 206) determine the genre as myth, as deliberative consensus, as divine right . . . : *Our Ancestors have always* . . . ; *By decision of* . . . , *we, the Assembly of representatives of the people* . . . ; *I, emperor by the grace of God, ordain* . . . . It cannot be otherwise since the tribunal that determines what a litigation is, which demands justice, and which thereby forgets, represses, and reactivates differends, must pronounce the sentences it passes, and must, first of all, found its authority upon the rules of a genre of discourse. At the same time, though, politics is not at all a genre, it bears witness to the nothingness which opens up with each occurring phrase and on the occasion of which the differend between genres of discourse is born.

200. In organizing itself around the empty center where deliberation takes place—namely, the conflict of phrases and their judgment—the Greek *polis* did not invent politics, it placed the dialectical and rhetorical genre or genres in the governorship of phrases, thereby allowing their differend to flow, in the form of litigations, right out into the (empty) milieu of political institutions. The Cashinahua put narration in that governorship, and the first French Republic the Idea, that is, dialectics in the Kantian sense, in particular the one whose stakes are in free causality (ethics). The Industrial Revolution gave the privilege of judging to the technical genre, whose stakes are in the maximizing of performance, that is, in obtaining the best input/output relation in the setting upon [*arraisonnement*], as Heidegger would say, of the referent whatever it be (the social included) by the will (or enjoyment) of the self. There are thus hegemonies of genres, which are like figures of politics. They fight over modes of linking. Capital gives political hegemony to the economic genre (Nos. 240ff.).

201. The terms of democracy, autocracy, oligarchy, monarchy, and anarchy (which designate modes of government) and those of republic and despotism (which designate modes of domination or authorization) belong to narrowly an-

thropological or politico-logical descriptions. What politics is about and what distinguishes various kinds of politics is the genre of discourse, or the stakes, whereby differends are formulated as litigations and find their "regulation." Whatever genre this is, from the sole fact that it excludes other genres, whether through interdiction (slaves and women), through autonymic neutralization, through narrative redemption, etc., it leaves a "residue" of differends that are not regulated and cannot be regulated within an idiom, a residue from whence the civil war of "language" can always return, and indeed does return.

202. To call this residue the "accursed part" [*part maudite*] is useless pathos. As for a politics centered on the emotions associated with sacrifice (Cashinahua Notice, § 7), on the pretext that it would constitute through suffering and jubilation the infallible index that a differend exists, and that no litigation could neutralize this differend, that would be human, all too human: as if humanity had some elected responsibility in safeguarding the occurrence! Bataille lacks the Hassidic or pagan sense of humor (and I know these two are not the same) in the greeting of the *Ereignis*. To govern in accordance with the feelings attendant upon sacrifice (or *Dienst*[service])(Heidegger, 1933: 476–78) that the differend would require would make for a politics of false supermen. In coddling the event, one puts on a Horrorshow *à la Grand Guignol*. One's responsibility before thought consists, on the contrary, in detecting differends and in finding the (impossible) idiom for phrasing them. This is what a philosopher does. An intellectual is someone who helps forget differends, by advocating a given genre, whichever one it may be (including the ecstasy of sacrifice), for the sake of political hegemony.

203. Authority is not deduced. Attempts at legitimating authority lead to vicious circles (I have authority over you because you authorize me to have it), to question begging (the authorization authorizes authority), to infinite regressions (*x* is authorized by *y*, who is authorized by *z*), and to the paradox of idiolects (God, Life, etc., designate me to exert authority, and I am the only witness of this revelation). The aporia of a deduction of authority, or the aporia of sovereignty, is the sign that the phrase of authorization cannot result from a phrase stemming from a different regimen. It is the sign of an incommensurability between the normative phrase and all others.

204. The question of authority is played out in the normative phrase. The norm is what turns a prescription into a law. *You ought to carry out such and such an action* formulates the prescription. The normative adds: *It is a norm decreed by x or y* (No. 155). It puts the prescriptive phrase in quotation marks. One may wonder whence *x* and *y* hold their authority. They hold it from this phrase, which situates them on the addressor instance in the universe authorizing the prescription. The referent for this universe is the prescriptive phrase, which is found to be authorized by that very fact.

205. One is tempted to describe the normative as a performative (No. 142). *The meeting is called to order, war is declared,* and this is thereby so. The addressor situated by the universe of these phrases is immediately the chair of the meeting or one of the belligerents; the addressee is immediately a member of the assembly coming to session or the adversary upon whom war is made. Thus the normative, *We decree that it is obligatory to carry out such or such an action,* would immediately situate the we in the position of sovereignty. —But what one vaguely calls these "effects" can be observed in all phrases, whatever their regimen, since they are simply the deployment of the instances of the universes they present and of their respective situations. The term performance is then so extended that it loses its ability to designate a specific phrase regimen. —It remains that no entity can have the authority to obligate unless it is the addressor of the normative that turns the obligation into a norm. This is a tautology. Nor do we see how, starting from non-narrative phrases, something could become that addressor if it is not already it. One phrase regimen is not engendered by another.

206. In its strictly ethical sense, obligation in and of itself does not need the authorization of a norm in order to take place, quite to the contrary (Nos. 155, 176; Kant Notice 2: § 1): by legitimating prescription, one suppresses the dissymmetry of the obligation, which is what distinguishes the regimen of prescriptive phrases. It is precisely a function, though, or at least an effect, of the normative to make the obligated one's situation symmetrical. By prefixing the prescriptive with *It is a norm decreed by y that x ought to carry out such and such an action,* the normative wrenches *x* from the anxiety of idiolect (Abraham or Schreber, Nos. 162, 164), which is also the marvel of the encounter with the other and a mode of the threat of *Ereignis.* This threat, this marvel, and this anxiety, namely the nothingness of a 'what-is-to-be-linked', are thus normalized. They are the same for other *x*'s, for the you's of the normed obligation. The normative, excluded as it is from the ethical, leads into the political. It constitutes a community of addressees of the prescriptive, who qua addressees of the normative, are advised that they are, if not necessarily equal before the law, at least all subject to the law. It does not make the obligation transitive, that's impossible (Kant Notice 2, § 6), it makes it common.

207. In its form, the normative entails the citation of a prescriptive (Nos. 45, 46). This prescriptive is autonymized. The normative is a phrase about a phrase, a metalanguage, but not a descriptive one. Truth is not what it has at stake, but justice. Its metalinguistic constitution marks the function of authority: to throw a bridge over the abyss between heterogeneous phrases. By declaring such and such a phrase permitted, such and such a phrase prohibited, and such and such a phrase obligatory, authority subjects them, whatever their heterogeneity might be, to a single set of stakes, justice. Singing undoubtedly relates to the beautiful, but it may be unjust if it is a certain song, at a certain time, in a certain place.

Learning relates to the true, but there again under certain conditions, etc. With the normative, whatever its supposed legitimation and whatever the form of this legitimation (myth, revelation, deliberation), one genre seizes upon heterogeneous phrases and subordinates them to the same set of stakes.

208. On the basis of this fact, if the addressee of the normative is also the addressee of the prescription that it norms, he or she is in the situation of meta-addressee with regard to the addressee of the prescription, even if both addressees bear the same name. We know that the notion of the citizen is "an abstraction" in relation to the "individual," that is, in relation to the entity who bears the same name and who is found situated in "current," heterogeneous phrase universes. What is true for the notion of the citizen, though, is also true for a member of the Cashinahua: the normative legitimating the distribution of names among sexes, generations, and moieties is respected because it is the law, and at the same time, this respect does not coincide with the phrases of object-languages, if we can say so, which correspond to the "activities" of "individuals" (Cashinahua Notice, § 3). The law should always be respected with humor because it cannot be completely respected, except at the price of giving credence to the idea that it is the very mode of linking heterogeneities together, that it has the necessity of total Being. This humor aims at the heterogeneity which persists beneath and despite legitimation. "The People," that impossible set of entities caught within incommensurable phrase universes, cannot believe that the law is the law because it is just, when it knows that the law is just (in the sense of instituting an impossible community of obligations) because it is the law (Pascal, 1670: fragments 66, 525). The "people" is not the sovereign, it is the defender of the differend against the sovereign. It is full of laughter. Politics is tragedy for the authorities, comedy for the people. The respecting of the event which comic laughter is should be granted its ontological dignity, and the tragic tear should be put back in its place, which is merely the highest one (Book II of the *Poetics* did this, only for that book then to be lost).

209. The normative also has among its addressees entities who are not the addressees of the prescription it legitimates. By legitimating the obligation incumbent upon x to carry out such and such an action, y also gives notice to a third party, z, that by linking onto the said action z will have to deal with y's authority. The normative is also a declarative. The gap between the normative prefix and the prescription creates the gap between the community of the obligated and whatever is outside this community but which should also be made aware of the law. But since the prescription is legitimated by the norm, how can it admit that others are not subject to what it prescribes? In the answer to this question lies the motive of imperialism: that all addressees of the normative also be addressees of the prescriptive. The Decree of Caracalla in 212 and the Edict of Constantine in 312 explicitly formulate this motive: all humans living within the *orbs romana* are Ro-

man citizens; all creatures, because they are called to the heavenly kingdom, belong to the earthly empire. Citizenship, or the fusion of the addressee of the prescriptive with the addressee of the normative, has no limit in principle (no Ideal limit), but only in fact. Nations, their languages, their customs, and their names are thrown back into the "empirical" as so many objects that the discourse of the Idea can refer to only negatively: they do not satisfy Ideal legitimation.

Declaration of 1789

1. This is a Declaration of rights, namely, the normative legitimation not of prescriptions to be executed but of limits to be respected by those prescriptions. In other words, a legitimation of essentially negative (limiting) prescriptions to be observed by the prescriptive authority itself. Not: It is a norm decreed by y that it is obligatory for x, etc.; but: It is a norm decreed by z that a norm decreed by y, making it obligatory for x, etc., is a norm only within the following limitations. The Declaration legitimates the legitimation of the prescriptive. It adumbrates a regression in the authorizations (No. 203) by passing to a rank of legitimacy above that of political (meta-normative) legitimacy. This passage is stirred by the imperialist principle of legitimation which impels it to universalize itself in the same movement by which it sets boundaries on the extension of legitimacies. This tension is resolved by the legitimation of the very bounds of legitimacy. The limits brought to bear on authority determine a political Constitution (Article 16). What authorizes the fixing of the said limits (the Declaration itself) is the Idea of man.

2. As the supreme authority, addressor, and sense of the meta-normative, man should have signed the Preamble of the Declaration. Such is not the case: "The representatives of the French people, organized in National Assembly, considering [. . .], have resolved to set forth in a solemn declaration the natural, inalienable, and sacred rights of man [. . .]. In consequence, the National Assembly recognizes and declares [. . .] the following rights of man and citizen." The signatory, the z who declares the norm that is to be imposed on the norms, is a community representative of a community, an assembly representing a people, who is named by a proper name: the French.

3. The world of names (No. 60) and history too return in the designation of the Declaration's author. They "return" because they were expulsed while the principle of authorization was extending its claims and passing from the metalinguistic rank to a higher rank (meta-metalinguistic, that is, meta-normative). What is indicated by this return is a heterogeneity. The addressor of the Declaration does not have a proper name in political history, but the French people does. The Declaration is a set of phrases obeying the speculative regimen, in the Kantian sense (the referents are objects of Ideas, which are not falsifiable through a process for establishing reality). If not ascribed to an addressor that can be named in the historical-political world, the Declaration remains what it is, a philosophical discourse, a "dialectical" one (in the Kantian sense). If the Declaration is signed by a nation, that is, by an entity which through its name alone stems—be it problematically—from the world of reality (in particular, historical-political reality), then the Declaration is itself a discourse, a set of phrases whose import is historical-political. By import, I mean to say that the linking which it calls forth on the addressee's part is not a

discussion about the truth or falsehood of its (dialectical) sense, but rather its acceptance or rejection by national communities (which bear names in the historical-political world) as the norm of norms. For the addressee thus situated by the mere signature of the addressor is him- or herself an entity subject to national, political laws. These laws are prescriptions, but they are not normed in accordance with the norm of norms (the rights of man and citizen). The addressee is thereby called upon to revise the norms authorizing the national laws to which he or she is subjugated, norms whose authority ought to appear badly authorized to her or him. After 1789, international wars are also civil wars.

4. Of course, the authority which the representatives of the French nation arrogate to themselves by speaking in the place of man is itself authorized by Article 3 of the Declaration: "The source of all sovereignty is essentially in the nation." If the nation is authorized in the Preamble to prescribe the Articles, and Article 3 in particular, it is because in that article the nation is declared to be authorized to prescribe in general. The Article names the sovereign, and the sovereign states the source that names him. But the sovereign had to begin his declaration before being authorized to do so by the Article he is going to declare, thus before being the authorized sovereign. The paradox is a trivial one in the legitimation of authority (No. 203), and we can't be all that shocked by it. (The same apparatus of self-authorization can be found in the *Communist Manifesto* or in the *Addresses* of the International Working Men's Association in 1870–1871. It can also be seen that their major difference from the apparatus of 1789 is that the instance by which these *Addresses* authorize themselves and to which they are addressed is not a historical-political one like a nation (which can always be named and therefore designated in the real world) but this instance is itself a problematic one, like the object of an Idea: the worker is a universal (like man). How can a transnational entity, the international organization of workers, have a historical-political reality when it ignores national proper names? The difficulties then and thereafter encountered by the workers' movement and its ultimate failure through its collapse back into national communities (at least since the socialist vote in favor of war budgets in 1914) would be a signal that the legitimation of communities through their names and traditional narratives resists their legitimation through an idea. These two legitimations stem from heterogeneous genres. Does the historical-political world irremediably belong to the former?)

5. I see in that sort of supplement/detriment to national authority given in the preamble a sign that the addressor of the meta-norm must be man: "The National Assembly recognizes and declares in the presence and under the auspices of the Supreme Being [. . .]." This Being of reason has no reason to authorize a particular nation. By soliciting its presence and by imploring its recommendation, the Assembly authorizes itself not only as French, but also as human. Here, the apparatus runs counter to the one described above. If the addressor has a political-historical name, his declaration has no import beyond that which corresponds to the extension of the name. If he must exceed this extension, and if the Declaration ought to extend to all names, then the addressor ought not to have any name proper to him. This is why he invokes the Supreme-Being, who is anonymous and whose creature, or whose token or an expression of whom he is (there were, among the members of the Constituent Assembly, several philosophies of this Being and of man's relation to Him), or, shall we say, whose equally anonymous existent he is. The splitting of the ad-

dressor of the Declaration into two entities, French nation and human being, corresponds to the equivocation of the declarative phrase: it presents a philosophical universe and co-presents a historical-political universe. The revolution in politics that is the French Revolution comes from this impossible passage from one universe to another. Thereafter, it will no longer be known whether the law thereby declared is French or human, whether the war conducted in the name of rights is one of conquest or one of liberation, whether the violence exerted under the title of freedom is repressive or pedagogical (progressive), whether those nations which are not French ought to become French or become human by endowing themselves with Constitutions that conform to the Declaration, be they anti-French. This confusion permitted by the members of the Constituent Assembly and assured its propagation throughout the historical-political world will turn every national or international conflict into an insoluble differend over the legitimacy of authority.

6. The members of the Constituent Assembly would have been prey to a "transcendental appearance" and even perhaps to a *dementia* (Kant Notice 4: § 4). They hallucinated humanity within the nation. Robespierre to the Convention on May 8, 1793: "If you allow patriots to have their throats slit one by one, then everything that is virtuous on Earth shall be exterminated. It's up to you to see whether you want to save the human race" (Kessel, 1969: 203). The nation, inasmuch as it is a community, owes the essential of its consistency and authority to the traditions of names and narratives (Cashinahua Notice). These traditions are exclusivist. They imply borders and border conflicts. The legitimacy of a nation owes nothing to the idea of humanity and everything to the perpetuation of narratives of origin by means of repeated narrations. Rightists never cease to make the most out of this. Leftists give credence to a counter-narrative, a history of the whole of humanity, the narrative of its emancipation, cosmopolitan, of international import, and without popular roots. They are always accused, though, of bringing the country to ruin, and yet they are always condemned to protect it on the occasion of civil, foreign or economic wars because authorization through myths, or immanent authorization (the heartland), does not yield to the authorization which resorts to the Ideal, transcendent meta-norm (the rights of man). There is no Supreme Being to reconcile these two authorizations.

210. In the deliberative politics of modern democracies, the differend is exposed, even though the transcendental appearance of a single finality that would bring it to a resolution persists in helping forget the differend, in making it bearable. The concatenation of genres of discourse and of phrase regimens at least allows itself to be taken apart, while in traditional narration the combination of various stakes—making believe, making known, convincing, making decide, etc. —defies analysis (so much is it inscribed in each phrase, and so much is the occurrence masked by the narrative form) (No. 219). The higher end is formulated, as in the ethical genre, by the canonical phrase (or the stakes) which is an interrogative prescriptive, *What ought we to be?*, but one weighted with possible senses: *happy, knowledgeable, free, equal, French, rich, powerful, artistic?* Philosophies of human history bring their answers to these questions. They are rarely debated within the enclosure of the political institution, where there reigns the confused presumption of an agreement concerning them. —The general feel-

ing is that a discussion (necessarily dialectical in the Kantian sense, that is, without term, and lacking in proof, since it is a matter of Ideas which cannot be decided upon through recourse to reality) could do no more than put the we back into question. The we is questioned by this interrogative prescriptive in its abstract generality, "we humans," but it is not questioned, it is presumed already resolved, in and through silence, insofar as it is a nameable particularity, "we French." By inquiring deep down into duty, one risks being surprised, for starters, that one ought to be French. For it is not obligatory to be French; at most, being French can probably be established as a reality. (Or else, a legitimation of the Cashinahua type would have to be admitted) (Cashinahua Notice). —Therefore, "we" ought to be a little of everything, rich, equal, free, etc., but wholly French: "we" are already that.

211. Onto the *What ought we to be?* there is linked a *What ought we to do in order to be that* (French, rich, free, equal, etc.)? This linking modifies the canonical phrase of the interrogative prescriptive genre. The introduction of *to do* and *in order to* into the question of duty makes duty pass into a hypothetical mode: if you want to be this, then do that. And *to do*, baptized as it is in the name of the practical, consists in a prescient calculation of phrases and of their effects, of their linkings that is, which are able to lead to the end that is sought for. But this "practical" calculation remains abstract, for lack of names, unless another genre of discourse inserts itself within the deliberative concatenation under the regimen of another canonical phrase: *What about the means?* This genre's end is the cognition of givens considered from the standpoint of their affinity, as means, with the supreme end. Analyses of the situation, inventories of available capacities, estimations of the capacities of adversaries and of allies, and definitions of respective interests, are effectuated through opinion polls, statistics, indexes, and information of all kinds. Realities are established, knowledge is what is at stake in this genre. The technoscience of specialists, experts, advisers, and consultants is put to use, but it remains subordinate to an interest that is not its own, that of rendering executory the supreme prescription (to be rich, free, etc.). The cognitive phrase is thus finalized by the prescriptive genre.

212. Once the givens are established, a new genre of discourse is required, one whose canonical phrase is *What can we do?* This phrase is not without analogy with what Kant calls an Idea of the imagination (intuitions without a concept) (*KUK*: 165–66, 189) or with what Freud calls free association. Today, these are called scenarios or simulations. They are narrations of the unreal, as in war games: what if they attacked our left flank? Then we would surround them by rapidly deploying our right flank. A multiplicity of possible, probable, and improbable stories are told heedless of their verisimilitude, in anticipation of what could be the case. One part of game theory consists in examining the ways games function and in looking for their rules. With the pronoun, *they, them,* the stress

is put on conflict with one or more opponents. There is presupposed on the opponent's part a set of abstract and "practical" ends, symmetrical to "our" ends even if they are different. It is still a question of "winning" (No. 181). These phrases of the imagination are anchored in possible reality by means of proper names: if there are opponents, it is because humanity has not realized itself, and because those legitimated by narratives and names remain present (No. 160; Cashinahua Notice: § 6).

213. Political deliberation properly called takes place in these scenarios. It obeys the dialectical and rhetorical genres. A scenario is refuted: *You are wrong* or: *He's wrong and this is why*. These are debates made of arguments aimed at silencing one's partner. Another end is mixed in, that of persuading him or her. This end is tied to another genre of discourse, the one Aristotle calls "deliberative" rhetoric and which is exchanged, for example, between two parties in front of the Assembly. The arguments (*logoi*) can be found described in the *Rhetorics* (II, 24), the *Topics* and the *Sophistical Refutations* (*passim*), and the commonplaces (*topoi*) are listed in the *Rhetorics* (II, 23). Commonplaces: Wouldn't it be criminal to . . . ?, I accuse *x* of . . . Apparent enthymemes: Since the government of Kabul or El Salvador has asked for Moscow or Washington's help, the presence of Soviet or American troops in the territory governed by Kabul or El Salvador is proof of the independence of those governments. In modern democracies, an important supplement to this genre is brought in from "forensic" type rhetoric where it is a question of persuading not the opponent but the third party who sits in judgment. This is public polemics, the campaign for public opinion, propaganda: the other is wrong, therefore I'm right; he or she is unworthy of your confidence (this is aimed at the opposing orator's ethos), he or she is leading you away from your true ends (this is aimed at the listener's pathos); such is not (therefore) the case with me.

214. Afterwards, comes the "decision," the "choice" of a scenario, along with the end that it implies: the resolution, the program, the result of the ballot, the judge's verdict. This scenario gives the answer which is the least bad (the principle of the lesser evil) (No. 197) to the question of means and ends. This is the judgment, the most enigmatic of phrases, the one which follows no rules, although in appearance it is linked to ends, to givens, to means, and to "consequences" (Kant Notice 3: § 3). It takes the form of resolutions, of programs, or of ballots.

215. The phrase of judgment still needs to be legitimated. That is the charge of normative discourse, of law in general, and of the law of the law (constitutional law). Then, it needs to be rendered executory (by decrees, edicts, laws, memoranda) and twistings of the law rendered legitimately condemnable (jurisdiction of infractions and punishments).

216. This concatenation (Nos. 210–15) seems entirely paradoxical, if one examines the linking of one phrase obeying a regimen and finalized by a genre with another phrase obeying another regimen or at least finalized by another genre. For example, the linking of *We ought to* with *We are able to* (Nos. 211, 212; Kant Notice 2: § 2) which poorly conceals the paralogism of the we. Or the linking *In consequence* (or: *Considering* . . .), *we decide* . . . , which conceals the fact that the phrase of judgment is not derivable without residue from phrases of a different regimen, and from cognitives in particular (Kant Notice 3). Or the linking of a normative with the prescription it legitimates (Nos. 204–9). Etc.

217. The deliberative is more "fragile" than the narrative (Nos. 219, 220, 230), it lets the abysses be perceived that separate genres of discourse from each other and even phrase regimens from each other, the abysses that threaten "the social bond." It presupposes and registers a profound dislocation of narrated worlds. The scientific genre, for example, whose canonical phrase is cognitive, which requires the establishment of realities, and which therefore implies their potential extermination (Referent Section), holds a place in deliberation that it does not in narration. Most especially, however, the unity of genres that make up the deliberative is under the sole guarantee, if it can be said, of the answer given to the canonical phrase of the prescriptive: *What ought we to be?* Within the narrative genre, this question is not formulated (we ought to be what we are, which is Cashinahua). In the deliberative, the answer remains uncertain, subject to a dialectic (in the Aristotelian or Kantian sense) between theses and antitheses. This dialectic has no end, since it concerns, if not "cosmological," then at least "anthropological" Ideas; or to speak again like Kant, "cosmo-political" (*weltbürgerliche*) Ideas. In a word: narrative is a genre; deliberation is a concatenation of genres, and that suffices to let the occurrence and differends sprout up within it.

The Sign of History

218. A phrase, which links and which is to be linked, is always a *pagus*, a border zone where genres of discourse enter into conflict over the mode of linking. War and commerce. It's in the *pagus* that the *pax* and the pact are made and unmade. The *vicus*, the *home*, the *Heim* is a zone in which the differend between genres of discourse is suspended. An "internal" peace is bought at the price of perpetual differends on the outskirts. (The same arrangement goes for the ego, that of self-identification.) This internal peace is made through narratives that accredit the community of proper names as they accredit themselves. The *Volk* shuts itself up in the *Heim*, and it identifies itself through narratives attached to names, narratives that fail before the occurrence and before the differends born from the occurrence. Joyce, Schönberg, Cézanne: *pagani* waging war among the genres of discourse.

219. Narrative is perhaps the genre of discourse within which the heterogeneity of phrase regimens, and even the heterogeneity of genres of discourse, have the easiest time passing unnoticed. On the one hand, narrative recounts a differend or differends and imposes an end on it or them, a completion which is also its own term. Its finality is to come to an end. (It is like a "round" in a tournament.) Wherever in diegetic time it stops, its term makes sense and retroactively organizes the recounted events. The narrative function is redeeming in itself. It acts as if the occurrence, with its potentiality of differends, could come to completion, or as if there were a last word. Felicitous or infelicitous in its meaning, the last word is always a good one [*un bon mot*] by virtue of its place. *Ultima verba*,

pacific happiness. On the other hand, the unleashing [*déchaînement*] of the now is domesticated by the recurrence of the before/after. The diachronic operator or operator of successivity is not called back into question, even when it is modulated. It "swallows up" the event and the differends carried along by the event. Narratives drive the event back to the border.

220. –Myth would be "the mimetic instrument par excellence" and would have an "identificatory force" for a society threatened with dislocation (Lacoue-Labarthe, 1980: 101–16). In this way, Nazism would have picked up, refashioned, produced, and represented the mythology of Nordic peoples in order to save a German identity sick from its "historical belatedness," from defeat and from economic crisis (Nos. 157, 158). –1. The identificatory force of myth is not debatable. It cannot be explained through the putting into place of a specular representation: a sick person does not get better by looking in the mirror. This force proceeds from the mere formal properties of the narrative tradition anchored as it is in a world of invariable names where not only the heroes but also the narrators and narratees are established and permutable, and thus identifiable respectively and reciprocally (No. 160, Cashinahua Notice). –2. Myth can be used only as an instrument by an instance which is not narrative-mythical. This is what is called Nazi cynicism. Myth would then be this monster: an archaic, modern politics, a politics of the community as a politics of humanity, a politics of the real origin as a politics of the ideal future. –3. If "mimetic" is understood as *imitative* or *representative*, then myth is not exceptionally mimetic. If *mimesis* signifies (Lacoue-Labarthe, 1975: 18–19, 20–21) that the presentation (*Darstellung*) can never be presented (Nos. 119, 124–27, 131), then myth–which is more of a genre of discourse whose stakes are in neutralizing the 'event' by recounting it, in appropriating what is absolutely improper, and in representing presentation–occults mimesis as much as it attests to it.

Cashinahua

1. "Among the Cashinahua, every interpretation of a *miyoi* (myth, tale, legend or traditional narrative) begins with a fixed formula: "Here is the story of . . . , as I've always heard it told. I am going to tell it to you in my turn, listen to it!" And this recitation invariably closes with another formula which says: "Here ends the story of . . . He who told it to you is . . . (Cashinahua name), or among the Whites . . . (Spanish or Portuguese name)" (d'Ans, 1978: 7). The ethnologist reports back to us (Whites) how the Cashinahua storyteller reports the story of the Cashinahua hero to his Cashinahua listeners. The ethnologist can do this because he is himself a (male) Cashinahua listener. He is this listener because he bears a Cashinahua name. By means of strict denomination, a ritual fixes the extension of myths and their recurrence. Every phrase contained in these myths is pinned, so to speak, to named and nameable instances in the world of Cashinahua names. Each universe presented by each of these phrases, no matter what its regimen, refers to this

world of names. The presented hero or heroes and places, the addressee, and finally the addressor are meticulously named.

2. Names of persons are distributed within a finite system with three variables: sex, generation, and "exogamic moiety." Two male "moieties," two female "moieties," and two age classes (same age or older than the ego, and younger) per moiety, make for a total of eight "kinship" groups. A. -M. d'Ans writes: "Considered on this plane, exogamic unions have the explicit function of transmitting *names*, of which each moiety, female as well as male, possesses two limited and immutable stocks corresponding to two alternating generations" (*Ibid.*: 35). "Kinship" relations are thus derivable from the system of names alone, without considerations of consanguinity or of marriage. Your personal name (be it through adoption) classifies you into one of the eight groups and thereby places you into certain defined relations with all the other Cashinahua depending upon each one's nominative group: obligatory phrases, permitted phrases, tolerated phrases, prohibited phrases. The prescriptions in question bear not only upon language, child rearing, and sexuality but also upon what you can sing, hunt, cook, grow, etc.

3. This is a regimentation in principle. It is not observed to the letter in the facts. The obligation concerns the distribution of the stock of names and their regular recurrence across the generations. They alone, thanks to their finite number, their permanence (rigidity), and their distribution, are what constitute the community's identity. For example, there is properly speaking no sexual taboo. Irregular marriages and cohabitations are numerous. Children born from these unions are nonetheless still distributed into the regular groups through the application of the rules for naming. And, if it happens that the child of a regular union can in principle indifferently receive the name either of the paternal group or of the maternal group, the final attribution is negociated. For example, each child of such a couple will be attributed in alternating order first to one, then to the other, of these groups. "When this negotiation comes to naught, abortion or even infanticide may take place: if the child has no name, he is nothing, he cannot exist" (*Ibid.*: 38). Human beings are named, or they are not human.

4. In order to hear the narratives, you have to have been named. (All males may listen as well as young girls prior to the age of puberty.) In order to tell them, the same applies (only men may tell them). And in order to be told about (referent), the same applies (all Cashinahua without exception may be told about). But the system of names does not engender and cannot engender narratives, it is a-chronic (generations are not considered otherwise than as classes of age) and by itself insignificant, since the namings are not descriptions (Nos. 57, 66, 74–77, 81). By inserting the names into stories, narration shelters the rigid designators of common identity from the events of the "now," and from the perils of its linkage. To be named is to be told about. There are two aspects to this: every narrative, even an apparently anecdotal one, reactualizes names and nominal relations. In repeating it, the community assures itself of the permanence and legitimacy of its world of names by way of the recurrence of this world in its stories. And from another standpoint, certain narratives explicitly tell stories of naming. Thus, the very origin of the "exogamic moieties" becomes the object of narrative 8 in d'Ans's collection; the origin of the Roa Bakë group, one of the male moieties, is recounted in narrative 9. These narratives

have particular value because, instead of telling a story to which one or more names are attached, they tell the story of the engenderment of names themselves.

5. The invention of the night (narrative 17): "At that time, our folk had no night in which to rest. Certainly, they had [. . .]. But as you know [. . .]. Our ancestors were quite annoyed about not being able to sleep [. . .]" (*Ibid.*: 185). The "current" narrator addresses the narratees and speaks to them about the Ancients. This narrative (in the French version) is told in free indirect style [*style indirect libre*]: the speech of the Ancients is "transposed," to use Genette's taxonomy (1972: 172; example: "I said to my mother: it was absolutely necessary that I marry Albertine"). The effect of this variation of narrative "distance" is that the attribution of the speech insofar as it is ascribed to one or another of the addressors remains equivocal: our ancestors were very annoyed, I'm telling you; or: our ancestors were very annoyed, they said (to themselves)? The declaration that serves as a prelude to the narration ("Here is the story [. . .]. I'm going to tell it to you [. . .]") (like the one that concludes the narration) strongly marks the instance of the "current" narrator in the entire narrative that follows (or precedes). The addressees, though, have undoubtedly forgotten him (or are about to forget him), "taken in as they are by the story" (this is a case for saying so). Most especially, the narrator himself declares that he has "always heard" this story. If every narrator has always declared this, then the story will have been reported with no discontinuity since the time of the Ancients, who were the first narrators as well as the heroes. There would be no gap, therefore, between the current narrator and the Ancients, except in principle a chronological one. Free, indirect style is faithful to this condensation of the extradiegetic instance (the current narrator) with the intradiegetic instance (the Ancients), a condensation characteristic of this kind of tradition. The "*in illo tempore*" of mythic time is no different from the time in which the narrating of it takes place. A "metalepsis" (Plato Notice, § 5) authorized by the constancy of proper names permits the passage from the time of day to the night of time.

6. Were we to raise in a positive way the question of the origin of tradition or of authority among the Cashinahua, we would find ourselves face to face with the usual paradox for these questions (No. 203). A phrase is authorized, one would think, only if its addressor enjoys some authority. What happens when the authority of the addressor results from the sense of the phrase? By legitimating the addressor that its universe presents, the phrase legitimates itself in the eyes of its addressee. The Cashinahua narrator's authority to tell his stories is drawn from his name. His name, though, is authorized by his stories, especially those that recount the genesis of names. This *circulus vitiosus* is a common one (No. 203). (Louis Marin finds it in the historiography of Louis XIV, which serves to legitimate the king's authority at the same time that this authority authorizes the history told by the king's historiographer) (1981: 49–107).

7. It sounds like a plateful of anecdotes [*historiettes*]. D'Ans doesn't talk about sacrifices among the Cashinahua, whom he presents instead as "secular." Couldn't it be said, though, that what is generally not consumable as anecdote and which has no place in the universe of narrative phrases–in short, the leftovers–is what is sacrificed? This is what I mean to say: the occurrence or event is not taken into account by legends, it would be sublimated in the strict sense of the term. It would be transformed into an airy element: smoke from sacrificial fires, the volatility of shaman spirits. The limit of the integrating capacity of nar-

ration and of naming would be recognized in this manner. And indetermination is what evaporates thereby. Why should that part be accursed? The sacrifice recognizes the differend which is not digested by the narration and acquits itself of it.

8. How can the war at the border (Clastres, 1977) be understood through this apparatus of integrated phrases? Is this too a sacrifice devoted to that major residue of indetermination which surrounds the world of narratives that is constitutive of the ethnic group's culture? But in this case, it is done in another mode. Could it be said that sacrifice represses occurrence, that it accepts it and integrates it the way a dream is able to do with a "movement of desire"? (In the absence of sacrifices, the Cashinahua men give themselves over to collective bouts with ayahuasca, a potent hallucinogen.) But that war forecloses occurrence at the boundaries of the narrative corpus constituting the social "body" the way paranoia allows the "movement of desire" to return from the outside, as "reality"?

221. What would be modern would be to raise the question of politics, the question of linkings, on the scale of the human, without recourse (in principle) to legitimation by names and narratives?–By narratives, at least in the sense of myths, tales, and rumors. The narrative form persists, however; and it undergoes the same sublimation as the story's hero. As he is no longer a Cashinahua, but man, so the narrative form no longer recounts "little stories" [*petites histoires*] but the story of History [*l'Histoire*]. The little stories received and bestowed names. The great story of history has its end in the extinction of names (particularisms). At the end of the great story, there will simply be humanity. The names humanity has taken will turn out to be superfluous, at best they will have designated certain stations along the way of the cross (Hegel Notice, § 3). This universalism and this pure teleology is not classical in the sense of Antiquity, but modern in the sense of Christianity. "Philosophies of history" are forged around a redemptive future. (Even capitalism, which has no philosophy of history, disguises its 'realism' under the Idea of an emancipation from poverty.)

222. A non-cosmopolitical (or "savage") narrative proceeds by phrases like *On that date, in that place, it happened that x, etc.* The question raised by cosmopolitical narrative would be the following: since this *x*, this date, and this place are proper names and since proper names belong by definition to worlds of names and to specific "savage" narratives, how can these narratives give rise to a single world of names and to a universal narrative?–The question may seem absurd: aren't these communities human ones?–No, they are "Cashinahua" and they call themselves the community of "true men," if not in exception to others, then at least in distinction from them (d'Ans, 1978: 11-13). The bond woven around "Cashinahua" names by these narratives procures an identity that is solely "Cashinahua." Were this identity already human in the cosmopolitical sense, it would not entail the excepting of other communities, or even the difference between them, and the universal history of humanity would consist in the simple extension of particular narratives to the entire set of human communities.

223. The objection may be made that narratives which result in a "savage" community, "despite everything," "already" have a cosmopolitical "import." It is sufficient to admit an equivocation in them: they present what they present (the "Cashinahua" world), but they also present what they don't present (the "human" world). –There is no objection in admitting this. The question is that of linkage: what genre of discourse governs the linking onto the "Cashinahua" narrative of a phrase discerning a "human" world therein which would stem from a universal history? What is not in doubt is that this genre, whichever one it is, "already" has universal human history for its referent, in order for it to be able to link onto "savage" narratives by placing them into that history. This linkage may be characterized as "projection." I would prefer to call it a begging of the question. If the "Cashinahua" story co-presents the universal history of humanity, it is because it is presented within a genre that presupposes a universal history of humanity. This genre allows for certain variants. The most explicit and most "impoverished" one consists in placing the Cashinahua story on the referent instance of phrases of historical (or anthropological) cognition. –This is always possible (any "object," if it satisfies the cognitive genre, can be situated on the referent instance in the universe of a phrase of cognition), but no proof results from this that the historical (or anthropological) cognition of the narrative of the community has been engendered, throughout the continuous trajectory of a universal history of humanity, from this narrative taken as origin. Yet this "engenderment" is what the concept of a universal history requires.

224. In the "impoverished" variant, the anthropologist-historian's relation to the Cashinahua (the West's relation to "savages") is solely "epistemological." The "archaic" narrative becomes the object of a genre of discourse, that of cognition, which obeys certain rules and which summons the "savage" narrative genre to appear only when these rules require that proofs (cases, that is to say, examples) be brought to bear upon an assertion relating to the "savage." The heterogeneity between the cognitive genre and its referent, the "savage" narrative genre, is not to be doubted (and in no way does it prohibit cognition). There is an abyss between them. The savage thus suffers a wrong on account of the fact that he or she is "cognized" in this manner, that is, judged, both he or she and his or her norms, according to criteria and in an idiom which are neither those which he or she obeys nor their "result" (Hegel Notice). What is at stake in savage narratives is not what is at stake in the descriptions of those narratives.

225. The historian of humanity will object that the epistemological linkage is not the one made by the genre of universal history. He or she invokes a "richer" variant of this linkage (No. 214). The equivocation that was supposed in the world presented by the "Cashinahua" narrative is, so it is said, intrinsic to that narrative. It becomes cognizable only when it has been deployed. It is then that the concept it contained, now fully disengaged, allows that equivocation to be retroactively

cognized. The historian adds that this concept, though, was implied in it "as the form of the oak tree is contained in an acorn." The symbol is not the concept, but it "gives something to think." –We recognize the speculative genre or one of its variations (hermeneutics, in particular). It requires that a self be supposed, which is neither the Cashinahua nor the historian, but the movement of an entity whose figures they are. They cannot be isolated. Man is this entity who only identifies himself in the referral of these moments to his end (as the sense of a movie shot depends upon its insertion into a sequence of shots, and the sense of the sequence upon the arrangement of the shots). –The rules for this "rich" linkage are those of the speculative genre (Hegel Notice) as applied to historical-political realities.

226. The universal history of humanity should be told in the narrative genre. Like all narratives, it would proceed by means of phrases like *On that date, in that place, it happened that x*, etc. But, as opposed to the savage narrative, it would be necessary that the onomastics of persons, places, and times, as well as the sense given the reported event, be accepted by all the addressees of the universal narrative (and even that these addressees be able to become in turn its addressors, if the stakes pursued by the narrative genre are indeed those of the narrative's recurrence), and that this community be the one to which those addressees belong. There would then need to be addressees who were themselves "universal." If one wants to escape the preceding question begging (No. 223), renewed here in this form, then in order for the history of humanity to be recounted, a universal, "human" narrator and corresponding narratee would have to be able to be engendered from "savage" ("national") narrators and narratees in their particularity and multiplicity.

227. The universalization of narrative instances cannot be done without conflict. Traditions are mutually opaque. Contact between two communities is immediately a conflict, since the names and narratives of one community are exclusive of the names and narratives of the other (principle of exception, vainglory and jealousy of names) (Nos. 93, 151). The conflict does not result from a problem of language, every language is translatable (this does not prevent linguistic differences from contributing on occasion to the exacerbation of a conflict). Nor is it a differend, since we have the same genre of discourse on each side: narration. It is thus a litigation over the names of times, places, and persons, over the senses and referents attached to those names (This place, this woman, this child, is not yours). This litigation, though, has no tribunal before which it can be presented, argued, and decided. For this tribunal would already have to be 'universal,' human, having an (international) law at its disposal, etc. (And nothing is said by saying at that moment that this tribunal is universal history unless it is to say that judgment is the very "course" of reality; for, if the end of time is awaited, there will no longer be enough time for a judgment) (Protagoras Notice; Nos. 17, 150). It is said that force is what decides. What is force, though, when

it is a question of deciding between phrases? Are some phrases and genres strong, and others weak (No. 231)?

228. You assert (No. 227) that between two particular narratives there is no differend, but only litigation, because they both belong to the same genre of discourse and are ruled by the same set of stakes. In order to judge in this way, you have therefore neglected the particular stories (diegeses) told by these narratives and singled out the form of narrative, which you declare to be identical in each. This distinction is the work of a genre of discourse, "critical" examination, which is not narrative. In declaring that there is a litigation, you have already passed judgment from a "universal" point of view, that of the analysis of genres of discourse. The interests put into play through this point of view are not those of the narrations. You too do them a wrong. What is at stake in them is not, as it is for you, that "language" knows itself, but rather that the occurrence be linked onto (No. 219). –As a matter of fact, the examination of phrases is but a genre, it cannot take the place of politics. For the philosopher to be at the governorship of phrases would be as unjust as it would be were it the jurist, the priest, the orator, the storyteller (the epic poet), or the technician. There is no genre whose hegemony over the others would be just. The philosophical genre, which looks like a metalanguage, is not itself (a genre in quest of its rules) unless it knows that there is no metalanguage. It thereby remains popular, humorous (No. 208).

229. Certainly, what is just is that "the people" be at the governorship of phrases, if it is true that "the people" is the totality of addressors, addressees, and referents of prose, which is not a genre, nor even a species of language, but the ungraded supply of phrases from all regimens and of linkages from all genres (including poetry). –Nevertheless, this mode of government is called demagogy. It is observed that the people contradicts itself, tears itself asunder, and annihilates itself, that it is trifling and enslaved to opinions. –It is not the people that is fickle, but "language." At each occurrence, the continuity between the phrase that happens and those that precede it is threatened, and the war between the genres is opened in order to assure its succession. Maybe prose is impossible. It is tempted on one side by despotism and on the other by anarchy. It succumbs to the seduction of the former by turning itself into the genre of all genres (the prose of popular Empire) and to the seduction of the latter by trying to be no more than an unregulated assemblage of all phrases (the vagabond's prose, Gertrude Stein?). But the unity of genres is impossible, as is their zero degree. Prose can only be their multitude and the multitude of their differends.

230. The multitude of phrase regimens and of genres of discourse finds a way to embody itself, to neutralize differends, in narratives (No. 220). There is a privileging of narrative in the assemblage of the diverse. It is a genre that seems able to admit all others (according to Marx, there is a history of everything).

There is an affinity between narrative and the people. "Language's" popular mode of being is the deritualized short story. Short because it is faithful to phrase regimens and to differends, which popular narratives do not seek to dissipate but only to neutralize. They contradict each other. They are resumed in maxims, proverbs, and morals that contradict each other. The wisdom of nations is not only their scepticism, but also the "free life" of phrases and genres. That is what the (clerical, political, military, economic, or informational) oppressor comes up against in the long run. Prose is the people of anecdotes.

231. Which has more "force" (No. 227), a narrative phrase or a critical phrase? Aryan myth or Kantian philosophy? A direct answer would presuppose that "language" is a unity, that it has only one interest, and that the force of a genre is measured by the closeness of its stakes to the interests of language. But genres are incommensurable, each has its own "interests." The "force" of a phrase is judged by the standard of a genre's rules, the same phrase is weak or strong depending upon what is at stake. That is why it is legitimate for the weaker argument to be the stronger one: the rules of the genre in which it is placed have been changed, the stakes are no longer the same. Aristophanes does not see that what is at stake for the sophists and for Socrates is not what is at stake in the popular tradition. The "ironic" phrase is a weak one in the tradition, and vice versa (Plato Notice, § 1). Language does not have a single finality, or, if it has one, it is not known. Everything is as if "language" were not.

232. At least, between two narratives belonging to the same genre, one can be judged stronger than the other if it comes nearer the goal of narratives: to link onto the occurrence as such by signifying it and by referring to it. The Christian narrative vanquished the other narratives in Rome because by introducing the love of occurrence into narratives and narrations of narratives, it designated what is at stake in the genre itself. To love what happens as if it were a gift, to love even the *Is it happening?* as the promise of good news, allows for linking onto whatever happens, including other narratives (and, subsequently, even other genres). Love as the principal operator of exemplary narrations and diegeses is the antidote to the principle of exception that limits traditional narratives. The authorization to tell, to listen, and to be told about does not result from a common affiliation with a world of names which are themselves descended from primordial narratives, it results from a commandment of universal attraction, *Love one another*, addressed to all heroes, all narrators, and all narratees. This commandment is authorized by the revelation (itself loving) of a primordial story in which we learn that the god of love was not very well loved by his children and about the misfortunes that ensued. This authorization remains in the circular form common to narratives, but it is extended to all narratives. The obligation to love is decreed by the divine Absolute, it is addressed to all creatures (who are none other than His addressees), and it becomes transitive (in an interested sense, be-

cause it is conditional): if you are loved, you ought to love; and you shall be loved only if you love.

233. Thanks to the precept of love, all of the events already told in the narratives of infidels and unbelievers can be re-told as so many signs portentous of the new commandment (the synoptic tables of the two Testaments). Not only are the narrative instances universalized, but occurrence is problematized. Christian narration not only tells what has happened, thereby fixing a tradition, but it also prescribes the *caritas* for what can happen, whatever it might be. This commandment orders the narrators and narratees to go to the forefront of the event and to make and carry out its narrative as if it told the story of a loving gift. Any referent can be signified as the sign of the good news announcing that "we" creatures are loved.

234. Inasmuch as it is a matter of ethics, obligation has, nonetheless, no need of an addressor, it is even in need of the contrary. At stake in it is: ought I to do this? The answer given the obligated one is that God wants it. S/he asks: is it really His will? The answer is that He declared His will at the beginning. The obligated one: but I don't feel it now, I don't understand what is prescribed by the authorized interpreters of the Scriptures, I feel the obligation for some other action (Joan of Arc's trial). The holding in suspicion of idiolects not only motivates witchcraft trials, but it already motivates the reception given the prophets, and still motivates the resistance to the Reformation. For his or her sake, though, the suspect holds the authority of tradition in suspicion. To belief in the narratives of love, he or she opposes faith in the signs of obligation. The latter is only actualized as the obligated one's feeling (the voice of conscience, respect for the moral law). The authority of the commandment to love is not necessarily called back into question, but the repetitive, narrative mode of its legitimation certainly is. To judge that one ought to do *this* thing because *that* thing has already been prescribed is to defy the occurrence and the addressee's responsibility before it. The time invoked by the free examination of one's conscience is no longer the before/after but the now. Narrative politics is shaken, including its way of receiving and neutralizing events, the commutability of addressors, addressees, and heroes (referents) that is constitutive of community, etc. The deliberative concatenation, which welcomes the competition between multiple genres of discourse to signify the event, and which favors judgment over tradition, has more affinity with obligation than with narrative (which passes to the rank of fictive scenario) (Nos. 210, 217).

235. Obligation cannot engender a universal history, nor even a particular community. Love supplied with its narrative of authorization can engender a universal history as progress toward the redemption of creatures. Relieved of the notion of revelation (the narrative of authorization in its beginnings, which determines its end), love persists in secular, universal history in the form of republican

brotherhood, of communist solidarity. Humanity is not made of creatures in the process of redeeming themselves, but of wills in the process of emancipating themselves. Authorization does not reside in a myth of beginnings, but in an Idea which exerts its finality upon phrases and which ought to allow for a way to regulate the differends between genres. The obstacle, though, to this finalization by the Idea of freedom persists in the form of "national" names and traditions, which are woven into popular prose. Peoples do not form into one people, whether it be the people of God or the sovereign people of world citizens. There is not yet one world, but some worlds (with various names and narratives). Internationalism cannot overcome national worlds because it cannot channel short, popular narratives into epics, it remains "abstract": it must efface proper names (Marx trying to rid the name of Alsace-Lorraine from the litigation between French and German socialists in 1870). Even the communist epic of workers' liberation splits off into national-communist epics. There is no differend between national narratives (unless one of them conceals the hegemony of another genre of discourse: the first French Republic up against the Austrian Empire); but the differend between the Idea of freedom and narratives of legitimation is inevitable.

Kant 4

1. Historical inquiry.

What reality is, in the historical-political as elsewhere, is that object for which intuitions of its concept can be presented, the phenomenon. Conditioned and conditioning, these objects furthermore form a diachronic series, which constitutes the history of humanity. This series is not given intuitively, it is the object of an Idea, and it falls beneath the blows of the same antithetical argument as the cosmological series in general. Cognition through the understanding, that is, the descriptive phrase taken within the scientific genre, is assuredly always possible for those sequences of the series for which there can be intuitive presentations. By definition, however, these sequences of conditioning and conditioned objects must be regular and therefore repeat themselves, and no becoming can be derived from them, be it progress, regression, or eternal return in stagnation (*Conflict*, § 3). The phrase signifying repetition in the series, whether this series is the object of an ascending or of a descending synthesis, is therefore legitimate on the condition that objects corresponding to it be presented in phenomena. "Man is an animal which [. . .] requires a master [. . .]. But then the master is himself an animal, and needs a master" (*Idea*, Sixth Thesis). "Man hates slavery, but a new slavery is needed in order to suppress it" (*Remarks*, in Vlachos: 92). Or again, in order to refute the hope of progress through education: "since they are also human beings who must effect this education, consequently such beings [. . .] themselves have to be trained for that purpose . . . " (*Conflict*: § 10). These regularities are not merely empirical laws; they can be established through statistics (*Idea*, Introduction) which make evident the *a priori* character of the categories used to synthesize givens into series, namely, the categories of causality and of reciprocal action.

The cognitive phrase, with its double criterion of pertinence with regard to negation (the principle of contradiction) and of pertinence with regard to intuitive presentation, is generally opposed in Kant to vain hopes, false promises, and prophecies. The cognitive phrase is the one used to refute the right of insurrection and to condemn the violent substitution of a new authority for a preceding one. The argument is the following: the existence of the common being (*das gemeine Wesen*) is the referent of a cognitive phrase (of the understanding) or, at best, of an objectively teleological one (finality in organized beings). This common being's proximity to the Good is judged in a subjectively teleological phrase (moral finality in reasonable beings). Revolution breaks apart (*Abbruch*) an existing common being; another one cannot not replace it (natural law). The heterogeneity of the two phrase families is not modified. Revolutionary politics rests upon a transcendental illusion in the political realm: it confuses what is presentable as an object for a cognitive phrase with what is presentable as an object for a speculative and/or ethical phrase; that is, it confuses schemata or exempla with *analoga* (Kant Notice 3). The progress of a common being toward the better is not judged according to empirical intuitions, but according to signs (*Theory and Practice*; *Perpetual Peace*; etc.).

In addition to the difficulty encountered by synthesis in the case of the ascending series (its totality and its beginning are not intuitable), the descending series has the further difficulty of linking together effects which are not yet there, and for which documents cannot be presented, as can be done for causes. Even worse: it can be admitted that the synthesis of descending series (that is, of phenomena to come) does not even require a speculative, transcendental Idea. The antinomy of the indefinite posed the problem of the beginning of cosmological series, but not of their end. Kant writes in the first *Critique*: "if we form an idea [. . .] of the whole series of all *future* alterations in the world, this is a being of reason (*ens rationis*) which is only arbitrarily thought, and not a necessary presupposition of reason" (*KRV*, 325). Despite its importance, there is no discussion here of the relation between an Idea (a concept without an intuition) and a Being of reason [*ens rationis*], which is an empty concept without an object, as it is examined on the last page of the Analytic in the first *Critique* (*KRV*, 295–96). Speculatively, there is nothing ahead of us, at least in cosmological time, *nothing*, either as an object, or even as a conceivable concept.

To these limitations on the presentation of the theoretical phrase about the human cosmological series, a final one is added, which Kant underscores with some solemnity in the article *Über den Gebrauch teleologischer Principien in der Philosophie* [*On the Use of Teleological Principles in Philosophy*] (1788), with regard to nature. He writes that a distinction must be made between the description of nature and its history, between physiography and physiogony. These two realms "are completely *heterogeneous*." The description of nature displays itself with all the splendor of a great system. The history of nature "for the moment, can only exhibit fragments or shaky hypotheses," "the outline of a science," where "a *blank* could be put for most questions." (There follows a long apology for Kant by Kant (against Forster) on the theme: I have taken scrupulous care to keep the sciences from encroaching on each other's frontiers) (1788b: 161–63). The issue, though, has to do with the regressive synthesis, in its movement back toward the beginnings of the history of the world. If some blanks ought to remain, we understand why: intuitions for all of the singular existences inscribed in the series must be able to be presented to the physiogonic phrase. Even exempla don't suffice here, and schemata even less so. The presentational requirement puts the tightest grip on sensation (documentation is needed for everything), and yet the series is only an Idea! The same would go for an anthropogony.

This is, in sum, what we have for the cognitive phrase: it doesn't have much to say about history which could be validated by the critical judge. In fact, it ignores the historical-political because it remains under the rule of intuitive presentation. There remain many other possible phrase families. Their presentational rules are different. We can expect to see analogies or, more generally, "passages" at work there.

2. The guiding thread.

The *Idea for a Universal History from a Cosmopolitical Point of View* (1784) argues the nature of discourse about the historical-political in the following fashion: if we stick to immediate, intuitive data, political history is chaos. It arouses an *Unwillen* (indignation, depression) because it suggests that this lamentable spectacle proceeds from an "aimless play of nature (*zwecklos spielende*)," such that "blind chance (*das trostlose Ungefähr*) takes the place of the guiding thread of reason" (First Thesis). But it is not just, in the critique's sense of the word, to stick to the gloom of this desolate randomness, that is, to the ascertaining of non-sense. Why? The disappointment accompanying the ascertainment is in itself a sign. Reason is the faculty of Ideas, in particular of the Idea of freedom. It is up to the Idea of freedom to realize itself (otherwise, the moral law remains without effect). On the other hand, one is allowed to suppose that nature has placed certain predispositions within the human species that have an affinity with the use of reason. If the history of humanity were but sound and fury, it would have to be admitted that this same nature that placed the "seeds" of reason in man also prohibits man, through its own disorder, from developing the effects of those seeds in reality. Which is contradictory. In other words, no passage would be possible between the cognitive phrase about history, which ascertains its chaos, and the speculative phrase, which awaits the progress of freedom.

The critical watchman is open to this sentimental protestation. He calls together the two parties, the one who says that human history is simply disorder, and the one who says it is organized by a providential nature. To the former, he repeats: if you stick to cognitive phrases, and if you can supply examples and counterexamples for every phrase in this family, then you may legitimately speak of disorder, but only within the previously indicated limits proper to the family of cognitives about history. With that, you may only carry out a pragmatic politics or politics of prudence supported by the fact that, as it is said in *Perpetual Peace*, "History furnishes us with contradictory examples from all governments (*Regierungsarte*)." You will be but a "political moralist," and not a moral politician (*Perpetual Peace*: 125, 119). To the other party, he says: you presuppose the Idea of a finality of nature designedly at work within human history and leading to a final end which only freedom can bring about (*KUK*: § 84). You are phrasing, therefore, not according to the rule of direct presentation proper to cognitives but according to the free, analogical presentation to which dialectical phrases in general are held. You can then call upon certain phenomena given through intuition, but they cannot, however, have the value of exempla or of schemata in your argument. By binding them together, you do not obtain a law of mechanical, or even organic, development, but only a guiding thread. As the *Critique of Judgement* explains, the guiding thread, which is reflective, owes nothing to and withdraws nothing from the subsumption of intuitions under concepts, namely, the rule of cognitive phrases. These are two heterogeneous, but compatible, phrase families. A single referent–say a phenomenon grasped in the field of human history–can be used qua example, to present the object of the discourse of despair, but also qua bit of guiding thread, to present analogically the object of the discourse of emancipation. And along with this guiding thread, one can undertake an analogically republican politics, and be a moral politician (*Conflict,* § 8; *KUK,* § 79, 83; *Idea,* Introduction, First and Ninth Theses).

3. The event.

The expression, *sign of history,* used in § 5 of the *Conflict of the Philosophy Faculty with the Faculty of Law* (1795) introduces a further degree of complexity into the "passages" needed to phrase the historical-political. The question raised (against the Faculty of Law, therefore) is whether it can be affirmed that the human race is constantly progressing toward the better, and if so, how this is possible. The difficulties proliferate: the better, progress, and the human race are objects of Ideas, with no possible direct presentation. Furthermore, we are dealing with a phrase whose referent is a part of human history that is still to come, a phrase therefore of *Vorhersagung,* of anticipation or prediction. Kant distinguishes this phrase from the phrase of the *Weissager* (of the soothsayer), by recalling that there can be (according to the rules for cognitives) no direct presentation of the object of this phrase, since it bears upon the future.

For the requested demonstration, it will be necessary to change phrase families. It will be necessary to seek in the anthropological realm, not an intuitive given (a *Gegebene*), which can never do anything more than validate the phrase that describes it, but what Kant calls a *Begebenheit,* an event or "act of delivering itself which would also be an act of deliverance, a *deal* [*une donne*], if you will (the Crakow manuscript, used to prepare the *Idea,* calls it *Ereignis*) (*KF*: 172, 173). This event would merely indicate (*hinweisen*) and not prove (*beweisen*) that humanity is capable of being both cause (*Ursache*) and author (*Urheber*) of its progress. More precisely, Kant explains, this *Begebenheit* which delivers itself into human history must indicate a cause such that the occurrence of its effect remains undetermined (*unbestimmt*) with respect to time (*in Ansehung der Zeit*): causality through freedom cannot be subordinated to the various diachronic series of the mechanical world (Kant Notice 2: § 4). And on account of that, it may intervene at any time (*irgendwann,* repeats the Crakow manuscript) (*KF*: 169, 170, 173) in the succession of events (*Conflict,* § 5).

But that's not all: this *Begebenheit* ought not to be in itself the cause of progress, but only its index (*hindeutend*), a *Geschichtszeichen.* Kant glosses this sign of history in this way: "*signum rememorativum, demonstrativum, prognosticon,*" a sign that recalls, shows, and anticipates. The sought-for *Begebenheit* would have the task of "presenting" free causality according to the three temporal directions of past, present, and future. What is this enigmatic, if not contradictory, "act of delivering itself"?

We might expect some momentous deed to be the sought-for "deal" that attests to the power of free causality. A momentous deed, however, is still only a given, one that certainly allows for several readings (the descriptive phrase, the dialectical phrase), but it is thereby but an equivocal object which may be grasped indifferently by one phrase or the other. Here, the exigency of the critical judge goes further than simple conciliation, to the point of appearing paradoxical. It is not sufficient for him to dismiss both the advocate of determinism and the advocate of freedom or finality through an arrangement that satisfies both, but rather he constrains them together and positively to exercise joint sovereignty over the sought-for event. If not given *by* experience, then at least given *in* experience, or "delivered," the *Begebenheit* ought to be the probative index of the Idea of free causality. With it, the rims of the abyss to be crossed over between mechanism and freedom or finality, between the realm of the sensible world and the suprasensible field, are almost closed without, however, suppressing the abyss, and that minute gaping is sufficient to fix the status (inconsistent and indeterminate perhaps but sayable and even "probative") of the historical-political. It can then be proven that humanity's natural predisposition to make use of speculative reason can indeed be realized, and that a constant progress toward the better can be anticipated in its history, without fear of error.

We have an event, Kant writes, which satisfies the givens of the problem. It is not at all a momentous deed, nor is it a revolution, "it is simply the mode of thinking (*Denksungsart*) of the spectators (*Zuschauer*) which betrays itself (*sich verrät*) publicly (*öffentlich*) in this game of great upheavals (*Umwandlungen*, such as revolutions), and manifests such a universal yet disinterested sympathy (*Teilnehmung*) for the players on one side against those on the other, even at the risk that this partiality could become very disadvantageous for them if discovered. Owing to its universality, this mode of thinking demonstrates (*beweist*) a character of the human race at large and all at once; and, owing to its disinterestedness, a moral (*moralisch*) character of humanity, at least in its predisposition (*Anlage*), a character which not only permits people to hope for progress toward the better, but is already itself progress insofar as its capacity is sufficient for the present." The recent revolution of a spirited (*geistreich*) people may well fail or succeed, it may accumulate misery and atrocities, but it "nonetheless finds in the hearts (*in den Gemütern*) of all spectators (who are not engaged in this game themselves) a wishful *participation* (*eine Teilnehmung dem Wunsche nach*) that borders closely on enthusiasm (*Enthusiasm*), the very expression of which is fraught with danger; this sympathy, therefore, can have no other cause than a moral predisposition in the human race" (*Conflict*, § 6).

4. Enthusiasm.

Enthusiasm is a modality of the feeling of the sublime. The imagination tries to supply a direct, sensible presentation for an Idea of reason (for the whole is an object of an Idea, as for example, in the whole of practical, reasonable beings). It does not succeed and it thereby feels its impotence, but at the same time, it discovers its destination, which is to bring itself into harmony with the Ideas of reason through an appropriate presentation. The result of this obstructed relation is that instead of experiencing a feeling for the object, we experience, on the occasion of that object, a feeling "for the Idea of humanity in our subject" (*KUK*: § 27). In this text, the feeling commented upon by Kant is that of respect. The analysis holds, though, for every sublime feeling insofar as it entails a "subreption": the substitution of a reconciliation [*réglage*] between the faculties within a subject for a reconciliation between an object and a subject.

In the case of the sublime, this "internal" reconciliation is a non-reconciliation. As opposed to taste, the adjustment of the sublime is good when it is bad. The sublime entails the finality of a nonfinality and the pleasure of a displeasure: "the displeasure in regard to the necessary extension of the imagination for accordance with that which is unbounded in our faculty of reason, viz. the idea of the absolute whole, and consequently the nonfinality [*Unzweckmässigkeit*, nonaffinity or incommensurability with the aim] of the faculty of imagination for rational ideas and the arousing (*Erweckung*) of them, are represented as purposive [. . .] and there accompanies the reception of an object as sublime a pleasure, which is only possible through the medium of a pain" (*KUK*: § 27).

The imagination, even at its most extended, does not succeed in presenting an object that might validate or "realize" the Idea. Whence the pain of the incapacity to present. What is the joy that is nonetheless grafted onto this pain? It is the joy of discovering an affinity within this discordance: even what is presented as very great in nature (including human nature and including the natural history of man, such as in a great revolution) is still and always will be "small in comparison with Ideas of reason" (§ 27). What is discovered is not only the infinite import of Ideas, its incommensurability to all presentation, but also the destination of the subject, "our" destination, which is to supply a presentation for the unpresentable, and therefore, in regard to Ideas, to exceed everything that can be presented.

Enthusiasm is an extreme mode of the sublime: the attempt at presentation not only fails, arousing the tension in question, but it reverses itself, so to speak, or inverts itself in order to supply a supremely paradoxical presentation, which Kant calls "a mere negative presentation," a kind of "abstraction," and which he boldly characterizes as a "presentation of the Infinite" (*KUK*, General Remark Upon the Exposition of the Aesthetical Reflective Judgment). What we have here is the most inconsistent possible "passage," the impasse as "passage." Kant even ventures to give some examples of it: "Perhaps there is no sublimer passage (*Stelle*) in the Jewish law than the command 'Thou shalt not make to thyself any graven image, nor the likeness of anything which is in heaven or in the earth or under the earth,' etc. This command alone can explain the enthusiasm that the Jewish people in their moral period felt for their religion, when they compared themselves with other peoples, or explain the pride which Mohammedanism inspires." And he goes on: "The same is true of the moral law and of the tendency to morality in us" (*Ibid*.). What is required for this abstract presentation, which presents what is beyond the presentable, is that the imagination be "unbounded" (*unbegrenzt*).

That extremely painful joy that is enthusiasm is an *Affekt*, a strong affection, and as such it is blind and cannot therefore, according to Kant, "deserve the approval of reason" (*Ibid*.). It is even a *dementia*, a *Wahnsinn*, where the imagination is "without bridle." As such, it is certainly preferable to *Schwärmerei*, to the uproar of exaltation. The latter is a *Wahnwitz*, an "*insanitas*," a going "without rule" of the imagination, a "deeply rooted illness," whereas enthusiasm is "a transitory accident which sometimes befalls the soundest understanding." The *Schwärmerei* is accompanied by an illusion: "seeing something beyond all bounds of sensibility," that is, believing that there is a direct presentation when there isn't any. It proceeds to a noncritical passage, comparable to transcendental illusion (cognizing something beyond the limits of all cognition). Enthusiasm, for its sake, sees nothing, or rather sees that what can be seen is nothing and relates it back to the unpresentable. Although ethically condemnable as pathological, "aesthetically, enthusiasm is sublime, because it is a tension of forces produced by Ideas, which give an impulse to the mind that operates far more powerfully and lastingly than the impulse arising from sensible representations" (*Ibid*.).

Historical-political enthusiasm is thus on the edge of dementia, it is a pathological outburst, and as such it has in itself no ethical validity, since ethics requires one's freedom from any motivating pathos; ethics allows only that apathetic pathos accompanying obligation that is respect. In its periodic unbridling, however, enthusiastic pathos conserves an aesthetic validity, it is an energetic *sign*, a tensor of *Wunsch*. The infinity of the Idea draws to itself all the other capacities, that is, all the other faculties, and produces an *Affekt* "of the vigorous kind," characteristic of the sublime. As can be seen, the "passage" does not take place, it is a "passage" in the course of coming to pass. Its course, its movement, is a kind of agitation in place, one within the impasse of incommensurability, and above the abyss, a "vibration," as Kant writes, that is, "a quickly alternating attraction toward, and repulsion from, the same object" (*KUK*: § 27). Such is the state of *Gemüt* for the spectators of the French Revolution.

5. The indeterminate norm and the human community.

Great changes, like the French Revolution, are not, in principle, sublime by themselves. Qua object, they are similar to those spectacles of (physical) nature on whose occasion the viewer experiences the sublime: "nature excites the ideas of the sublime in its chaos or in its wildest and most irregular disorder and desolation, provided size and might are perceived" (*KUK*: § 23). The sublime is best determined by the indeterminate, by the *Formlosigkeit* (§ 24): "the sublime in nature [. . .] may be regarded as quite formless or devoid of figure" (§ 30); "no particular form is represented in nature" (§ 23). The same ought to apply for a revolution, and for all great historical upheavals: they are what is formless and without figure in historical human nature. Ethically, they are nothing validatable. They fall, on the contrary, under the sway of the critical judgment. They result from a confusion (which is *the* political illusion) between the direct presentation of the phenomenon of the *gemeine Wesen* and the analogical presentation of the Idea of a republican social contract.

The *Begebenheit* which ought to make a sign of history could be found only on the side of the audience watching the spectacle of the upheavals. On stage, among the actors themselves, interests, ordinary passions, and the whole pathos of empirical (psychical, sociological) causality are forever inextricably bound up with the interests of pure moral reason and with the call of the Idea of republican law. The spectators, placed on other national stages, which make up the theater hall for the spectacle and where absolutism generally reigns, cannot on the contrary be suspected of having empirical interests in making their sympathies public (*öffentlich*), they even run the risk of suffering repression at the hands of their governments. That itself guarantees the–at least aesthetic–value of their feelings. It must be said of their enthusiasm that it is an aesthetic analogue of pure, republican fervor.

To this is added a second argument in the audience's favor. It may be that the revolutionaries' activity is directed not only toward a French political constitution under the authority of the sole legitimate sovereign *de jure* (the people, that is) but also toward a federation of States in a peace project, which then concerns all of humanity. It doesn't matter that their action remains localized on the French scene, and that, as Kant puts it, the foreign spectators watch it "without the least intention of assisting" (*ohne die mindeste Absicht der Mitwirkung*) (*Conflict*: § 6).

The *Teilnehmung* through desire is not a participation in the act. But it is worth more, because the feeling of the sublime, for its sake, is in fact spread out onto all the national stages. Potentially, at least, it is universal. It is not universal the way a well-formed and validated cognitive phrase may be; a judgment of cognition has its determinative rules "in front of it," while the feeling of the sublime judges without a rule. Like the feeling of the beautiful, though, it does have an *a priori* which is not a rule that is universally recognized but a rule awaiting its universality. It is this universality in abeyance or in suspense that is invoked by the aesthetic judgment. Kant calls it this universality *sensus communis*, or "the Idea of a *gemeinschaftlichen Sinn*, of a communal sense [*sens communautaire*]" (*KUK*: § 20–22, 40). He specifies this as "a faculty of judgment which, in its reflection, takes account (*a priori*) of the mode of representation of all other men" (*KUK*: § 40). This common or communal sense does not guarantee that "everyone *will* agree with my judgment, but that he *ought*" (§ 22). It is merely an "ideal norm," an "indeterminate norm" (*Ibid.*) If the enthusiasm of the spectators is a probative *Begebenheit* for the phrase which says that humanity is progressing toward the better, it is because enthusiasm, as a pure aesthetic feeling, requires a common sense, and calls upon a consensus which is nothing more than a *sensus* which is undetermined, but *de jure*; it is a sentimental anticipation of the republic.

The indeterminacy of this *a priori* expected universality in the aesthetic judgment is the trait thanks to which the antinomy of taste is removed in the Dialectic of the Aesthetical Judgment (*KUK*: § 56 ff.). This judgment must not be based on concepts, for otherwise it would admit of controversy–so observes the thesis. It must be based on concepts, for otherwise we could not even discuss whether it can lay claim to universality–retorts the antithesis. This antinomy is removed by introducing the notion of a concept "in itself undetermined and undeterminable" (§ 57). The phrase of cognition requires the presentation of a corresponding intuition: the concept is then determined by means of the presentation that suits it, namely the schema. The phrase of aesthetic judgment, on the contrary, "cannot be determined through intuition," "we know nothing, and consequently it can *supply no proof* for the judgment of taste" (*Ibid.*).

There is a transcendental appearance (a *Schein*) in the aesthetic phrase as there is one in the speculative phrase, and there is a corresponding illusion, which cannot be evaded, but which is not insoluble. In its theoretical use, the illusion consists in extending the validity of the cognitive beyond the determination of the phrase through an intuitional presentation. In its aesthetic use, the critical watchman declares that the aesthetic phrase is the phrase par excellence of the faculty of presentation, but that it has no concept for which to present its sensible or imaginative intuition, it cannot therefore determine a realm, but only a field. Moreover, that field is only determined to a second degree, reflectively, so to speak: not by the commensurability between a presentation and a concept, but by the indeterminate commensurability between the capacity for presenting and the capacity for conceptualizing. This commensurability is itself an Idea, its object is not directly presentable. It results from this that the universality invoked by the beautiful and the sublime is merely an Idea of community, for which no proof, that is, no direct presentation, will ever be found, but only indirect presentations.

In the solution to the Dynamical Antinomies, which are differends par excellence, not only is the validity of the conflicting phrases in play but also the situation of the addressors and addressees presented by these phrases. In regard to aesthetic feeling, the partisan of the universality of the beautiful requires a consensus identical to the one obtainable for the true, and his opponent, by showing that this is impossible (because there is no concept corresponding to an aesthetic presentation), seems to forgo any universality. The Kantian solution calls upon the feeling itself that both parties necessarily have, without which they would not even be able to agree that they disagree. This feeling proves that there is a bond of "communicability" between them (*KUK*: § 40). This sentimental bond cannot become the object of a concept, as one side wishes, nor is this feeling the absence of a bond, as the other side claims. This bond must retain the status of a feeling, at the same time as it aims to transform itself into an explicit consensus over what motivates it, the Idea of the beautiful. The phrase of taste is a phrase in suspense or in suspension (No. 22) onto which each of the interlocutors links in a heterogeneous way, but a phrase whose sense each ought to try to formulate completely. Communicability is thereby required "as a duty, so to speak," and taste is the faculty that judges it *a priori* (*Ibid.*).

The *sensus communis* is thus in aesthetics what the whole of practical, reasonable beings is in ethics. It is an appeal to community carried out *a priori* and judged without a rule of direct presentation. However, in the case of moral obligation, the community is required by the mediation of a concept of reason, the Idea of freedom, while in the phrase of the beautiful, the community of addressors and addressees is called forth immediately, without the mediation of any concept, by feeling alone, inasmuch as this feeling can be shared *a priori*. The community is already there as taste, but it is not yet there as rational consensus.

Enthusiasm as an "event of our time" thus obeys the rule of the aesthetic antinomy. And it is the most contradictory of aesthetics, that of the most extreme sublime. First of all, because the sublime is not only a disinterested pleasure and a universal without a concept, such as taste, but also because it entails a finality of antifinality and a pleasure of pain, as opposed to the feeling of the beautiful whose finality is merely without an end and whose pleasure is due to the free agreement of the faculties with each other. With the sublime, Kant advances far into heterogeneity, so much so that the solution to the aesthetic antinomy appears much more difficult in the case of the sublime than it does in the case of the beautiful.

6. Culture.

And all the more so when we are dealing with enthusiasm, which is at the furthest extremes of the sublime. Kant recognizes this: "That the mind be attuned to feel the sublime postulates *eine Empfänglichkeit* for Ideas," a susceptibility of the mind for Ideas, a sensitivity to Ideas (*KUK*: § 29). And further on: "the judgment upon the sublime in nature [in human nature also, for that matter] needs culture" (*Ibid.*), which is not to say that the judgment is produced by culture, for "it has its root in human nature." This allusion to culture finds its elucidation in the paragraph of the Critique of Teleological Judgment which bears upon the ultimate end of nature. There, Kant refutes, as he does in many of his political opuscules, the thesis that this end might be the happiness of the human race, and demonstrates that it can only be its culture. "The production of the aptitude of a rational being for arbitrary ends in general (consequently in his freedom) is culture" (*KUK*: § 83). Culture is the ultimate end pursued by nature in the human race because culture is what makes men more "susceptible to Ideas," it is the condition that opens onto the thought of the unconditioned.

In the same paragraph, Kant distinguishes between the culture of skill and the culture of will, and, within the former, between the material and the formal culture of skill. But this formal development of the culture of skill requires the neutralization of conflicts between freedoms, carried out on the level of individuals through a "lawful authority in a whole, which we call *bürgerliche Gesellschaft*, civil society." And, if men succeed in outpacing the plan of natural providence, then the development of the culture of skill requires the same neutralization, but this time at the level of States through "a cosmopolitical whole, *ein weltbürgerliche Ganzes*," which would be a federation of States (§ 83). In this way, the enthusiasm which publicly betrays itself on the occasion of the French Revolution, first because it is an extreme feeling of the sublime, then because this feeling already requires a formal culture of skill, and finally because this culture in turn has civil and perhaps international peace as its horizon–this enthusiasm by itself–"not only permits people to hope for progress toward the better, but is already itself progress insofar as its capacity is sufficient for the present" (*Conflict:* § 6).

So it is not just any aesthetic phrase, but that of the extreme sublime which is able to supply the proof (*beweisen*) that humanity is constantly progressing toward the better. The beautiful is not sufficient, it is merely a symbol of the good. But, because the feeling of the sublime is an affective paradox, the paradox of feeling publicly and as a group that something which is "formless" alludes to a beyond of experience, that feeling constitutes an "as-if presentation" of the Idea of civil society and even of cosmopolitical society, and thus an as-if presentation of the Idea of morality, right where that Idea nevertheless cannot be presented, within experience. It is in this way that the sublime is a sign. This sign is only indicative of a free causality, but it nonetheless has the value of a proof for the phrase which affirms progress, since the spectating humanity must already have made cultural progress in order to make this sign by its "mode of thinking" about the Revolution. This sign is progress in its present state, it is as much as can be done, even though civil societies are nowhere near republican in their regime nor States anywhere near world federation (far from it!).

The faculty of judgment at work in critical philosophy (in Kant as he writes the *Conflict*) sees a sign of history in peoples' enthusiasm for the Revolution because that enthusiasm is a proof of progress in the faculty of judgment for the whole of humanity taken as a natural species. This sign is indicative when it is evaluated according to the standard of the presentational rule for phrases of historical cognition, a mere event amid intuitable historical givens. Within the strange family of phrases of judgment, though, this sign is a proof for the Kantian phrase which judges that there is progress, since this sign is itself this (popular) phrase, certainly not "said," but publicly expressed as a feeling in principle able to be shared, and felt on the occasion of an "abstract" given. Kant's *There is progress* does no more than reflect the peoples' *There is progress*, which is necessarily implied in their enthusiasm.

Kant can, with some solemnity, thereby make links: "Now I claim to be able to predict (*vorhersagen*) to the human race–even without prophetic insight–according to the aspects and omens (*Vorzeichen*) of our day, the attainment (*Erreichung*) of this end. That is, I predict its progress toward the better which, from now on, turns out to be no longer completely reversible. For such a phenomenon in human history *is not to be forgotten* (*vergisst sich nicht mehr*)" (*Conflict:* § 7). No politician (the politician of politics, the one Kant calls the "political moralist"), "affecting wisdom, might have conjured out of the course of things hitherto existing" this capacity for the better that enthusiasm has discovered in human nature. He adds that this is something which "nature and freedom alone, united in the human race in conformity with inner principles of right, could have promised [*verheissen*]. But so far as time is concerned, it can promise this only indeterminately and as a contingent *Begebenheit.*" Intemporality and fortuitousness show up to recall the necessarily, determinately, indeterminate character of the "passage" between nature (the Revolution and the pathological aspect of the feeling it arouses) and freedom (the tendency toward the moral Idea of the Absolute Good, which is the other aspect–universal and disinterested–of the same feeling).

"There is progress": the critical watchman can legitimate this phrase every time he is able to present a sign which serves as a referent for that assertion. But he cannot say when such "objects" will present themselves; the historical sequences that form series give the historian only data (which are, at best, statistically regular), but never signs. The historical-political makes itself present to the assertion only through cases, which operate not as exempla and still less as schemata, but as complex hypotyposes, the more complex ones being the surer. The popular enthusiasm for the Revolution is a very validating case for the historical-political phrase, and thus allows for a very sure hypotyposis. This is for the simple reason that it is itself a very improbable hypotyposis (the recognition of the Idea of the republic in a "formless," empirical given). As for the philosophy of history, about which there can be no question in a critical thought, it is an illusion born from the appearance that signs are exempla or schemata.

236. Marxism has not come to an end, but how does it continue? Marx in 1843: "a class with radical chains, a class of bourgeois society which is not a class of bourgeois society, a sphere which has a universal character by its universal suffering and claims no particular right because no particular wrong but wrong generally (*ein Umrecht schlechthin*) is perpetrated against it (Marx, 1843: 186). The wrong is expressed through the silence of feeling, through suffering. The wrong results from the fact that all phrase universes and all their linkages are or can be subordinated to the sole finality of capital (but is capital a genre?) and judged accordingly. Because this finality seizes upon or can seize upon all phrases, it makes a claim to universality. The wrong done to phrases by capital would then be a universal one. Even if the wrong is not universal (but how can you prove it? it's an Idea), the silent feeling that signals a differend remains to be listened to. Responsibility to thought requires it. This is the way in which Marxism has not come to an end, as the feeling of the differend.

237. Marx tries to find the idiom which the suffering due to capital clamors for. In suffering and in class struggle, which is a referent for cognitive phrases (the phrases of the historian, the socialist, and the economist), he thinks he hears the demand of the proletariat, which is the object of an Idea, an ideal of reason, namely an emancipated working humanity. The proletariat demands communism, the free linking of phrases, the destruction of genres: the *gemeine Wesen*. This finality is signaled by signs of history, by the enthusiasm which workers' struggles can arouse: "No class of bourgeois society can play this role [of emancipation] without arousing a moment of enthusiasm in itself and in the masses, a

moment in which it fraternizes and merges with society in general, becomes confused with it and is perceived and acknowledged as its general representative" (*Ibid.*: 184). –A prisoner of the logic of result (Hegel Notice) and its presupposition of a self, Marx understands the feeling of enthusiasm as a request emanating from an (ideal, emancipated) self. The referent of the Idea of communism is transcribed as a subject (addressor) who prescribes communism. The common being wants itself. This can be formulated only within the speculative genre.

238. In historical-political reality, it is necessary to "let this subject speak." –Aren't its phrases the signs in question (No. 236): suffering, class anger and hatred, enthusiasm and solidarity? And only these signs?–But if these signs have a universal value, they are on the side of the audience (Kant Notice 4: § 5), they have an aesthetic and not a "practical" value. They are awaited, they come at any time, they are evaluations not actions, they threaten only in an aleatory way the permanence of the linking of capital, which renews itself after every storm. To let the proletariat "speak" is to endow it with a historical-political reality. Marx built the International Association of Working Men. He interprets the sign that is the enthusiasm aroused by the Commune as if it signaled the political project of the real class and as if it outlined the organization of a real party. This is a second illusory "passage": the first (No. 237) passes from the sign that is solidary enthusiasm to the ideal of a revolutionary subject, the proletariat; the second passes from this ideal to the real political organization of the real working class.

239. The party must supply the proof that the proletariat is real, but it cannot, no more than one can supply the proof for an ideal of reason. It can only give itself as proof and undertake a realist politics (a Machiavellian one, one that remains attached to proper names and to the narratives of real communities). The referent of its discourse remains unpresentable in any direct way. It is non ostensible, and only manifests itself through signs. The party is constrained to mistake the proletariat–a referent of the dialectical genre (in the Kantian sense), namely, the ideal object (and perhaps subject) of the Idea of emancipated working humanity–for the real working classes, the multiple referents of "positive" cognitive phrases. In order to mask the differend between the genres of discourse that argue over the sense of the referent (the scientific genre having its stakes in the attestability of the latter's definition, the "dialectical" genre in the complete development of its concept without the worry of supplying sensible proofs), the party assumes a monopoly over the procedures for establishing historical-political reality. It exerts the threat of the dilemma over and against whatever contests this monopoly (No. 4). The repressed differend returns within the workers movement, especially in the form of recurrent conflicts over the question of organization (that is, over the question of the monopoly). But even the differend between centralists and spontaneists is masked as a litigation (the spontaneists don't aspire to be less

realistic than the centralists, they aspire to be more realistic)*. This litigation is always regulated to the advantage of centralism, that is to the advantage of the monopoly, since the tribunal (the politburo) which decides the litigation derives its authority from that monopoly. This regulation, however, does no more than engender the differend anew, on the confines of the organization (outside and inside).

240. Phrase 1: (addressor) x cedes to (addressee) y referent a, this (ostensible) thing. Phrase 2: (addressor) y cedes to (addressee) x referent b, that (ostensible) thing. The economic genre: the cession of that thing ought to annul the cession of this thing. Phrases 1 and 2 are linked together with a view (the stakes or finality of the genre) to "freeing" the two parties, to unbinding them. What this or that thing is, what their senses are, is important only to a phrase that seeks to describe this thing and that thing correctly (the phrase of the anthropologist, the economist, the sociologist, or the psychoanalyst). In the economic phrase (which is not the phrase of the economist), sense is not the sense of the exchanged objects, exchange is the sense. Through phrase 1, x is immediately placed into the situation of creditor and y into the situation of debtor. Phrase 2 annuls these situations, and in the economic genre it is the one called forth by phrase 1. The linking of 2 onto 1 constitutes the exchange itself. Without 2, 1 does not take place. Thus, time $t + 1$ (the occurrence of 2) is the condition for time t (the occurrence of 1). A didactic phrase "expects" its acquiescence, namely, another phrase, but the latter phrase is not the condition for the former. A prescriptive expects its execution, but that execution is not the prescriptive's condition, etc. The economic phrase of cession does not expect the phrase of acquittal (counter-cession), it presupposes it.

241. The economic genre is ruled by the rules of parity for the referents and of permutability for the addressors and addressees. After a turn (phrases 1 and 2), the sum of the exchanges is null. If this sum is not null, then the positive or negative balance is credited to x or y's account for the following turn, up until he or she is freed of it. Once he or she is freed of it, another round may begin, but not necessarily. It would be necessary if the economic genre were necessary not as a linking of phrases, but as a linking of "rounds." But how do you prove that a genre is necessary? Some call upon the social bond, etc.; some indulge in Robinsonades. All of which is vainly anthropomorphic.

242. How do you know that y's debt to x is acquitted when he cedes b against the a he or she received? When a and b are of the same value? First hypothesis: when x values b to the same degree that y values a. Use value, need, marginal

---

*Spontaneism refers to Rosa Luxemburg's critique of Lenin's (centralist) view of the Party as the organizing agent for the proletariat in revolutionary struggle.–tr.

utility, symbolic value, etc. But this anthropological hypothesis presupposes a debate over parities and a consensus on a scale of values, within which the question remains unchanged: how can y know that x values b as he or she values a? Raised in this way, the question is that of the incommensurability of idiolects (needs, desires, uses, etc.) (No. 56). Recourse to their price (to their value as a quantity of money) does not resolve the question. Prices are to values as thermometer degrees are to heat. Marx's answer is that the common measure is the mean amount of social time incorporated into a and b. It then has to be presupposed that a and b are "produced." The danger here is that of a metaphysics of production (*energeia*), capped by a metaphysics of the capacity to produce (*dunamis*, labor power) borrowed, by Marx's own avowal (*Grundrisse*), from Aristotle's metaphysics and transferred over to the account of a human subject. On the other hand, the consideration solely of time is pertinent, since time is included in the formation of the economic phrase to the extent that this phrase requires its subordination to the occurrence of a latter phrase which will annul it (No. 240). (We are dealing with an arithmetical time, the one Kant says is implied as a schema in the formation of the series of natural numbers, or, better yet, an algebraic time, Wittgenstein's *And so on* (No. 95). Countable time.)

243. In and of itself, work does not belong to exchange, to the economic genre. It is a concatenation of genres of discourse. An addressor (whatever his or her nature, human, divine, or animal) is presumed to ask for a given object: an idea of the imagination, one of the phrases necessary for the productive genre. The other required phrase is the quest for objects and their transformation according to the required model. Objects are taken as materials, that is, they are negated in terms of their given finality and diverted to another end, the one proposed by the model. This phrase is a "metaphorical" one, it transports the referent from one destination toward another. This metaphor is on the condition, though, that the result remain ostensible: this is the object requested by the initial addressor. Techniques improve the phrases of transformation with regard to their stakes; culture (?), genius (?) improve the phrases of the imagination with regard to their stakes. The result of the latter can act as the referent of an exchange (a patent), if it is ostensible.

244. The time for the production of a commodity is not economic time, if it is true that the economic genre obeys the rules of exchange. Production takes time and this time is subtracted from the exchange. Time accumulates during production, it is stocked up in products, up until these are presented for exchange. The qualifications of a seller of services are measured in terms of the amount of training time. The same goes for determining the price of a commodity. The mere fact that it remains in stock raises its cost. The same goes for a national economy: its development is proportional to the amount of time accumulated in basic equipment and in means of production (invested fixed capital). Work is not an expendi-

ture of energy, but an expenditure of time. It doesn't put delays on enjoyment (within the economic genre, enjoyment is inessential, it is a destruction of objects that takes place in-between two "rounds" and is entirely subordinate to the exchange). The exchange is what delays enjoyment. But production puts delays on the exchange. Lots of time to produce, lots of delays to make up and of (lost) stocked-up time to annul, lots of value to be realized.

245. Between the phrases of imagination on the one hand, the phrases of technical effectuation on the other, and finally the phrases that follow the rules of the economic genre, there is heterogeneity. Capital subordinates the first two regimens to the third. Inventing and executing, along with the stakes proper to them, are treated as so much lost time with regard to the concatenation phrase 1-phrase 2. This loss of time ought to be annulled in the exchange of products. The accelerating rhythm and, in general, the saturated scheduling of time in communities result from the extension of the economic genre to phrases not under the rule of exchange: namely, the subordination of current phrase 1 to a phrase 2 which will annul the cession and 'free' the exchanging partners. All debts (for love, for an opus, for life itself) are reputed to be repayable. For example, in dying, x will leave some incompleted cycles of exchange, that is, he or she will die before the annulation of the cessions he or she is implicated in has taken place. By insuring his or her life, a society relays his or her capacity to discharge his or her debts. One does not owe one's life to the gods or to one's family, but to the insurance company, that is, to exchange.

246. Money is not the general equivalent for the referents of exchanges (a, b, commodities). It cannot, like them, be withdrawn from circulation (consumed). And its face value is independent of the time incorporated into its "production" (this time is the same for a $1 bill as for a $20 bill). It ought, however, to be the (more or less faithful) equivalent of the time incorporated into commodities and lost in their production until they are exchanged. In the counter-cession or buying (phrase 2), it may be substituted for any b. It discharges the time lost by x in the production of a. It makes evident the fact that the enjoyment or the ownership of objects is inessential, but that exchange is a negotiation of time. Whatever its nature, a monetary sign is "abstract" accumulated time. Detached from "actual" exchanges of ostensible (*hic et nunc*) commodities, it is able to transfer the bundle of time whose sign it is onto any moment of these exchanges.

247. One's fortune is proportionate to one's disposing of more passed time than the other parties in exchange. One has capital proportionate to one's putting this time back into circulation through exchange. Putting time into the time of exchange, the time separating phrase 1 at moment t from phrase 2 at moment $t + 1$, is not only the ability to buy commodities which themselves contain even more time, but also the ability to lengthen the interval between the two instants. –There

are those who have nothing to sell but "their" time (*hic et nunc*), and those who, in possession of some disposable accumulated time, can cede some of it. And, in between these two, there are those who are a little ahead, but not enough to . . .

248. Money can make advances in time because it is stocked-up time. Consumer credit (intended for the buyer) allows one to anticipate the time of enjoyment; circulating credit (intended for the merchant) to anticipate the time of payment (to the suppliers); investment credit (intended for the entrepreneur) to anticipate the time of production; creditor's credit (intended for the banker) to anticipate the time of the debtor's amortizing the debt. The lender gives time, suppressing for the debtor the delay of time necessary to realize his or her transaction. Money (time in other words) is then itself taken as an "as-if commodity." Under the rule of exchanges, the cession of money presupposes, as always, a counter-cession. Here, what is ceded by the creditor is an advance of time. The assumption is that the counter-cession, the reimbursement of the advance, is deferred for several exchange cycles (short, mean, or long term). Otherwise, there wouldn't be any advance. However, the time of the exchanges during which the money is thereby blocked in the form of credit is so much time lost in relation to effective exchanges (*hic et nunc*), just as when it is blocked during production. This lost time in turn must be made up and annulled until the credit reaches its term. Interest discharges what is deferred, the time lost by the lender.

249. If work is considered as so much time lost for exchange, then it must be reduced as much as possible. Exploitation, in the Marxian sense (the extraction of relative surplus-value, the only one pertinent to the economic genre), is one of the means of obtaining this reduction. There are others. But we see what the ideal of the genre is: to make up the lost time immediately, to anticipate, for example, the time lost in credit. To have the interest on a loan paid right away, as if the cycles to be traversed up until its term had already passed by. This is also, for example, what is realized by self-financing business ventures: the profits earned from the sale of commodities are incorporated back into the starting costs. They may be put back into the next circuit of exchange before the preceding one is completed. The smallest gap between phrase 1 and phrase 2 is sought after, but by making *a* paid for as if the gap were great, as if dead time had to be advanced for the payment of *a* and as if *y* were supposed to acquit him- or herself not only for the time incorporated into *a* but also for the time lost through the extending of the credit.

250. Work is twice subject to the rule of exchange. Working conditions in a capitalist system all result from the hegemony of the economic genre, in which the issue is to gain time. By itself, work ignores these stakes (Nos. 243, 244). There is an insoluble differend between working and gaining time. The feelings (sadness, anger, hatred, alienation, frustration, humiliation) that accompany the

said working conditions are born from this differend and signal it. -The subordination of work to exchange is also called wage-earning. The economic genre presents this as a contract between a buyer and a seller of "services." There is a difference, though, which has to do with 'real' time (Referent Section). A moment is said to be real when it is now and when it is chrononymically nameable (day, hour, minute). In the commodity/money exchange, only the moment of exchange is real: objects, which are so much abstract time, are exchanged now, on such a day, at such an hour. In the "work contract," the "service," which in principle is the exchanged object, is defined not only in abstract time (the time of the wage-earner's past qualifications and the time of his or her future well-being and upkeep), but also in real time. The wage-earner will be here (at his or her workpost) and now (for every moment between such and such an hour, so many days per week, so many weeks per year). Partners in exchange may hope to gain time, one by selling, the other by buying, because they are exchanging abstract time, which is mobile in "real" chronology and exchangeable at the right moment. In ceding real time, however, the wage-earner, remains riveted to the deictics of the employer's phrase (*Yes, s/he's there*) and to the calendar (*Yes, s/he arrived at eight o'clock*). Real time cannot be moved about. Even if we suppose that the wage-earner gains more abstract time (as money) than he or she spends in real time to gain it (is this possible?), it seems improbable that he or she would have the (real) time to spend the accumulated time. The problem seems analogous to the problem of narration in *Tristram Shandy* or in Butor's *Passing Time*: it takes more time to tell the life of the narrator (as the hero of the story) than this life has really taken. It can only be hoped that the time stocked up in an opus is not lost for everybody.

251. With capital, there is no longer a time for exchange. Exchange is the exchange of time, the exchange in the least possible time ("real" time) for the greatest possible time ("abstract" or lost time). Anything at all may be exchanged, on the condition that the time contained by the referent and the time required for the exchange are countable. In communication theory, a unit countable in Boolean algebra has been determined for phrases in general, the bit of information. Under this condition, phrases can be commodities. The heterogeneity of their regimens as well as the heterogeneity of genres of discourses (stakes) finds a universal idiom in the economic genre, with a universal criterion, success, in having gained time; and a universal judge in the strongest money, in other words the most creditable one, the one most susceptible of giving and therefore of receiving time. Currency speculation, which short-circuits production, is revealed to be the quickest procedure for accumulating time through exchange: you buy weak money on Friday and you sell it on Tuesday when it is steady, or simply because it has not been devaluated.

252. The differends between phrase regimens or between genres of discourse are judged to be negligible by the tribunal of capitalism. The economic genre with its mode of necessary linkage from one phrase to the next (Nos. 240, 241) dismisses the occurrence, the event, the marvel, the anticipation of a community of feelings. "You'd never be done" taking into consideration the incommensurability of the stakes and the void this incommensurability opens between one phrase and the next. Time is at its fullest with capitalism. But if the verdict, always pronounced in favor of gained time, puts an end to litigations, it may for that very reason aggravate differends.

253. The economic genre's hegemony over the others can certainly put on the garb of an emancipatory philosophy of history. More wealth, more security, more adventure, etc., there's our answer to the canonical phrase of political ethics: *What ought we to be?* (No. 210; Kant Notice 4; § 2). This ethical question is not asked, however, in the economic genre. In it, you don't gain (you don't grab onto the stakes) because you listened to the obligation and welcomed it, but because you've gained some time and are able to gain even more. Thus, the economic genre of capital in no way requires the deliberative political concatenation, which admits the heterogeneity of genres of discourse. To the contrary, it requires the suppression of that heterogeneity. It only tolerates it to the degree that the social bond is not (yet) entirely assimilated to the economic phrase alone (cession and counter-cession). If this is one day the case, political institutions will be superfluous, as national narratives and traditions already are. But then, without the deliberative concatenation where the multiplicity of genres and their respective ends can in principle be expressed, how could the Idea of a humanity, which is not the master of "its" ends (a metaphysical illusion), but which is sensitive to the heterogeneous ends implied in the various known and unknown genres of discourse, and capable of pursuing them as much as possible, maintain itself? And without this Idea, how would a universal history of humanity be possible?

254. In an exchange, the debt must be canceled, and quickly. In a narrative, it must be recognized, honored, and deferred. In a deliberation, it must be questioned, and therefore also deferred. (And the differend accordingly comes to light in deliberation, and even in narrative, or around it). Communities woven through narration must be destroyed by capital: "backward mentality." And the questions that other ("developed") communities ask themselves by means of deliberative institutions must be abbreviated ("chit-chat," "playing to the gallery": anti-parliamentarianism) and brought back down to the canonical question of exchange: what is the *a* that *x* ("we," France, Europe, subway conductors, etc.) must cede to *y* ("them," Germany, the United States, the ministry in charge, etc.) in order to obtain *b*? Beneath all this, the following is understood: without irreparably indebting "us," without "us" having to say thanks, so "we" can enter the next round in a good position, etc. Can the differend, the *And?* (No. 100), the nothing-

ness that suspends and threatens the linkage from one phrase to the next, be covered over in this way, by negotiation? Can the *Come back* implied in the rule of parity for cessions and counter-cessions neutralize the *Is it happening?* (Nos. 131, 132) in such a way that nothing else but the negotiable happens?

255. Capitalism does not constitute a universal history, it is trying to constitute a world market (while deferring it, since it also needs the gaps between national communities). If there is something like a universal history, it would be signaled by signs of history. These signs would be feelings which would in principle be able to be universally shared, disinterested, and "vigorous," and which would manifest themselves publicly on the occasion of events (Kant Notice 4). Kant cites, by way of a sign of history, the enthusiasm aroused by the French Revolution. Other names are now part of our history. One question would be: do feelings identical to that enthusiasm, if not in content, then at least in terms of the formal traits recalled above, attach themselves to these names or to certain ones among them? (But the preliminary question would be: are 'we' today still able to give credence to the concept of a sign of history?)

256. Kant following Burke recognizes sublime feelings other than enthusiasm. Besides respect, of course, and admiration, sorrow (*der Kummer*) also counts among the "vigorous emotions," if it is grounded in moral Ideas (*KUK*: 117). The despair of never being able to present something within reality on the scale of the Idea then overrides the joy of being nonetheless called upon to do so. We are more depressed by the abyss that separates heterogeneous genres of discourse than excited by the indication of a possible passage from one to the other. –Would a vigorously melancholic humanity be sufficient thereby to supply the proof that it is "progressing toward the better"?

257. The "philosophies of history" that inspired the nineteenth and twentieth centuries claim to assure passages over the abyss of heterogeneity or of the event. The names which are those of "our history" oppose counter-examples to their claim. –Everything real is rational, everything rational is real: "Auschwitz" refutes speculative doctrine. This crime at least, which is real (Differend and Referent Sections), is not rational. –Everything proletarian is communist, everything communist is proletarian: "Berlin 1953, Budapest 1956, Czechoslovakia 1968, Poland 1980" (I could mention others) refute the doctrine of historical materialism: the workers rose up against the Party. –Everything democratic is by and for the people, and vice-versa: "May 1968" refutes the doctrine of parliamentary liberalism. The social in its everydayness puts representative institutions in check. –Everything that is the free play of supply and demand is favorable for the general enrichment, and vice-versa: the "crises of 1911 and 1929" refute the doctrine of economic liberalism. And the "crisis of 1974–1979" refutes the post-Keynesian revision of that doctrine. The passages promised by the great doctrinal

syntheses end in bloody impasses. Whence the sorrow of the spectators in this end of the twentieth century.

258. Worse than sorrow–which is a negative feeling but one that can reach the level of the sublime and attest to the heterogeneity between Ideas and realities–is the disillusioned feeling (*ressentiment?*). Reformism accepts the stakes of the economic genre (capitalism) even while priding itself on redistributing the result of the exchange more equitably.* It wants time to be gained, but for everyone. For those who have a lot, to cede some of it without recompense to those who have only a little. Now, first of all, the project is inconsistent with respect to its genre: either this genre is the genre of exchange (No. 241), and every cession presupposes its counter-cession; or else, if there is no counter-cession, then it is not the genre of exchange, and revolution is brought to the economic genre's hegemony over the others. So it's without exerting any blackmail and by conforming to the stakes of his genre, that the banker refutes the timid reformist endeavor: if I advance you some time (credit), you must pay me back (with interest); if you don't pay me back, I won't advance it to you, I'll spend it (by consuming "my" gained time, and the decadence of the economic genre won't have to wait). Second, the reformist project is ethically debatable: the social community does not in principle coincide with the set of partners situated by the economic phrase. To assign it the end of happiness, that is, the equitable distribution of gained time, is to confuse one with the other, to put the you of obligation in the place of the *I* of enjoyment (Obligation Section). –In principle, reformism cannot make anybody happy. But just as the hope surrounding its birth was not vigorous, so the disillusionment linked to its decline is not a sublime feeling either. Sulking, we go back to exchange.

259. If humanity were progressing toward the better, it would not be because "things are getting better" and because the reality of this betterment could be attested through procedures for establishing reality, but because humans would have become so cultivated and would have developed an ear so attuned to the Idea (which is nonetheless unpresentable) that they would feel its tension on the occasion of the most apparently impertinent, with regard to it, facts and that they would supply the very proof of progress by the sole fact of their susceptibility. This progress could therefore be compatible with the general feeling that "things are getting worse." In its aggravation, the gap between Ideas and observable historical-political reality would bear witness not only against that reality but also in favor of those Ideas.

---

*The allusion is to Keynesian economics but also and more broadly to the liberalist gesture of introducing reforms *within* a system in an attempt to assuage the threat or necessity of full-scale revolution.–tr.

260. But what assurance is there that humans will become more cultivated than they are? If culture (culture of the mind, at least) requires work and thus takes time, and if the economic genre imposes its stakes of gaining time on the greater part of phrase regimens and genres of discourse, then culture, as a consumer of time, ought to be eliminated. Humans will thereby no longer feel even sorrow before the incommensurability between realities and Ideas, since they will lose their capacity to have Ideas. They will become more and more competent at strategies of exchange, but exclusively so. The word *culture* already signifies the putting into circulation of information rather than the work that needs to be done in order to arrive at presenting what is not presentable under the circumstances [*en l'occurrence*].

261. And how can it still be supposed (No. 255) that in human history–assuming that the economic genre has not destroyed it–a providence, under the name of Nature, continues to signal, to make signs, to hold out guiding threads? Providence is finality, and finality is deferred accomplishment, expectation, suspense. What finality could maintain itself if hegemony were left to exchange, within which the time of payment on the debt must be abridged? And within which, it goes without saying that there is nothing to wait for–there is no sign whatsoever–from anyone other than oneself.

262. The resistance of communities banded around their names and their narratives is counted on to stand in the way of capital's hegemony. This is a mistake. First of all, this resistance fosters this hegemony (No. 255) as much as it counters it. Then, it puts off the Idea of a cosmopolitical history and generates the fear of falling back onto legitimation through tradition, indeed onto legitimation through myth, even if that legitimation also gives shape to the resistances of peoples to their extermination. Proud struggles for independence end in young, reactionary States.

263. The only insurmountable obstacle that the hegemony of the economic genre comes up against is the heterogeneity of phrase regimens and of genres of discourse. This is because there is not 'language' and 'Being,' but occurrences. The obstacle does not depend upon the "will" of human beings in one sense or in another, but upon the differend. The differend is reborn from the very resolutions of supposed litigations. It summons humans to situate themselves in unknown phrase universes, even if they don't have the feeling that something has to be phrased. (For this is a necessity and not an obligation.) The *Is it happening?* is invincible to every will to gain time.

264. But the occurrence doesn't make a story, does it?–Indeed, it's not a sign. But it is to be judged, all the way through to its incomparability. You can't make a political "program" with it, but you can bear witness to it. –And what if no one hears the testimony, etc. (No. 1ff.)? –Are you prejudging the *Is it happening?*

Works Cited

Works Cited

(Note: In accordance with the author's wish to simplify the bibliography, accessible English translations of foreign works are indicated below and have served as the *basis* for rendering his citations from them. When necessary, however, these translations have been modified to respect the particularity of his own reading of a passage or to prevent the lexical confusion that may arise from our reliance on the manifestly different ways in which the wide array of authors and texts cited by Lyotard have been translated. — tr.)

Theodor W. Adorno 1966, *Negative Dialectics* (tr. E. B. Ashton), New York, 1973.

Aeschylus, *Agamemnon*, in *Aeschylus* (tr. H. W. Smyth) Cambridge, Mass., and London, 1957.

André-Marcel d'Ans 1978, *Le dit des Vrais Hommes*, Paris.

Karl Otto Apel 1981, "La question d'une fondation ultime de la raison," *Critique* 413.

Aristotle, "De interpretatione" (tr. J. L. Ackrill), in *The Complete Works of Aristotle*, ed. J. Barnes, Oxford, 1984.

——, *Metaphysics* (tr. W. D. Ross), in *Complete Works*.

——, *Physics* (tr. R. P. Hardie and R. K. Gaye), in *Complete Works*.

——, *Sophistical Refutations* (tr. W . A. Pickard-Cambridge), in *Complete Works*.

——, *Rhetoric* (tr. W. Rhys Roberts), in *Complete Works*.

——, *Topics* (tr. W. A. Pickard-Cambridge), in *Complete Works*.

Pierre Aubenque 1966, *Le Problème de l'être chez Aristote*, Paris.

Erich Auerbach 1946, *Mimesis. The Representation of Reality in Western Literature* (tr. W. Trask), Princeton, 1953.

Renford Bambrough 1961, "Universals and Family Resemblances," in Pitcher, ed., *Wittgenstein. The Philosophical Investigations*, New York, 1966.

Robert Blanché 1955, *Axiomatics* (tr. G. B. Keene), New York, 1962.

Bernard Bourgeois 1970, *Hegel à Francfort, ou Judaïsme, Christianisme, Hegelianisme*, Paris.

Jacques Bouveresse 1980, "Frege, Wittgenstein, Dummett et la nouvelle 'querelle du réalisme'," *Critique* 399-400.

Martin Buber 1938, *I and Thou* (tr. R. G. Smith), New York, 1958.

―― 1953, *For the Sake of Heaven* (tr. L. Lewisohn), Philadelphia.

M. F. Burnyeat 1976, "Protagoras and Self Refutation in Later Greek Philosophy," *The Philosophical Review* LXXXV, I.

F. D. Caizzi 1964, *Antistene*, Urbino.

―― 1966, *Antisthenis Fragmenta*, Milan.

A. Capizzi 1955, *Protagora, Le Testimonianze e i frammenti*, Florence.

François Châtelet 1981, *L'Etat savant*, unpublished typescript, Paris.

Pierre Clastres 1977, "Archéologie de la violence," *Libre* 1.

Jacques Derrida 1968a, "The Pit and the Pyramid. Introduction to Hegel's Semiology," in *Margins — of Philosophy*, Paris, 1972 (tr. A. Bass) Chicago, 1982.

―― 1968b, "Ousia and Grammé. Note on a note from *Being and Time*," in *Margins — of Philosophy*.

Descartes 1641, *Meditations on First Philosophy* (ed. and tr. E. Anscombe and P. T. Geach) in *Descartes' Philosophical Writings*, Indianapolis, 1971.

J.-P. Desclès and Z. Guentcheva Desclès 1977, "Métalangue, métalangage, métalinguistique," in *Documents de travail* 60-61, Urbino.

Vincent Descombes 1977, *L'inconscient malgré lui*, Paris.

―― 1981a, "La Philosophie comme science rigoureusement descriptive," *Critique* 407.

―― 1981b, "La guerre prochaine," *Critique* 411-12.

Edouard des Places 1970, *Lexique platonicien*, 2 vols., Paris.

Marcel Detienne 1963, *La notion de Daïmôn dans le pythagorisme ancien*, Paris.

―― 1967, *Les Maîtres de vérité dans la Grèce archaïque*, Paris.

Hermann Diels and Walther Kranz 1952, *Die Fragmente der Vorsokratiker*, vols. I and II, Berlin.

Oswald Ducrot 1977, "Présupposés et sous-entendus," in *Stratégies discursives*, Lyon.

Pascal Engel 1981, "Davidson en perspective, *Critique* 409-410.

Paolo Fabbri 1980, Private conversations.

―― and Marina Sbisa 1980, "Models (?) for a Pragmatic Analysis," *Journal of Pragmatics* 4.

Emil Fackenheim 1970, *God's Presence in History: Jewish Affirmations and Philosophical Reflections*, New York.

Paul Feyerabend 1975, *Against Method*, London.

Gottlob Frege 1892, "On Sense and Reference" (tr. M. Black) in *Translations from the Philosophical Writings*, ed. P. Geach and M. Black, Oxford, 1960.

Sigmund Freud 1905, *Jokes and Their Relation to the Unconscious* (ed. and tr. J. Strachey), New York, 1963.

Jean-Louis Gardies 1975, *La logique du temps*, Paris.

Gérard Genette 1972, *Narrative Discourse* (tr. J. Lewin), Ithaca and London, 1982.

―― 1976, *Mimologiques*, Paris.

Gorgias, *On Not-Being, Péri tou mè ontos*, in 1° Anonymous, "De melisso, Xenophane et Gorgia" (ed. B. Cassin) in Barbara Cassin, *Si Parménide*, Lille 1980; 2° "Sextus Empiricus, Adversos Mathematicos," 65 Janacek, in Diels-Kranz, 82 B 3.

Pierre Guyotat 1975, *Prostitution*, Paris.

Jürgen Habermas (with N. Luhmann) 1971, *Theorie der Gesellschaft oder Sozialtechnologie — Was leistet die Systemforschung?*, Frankfurt.

François Hartog 1980, *Le miroir d'Hérodote*, Paris.

Georg W. F. Hegel 1802, "Verhältnis des Skeptizismus zur Philosophie,"in *Werke in zwanzig Bänden* II, Frankfurt, 1970.

―― 1804 (?), *First Philosophy of Spirit* (ed. and tr. H. S. Harris), Albany, 1979.

—— 1806, *Phenomenology of Mind* (tr. J. B. Baillie) New York, 1967. (*PhG*)

—— 1809, *Texte zur Philosophischen Propädeutik* in *Werke* IV (as 1802).

—— 1816, *Science of Logic* (tr. A. V. Miller) London, 1969. (*WL*).

—— 1829, *Aphorismen über Nichtwissen und absolutes Wissen im Verhältnisse zur christlichen Glaubenserkenntnis. Von Karl Friedrich Göschel*, in *Werke* XI (as 1802).

—— 1830, *Encyclopaedia of the Philosophical Sciences*, Part One (tr. W. Wallace) Oxford, 1975.

—— 1835, *Aesthetics* (tr. T. M. Knox) 2 vols., Oxford, 1975.

Martin Heidegger 1929, *Kant and the Problem of Metaphysics* (tr. J. Churchill) Bloomington, 1962.

—— 1933, "The Self-Assertion of the German University" (tr. K. Harries), *Review of Metaphysics* XXXVIII, 3.

—— 1953–1954, "A Dialogue on Language" (tr. P. Hertz), in *On the Way to Language*, San Francisco, 1971.

—— 1962, *On Time and Being* (tr. J. Stambaugh) New York, 1972.

Herodotus, *Histories* (tr. A. de Sélincourt), Harmondsworth, 1954.

Gilbert Hottois 1981, "Logique déontique et logique de l'action chez von Wright," in *Revue Internationale de philosophie* 135.

David Hume 1739, *A Treatise of Human Nature* (ed. L. A. Selby-Bigge), Oxford, 1888.

Hans Jonas 1958, *The Gnostic Religion*, Boston, 1963.

Laurence Kahn 1978, *Hermès passe*, Paris.

G. Kalinowski 1972, *La logique des normes*, Paris.

Immanuel Kant 1764, *Observations on the Feelings of the Beautiful and Sublime* (tr. J. Goldthwait), Berkeley, 1960.

—— 1781 and 1787, *Critique of Pure Reason*, First and Second edition (A and B) (tr. N. K. Smith) New York, 1929. (*KRV*)

—— 1784a, "Idea for a Universal History from a Cosmopolitan Point of View," (tr. L. W. Beck) in *On History* (ed. L. W. Beck), Indianapolis, 1963. (*Idea*).

—— 1784b, "What is Enlightenment?" (tr. L. W. Beck), in *On History* (as 1784-a).

—— 1785, *Foundations of the Metaphysics of Morals* (tr. L. W. Beck), Indianapolis, 1956.

—— 1788a, *Critique of Practical Reason* (tr. L. W. Beck), Indianapolis, 1956. (*KPV*).

—— 1788b, "Uber des Gebrauch teleologischer Principien in des Philosophie," in *Gesammelte Schriften* (ed. Königlich Preussischen Akademie des Wissenschaften), VIII, Berlin and Leipzig, 1923.

—— 1790, *Critique of Judgement* (tr. J. H. Bernard) New York and London, 1951. (*KUK*).

—— 1791, *What Real Progress has Metaphysics made in Germany since the Time of Leibniz and Wolff?* (tr. T. Humphrey) New York, 1983.

—— 1793, *On the Old Saw: That May be Right in Theory but It Won't Work in Practice* (tr. E. B. Ashton) Philadelphia, 1974. (*Theory and Practice*).

—— 1795, "Perpetual Peace," (tr. L. W. Beck), in *On History* (as 1784-a). (*Project*)

—— 1796, "Verkündigung des nahen Abschlusses eines Traktats zum ewigen Frieden in der Philosophie," in *Gesammelte Schriften* VIII (as 1788b).

—— 1798a, *Anthropology From a Pragmatic Point of View* (tr. M. Gregor), The Hague, 1974.

—— 1798b, "An Old Question Raised Again: Is the Human Race Constantly Progressing?" (Part Two of "The Conflict of the Faculties) (tr. R. Anchor), in *On History* (as 1784a). (*Conflict*)

—— 1959/60, "Krakauer Fragment zum 'Streit der Fakultäten'," in *Politische Schriften* (Van der Gablentz, ed.), Cologne and Opladen, 1965. (*KF*)

Pierre Kaufmann 1967, *L'expérience émotionnelle de l'espace*, Paris.

Patrick Kessel 1969, *Les gauchistes de 89*, Paris.

Sören Kierkegaard 1843, *Fear and Trembling* (tr. W. Lowrie), New York, 1954.

Alexandre Koyré, 1947, *Epiménide le menteur*, 1947.

Saul Kripke 1980, *Naming and Necessity*, Cambridge, Mass.

Philippe Lacoue-Labarthe 1975, "Mimesis and Truth" *Diacritics* 8 (No. 1: Spring, 1978).

—— 1980, "Le mythe nazi" (with J.-L. Nancy), in Colloque de Schiltigheim, *Les mécanismes du fascisme*, unpublished typescript.

Bruno Latour 1981, *Irréductions. Tractatus scientifico-politicus*, unpublished typescript, Paris.

John Lawler 1977, "Quelques problèmes de référence," *Langages* 48.

Gérard Lebrun 1972, *La patience du concept. Essai sur le discours hégélien*, Paris.

Gottfried W. Leibniz 1686, "Discourse on Metaphysics," in *Philosophical Papers and Letters* (tr. and ed. L. Loemker), vol. 2, Dordrecht, 1969.

—— 1714, "The Principle of Nature and of Grace, Based on reason," in *Philosophical Papers* (as 1686).

Emmanuel Levinas 1961, *Totality and Infinity* (tr A. Lingis), Pittsburgh, 1969.

—— 1968a, *Quatre lectures talmudiques*, Paris.

—— 1968b, "Humanisme et anarchie," in *Humanisme de l'autre homme*, Montpellier, 1972.

—— 1974, *Otherwise Than Being, or Beyond Essence* (tr. A. Longis), The Hague, 1981.

—— 1976a, *Noms propres*, Montpellier.

—— 1976b, *Difficile liberté*, Paris.

—— 1977, *Du sacré au saint. Cinq nouvelles lectures talmudiques*, Paris.

Nicole Loraux 1974, "Socrate contrepoison de l'oraison funèbre. Enjeu et signification du *Menexenus*," *L'Antiquite classique* 43.

—— 1981, *L'invention d'Athènes*, Paris–La Haye–New York.

John L. Mackie 1964, "Self Refutation, a Formal Analysis," *Philosophical Quarterly* XIV.

Louis Marin 1981, *Le Portrait du roi*, Paris.

Karl Marx 1843, "Contribution to the Critique of Hegel's Philosophy of Law. Introduction," in *Collected Works of Karl Marx and Frederick Engels*, New York, 1975.

Jean-Luc Nancy 1983, *L'impératif catégorique*, Paris.

Pascal 1670, *Pensées* (ed. L. Lafuma) (tr. A. J. Krailsheimer), Harmondsworth, 1966.

Robert Pinget 1980, *L'apocryphe*, Paris.

Plato, *Apology* (tr. H. Tredennick), in *Collected Dialogues* (ed. E. Hamilton and H. Cairns), Princeton, 1961.

——, *Cratylus* (tr. B. Jowett), in *Collected Dialogues*.

——, *Euthydemus* (tr. B. Jowett), in *Dialogues I*, New York, 1937.

——, *Gorgias* (tr. W. D. Woodhead), in *Collected Dialogues*.

——, *Laws* (tr. A. E. Taylor), in *Collected Dialogues*.

——, *Letters* (tr. L. A. Post), in *Collected Dialogues*.

——, *Menexenus* (tr. B. Jowett),in *Collected Dialogues*.

——, *Phaedrus* (tr. R. Hackforth), in *Collected Dialogues*.

——, *The Republic* (tr. P. Shorey), in *Collected Dialogues*.

——, *The Sophist* (tr. F. M. Cornford), in *Collected Dialogues*.

——, *The Statesman* (tr. J. B. Skemp), in *Collected Dialogues*.

——, *Theaetetus* (tr. F. M. Cornford), in *Collected Dialogues*.

Jean-Benoît Puech 1982, *L'Auteur supposé*, unpublished typescript, Paris.

Nicholas Rescher 1967, *Temporal Modalities in Arab Logic*, Dordrecht.

Josette Rey-Debove 1978, *Le métalangage*, Paris.

Clement Rosset 1976, *Le réel et son double*, Paris.

David Rousset 1979, *Le pitre ne rit pas*, Paris.

Bertrand Russell 1903, *Principles of Mathematics*, London.

—— 1959, *My Philosophical Development*, London.

Jean-Michel Salanskis 1977, "Paradoxes, singularités, systèmes," *Critique* 361–62.

Jean Schneider 1980, "La logique self-référentielle de la temporalité," unpublished typescript, Paris.

Gertrude Stein 1931, *How to Write* (ed. P. Meyerowitz), New York, 1975.

Lawrence Sterne 1678, *Tristram Shandy* (ed. I. Ross), Oxford, 1983.

Alfred Tarski 1944, "The Semantic Conception of Truth and the Foundations of Semantics," *Philosophy and Phenomenological Research* IV.

Serge Thion 1980, *Vérité historique ou vérité politique?* Paris.

Elias Tsimbidaros 1981, "La logique du signe. Commentaire sur les aphorismes du *Tractatus* de Wittgenstein et textes connexes," unpublished typesecript, Paris.

Pierre Vidal-Naquet 1981, "A Paper Eichmann" (tr. M. Jolas), *Democracy* I, 2.

Georges Vlachos 1962, *La pensée politique de Kant*, Paris.

Hayden White 1982, "The Politics of Historical Interpretation: Discipline and De-Sublimation," *Critical Inquiry* 9 (September 1982).

Ludwig Wittgenstein 1914–1916, *Notebooks* (ed. and tr. G. E. M. Anscombe and G. H. von Wright), Oxford, 1979. (*TB*)

—— 1921, *Tractatus Logico-Philosophicus* (tr. D. Pears and B. McGuinness) London, 1961. (*TLP*)

—— 1929–1930, "Lecture on Ethics," *The Philosophical Review* LXXIV, 1.

—— 1945, *Philosophical Investigations* (tr. G. E. M. Anscombe) New York, 1958. (*PhU*)

—— 1945–1948, *Zettel* (tr. and ed. G. E. M. Anscombe and G. H. von Wright) Oxford, 1967.

—— 1950–1951, *Remarks on Colour* (ed. G. E. M. Anscombe; tr. L. McAlister and M. Schättle) Berkeley and Los Angeles, 1977.

G. H. von Wright 1967, "Deontic Logics," *American Philosophical Quarterly* 4, 2.

Alexander Zinoviev 1977, *The Yawning Heights* (tr. G. Clough), New York, 1978.

Glossary of French Terms

Glossary of French Terms

Actuel: current; in French, the adjective *actuel* means both what is actual or real (as opposed to what is merely potential) and what is current or occurring "now." Both senses are implied in Lyotard's use of the word, but in order just to maintain the latter sense in English, I have had to translate *actuel* as "current" since "currentness" still implies an actualization, whereas English "actual" does not necessarily imply the notion of what is happening "now."

Agencement: concatenation; an arrangment or articulation of phrases in accordance with the finality imposed by a genre of discourse.

Arraisonner: to set upon; a technical term which refers to the boarding of a ship by customs officials to check for and if need be, to seize contraband; the term is also the standard French translation of the Heideggerian notion of *das Gestell*, traditionally rendered into English as "enframing": "Enframing means the gathering together of that setting-upon that sets upon man, i.e., challenges him forth, to reveal the real, in the mode of ordering, as standing-reserve" [Martin Heidegger, "The Question Concerning Technology," tr. W. Lovitt, in D. Krell, ed. *Basic Writings* (New York: Harper and Row, 1977), p. 302].

Arrive-t-il?: Is it happening?; translates German *Ereignis*; the French verb *arriver* means "to arrive" as well as "to happen." While the latter sense predominates in the expression "arrive-t-il?," Lyotard often plays on the sense of what happens as what comes or arrives (see especially, No. 172 and the last paragraph of the "reading dossier").

Belle Mort: Beautiful Death; heroic death, in which mortality is traded for immortality.

Comme si: as if; translates German *als ob*.

Connaissance: most often translated as "cognition" (but occasionally as "knowledge") to distinguish it from *savoir*, translated uniformly as "knowledge"; translates German *Erkenntnis*.

Demande: request.

Destinataire: addressee.

Destinateur: addressor.

Différend: differend; the French term has been retained in lieu of one of its English equivalents (dispute, conflict, disagreement, difference of opinion, quarrel, or dissension) in order to allow the particular, technical sense Lyotard is attributing to it.

Discours (genre de): genre of discourse.

Dispositif: apparatus.

Dommage: damages; understood in the legal sense of an injury for which legitimate grievance can be sought.

Enchaîner, enchaînement: to link, a linking or linkage; derived from the metaphor found in Kripke (see No. 57) of a "chain of communication" whereby utterances are linked or hooked onto each other as the situation of enunciation changes or develops.

Enjeu: stakes; what one bets on, and, presumably, banks on.

Enoncé (sujet de l'): subject of the utterance.

Enonciation (sujet de l'): subject of the uttering. The important semiotic distinction between *énoncé* and *énonciation* goes back, of course, to Emile Benveniste.

Etant: existent; translates German *Seindes*; I have disregarded the frequent translation of this term by entity since the latter is also part of Lyotard's vocabulary.

Etre: Being; translates German *Sein*.

Fin: end; both aim and termination.

Finalité: finality; translates German *Zweckmässigkeit*; the determination of something in terms of its "end" or *fin*.

Fois: time; time as occurrence in expressions like "one at a time" or "one time only"; to be distinguished from *temps* or time as temporality.

Genre de discours: genre of discourse.

Je: I.

Litige: litigation.

Merveille: marvel.

Moi: the ego; in the phenomenological as well as the Freudian sense.

Nom propre: proper name.

Oubli: oblivion or forgetting.

Phrase: phrase; the English cognate has been used throughout rather than the semantically more correct *sentence* for a number of reasons. The term, as Lyotard develops it here, is *not* a grammatical—or even a linguistic—entity (it is not the expression of one complete thought nor the minimal unit of signification), but a *pragmatic* one, the concern being with the possibility (or impossibility) of what can (or cannot) be "phrased," of what can (or cannot) be "put into phrases." The value of the term *phrase* is thus increased by its ability to be used (in French as well as in English) either as a noun or as a verb with no appreciable semantic difference. *Phrase* is also a term of very wide extension which encompasses utterances at various levels between word and sentence, and which is even available for designating units of nonlinguistic signification such as gestures, signals, or notes of music. A phrase is defined by—as it, in fact, defines—the situating of its instances (addressor, addressee, referent, sense) with regard to one another. Rather than defining a grammatical or semantic unit, a *phrase* designates a particular constellation of instances, which is as contextual as it is textual—if it is not indeed precisely what renders the "opposition" between text and context impertinent.

Puissance: potency or potentiality; as opposed to *pouvoir*, translated as power.

Régime (de phrase): phrase regimen; the political, as well as the dietary, senses of the French word, *régime*, should be kept in mind in addition to its linguistic sense.

Relève, relever: sublation, sublate; translates German *Aufhebung*, *aufheben*; Lyotard is here following Jacques Derrida's translation of Hegel's term; see *Margins − of philosophy*, especially pp. 88–95.

Savoir: knowledge; see note on *connaissance* above.

Sens: sense; often with the sense of "meaning"; used in conformity with Frege's important distinction between "sense" and "reference"; Frege's article has been crucial in Lyotard's thinking since at least *Discours, figure* (Paris: Klincksieck, 1971), especially pp. 105–16.

Sentiment: feeling.

Soi: self.

Souffrance (en): in abeyance; the idiom is used to refer to the suspense or suspension within which the not-yet actualizable phrase is held, but Lyotard also manifestly plays on the non-idiomatic connotation of what "suffers" from its not being able to be put into phrases: see especially no. 93.

Témoigner: to bear witness to or to testify.

Témoin: witness; in no. 47, the racing context induced the term "baton" (itself a borrowing from French) for *témoin* as the object passed from runner to runner in a relay race.

Temps: time; see note on *fois* above.

Tiers: third party.

Tort: wrong; the word is initially defined by Lyotard (No. 7) in terms similar to the technical use of the word tort in English jurisprudence, but it acquires a wider, more broadly ethical connotation.

Tu: you; for the sake of consistency, I have maintained this translation of the second-person pronoun throughout, although it is often to be understood as well (especially in the Levinas Notice) in the sense of Buber's *thou*.

Univers (de phrase): phrase universe.

Index of Names

Index of Names

Note: The references are to numbers in the text (not to pages in the book). To locate the references to the Notices, see the table of contents.

Index of Terms

Index of Terms

Abyss: 178, 181, 207, 217, 256, 257; Notices: Kant 2, §§ 3 and 5; Kant 4, § 3; see Heterogeneous.

Addressor, addressee (*destinateur, destinataire*): 18, 25, 53, 91, 164, 165, 172, 173, 208, 209, 226, 241; Notices: Kant 1; Levinas, § 1; Kant 2, § 2; Declaration of 1789; Cashinahua, §§ 1 and 5; see Universe (of phrase).

Archipelago: Kant Notice 3, § 1.

As if (*comme si*): 248; Notices: Kant 2, § 4; Kant 3, §§ 2 and 4; Kant 4, § 6.

Autonomy: 45, 46, 201, 207; Notices: Levinas, § 3; Kant 2, § 1.

Authorization: 155, 157, 197, 201, 203–205, 207, 209; Notices: Declaration of 1789; Cashinahua, § 6.

Being (*être*): 113, 114, 117, 127, 190, 197, 263; Notices: Gorgias; Hegel, § 2; see *Is it happening?*; Occurrence.

Body (*corps*): 144, 145.

Capital: 191, 221, 245, 247, 250–252, 255, 262.

Case: see Time (*fois*).

Category: 117.

Chagrin: 256–258, 260.

Citizen: 200, 208, 209; Declaration of 1789 Notice.

Cognitive: 28, 30, 34, 36, 61, 64, 67, 68, 76, 77, 81, 85, 176, 211, 217, 237; Kant Notice 4, § 1.

Color: 59, 61; Gorgias Notice.

Commentary: 165, 177, 196; Notices: Levinas, §§ 1, 2, and 3; Kant 2, § 1.

Communist: 4, 235–237, 239, 257.

Context: 141–143.

Contingency: see Necessity.

Culture: 260, Kant Notice 4, § 6.

Death: 11, 16, 17, 93, 152, 153, 156, 157.

Death (Beautiful) (*Belle Mort*): 153, 156, 160, 168; Plato Notice, § 1.

Declarative (genre): 209; Declaration of 1789 Notice.

Note: The references are to numbers in the text (not pages in the book). To locate references to the Notices and their paragraphs, use the table of contents.

205

Theory and History of Literature

Jean-François Lyotard is professor emeritus of philosophy at the Université de Paris VIII and professor at the University of California, Irvine. He has been a visiting professor at numerous universities, including Johns Hopkins, the University of California, Berkeley and San Diego, the University of Minnesota, the Université de Montréal, Canada, the Universität Siegen, West Germany, and the University of Saõ Paulo, Brazil. He is author of *Discours, figure, Economie libidinale, Driftworks, Peregrinations, The Postmodern Condition*, and with Jean-Loup Thébaud, *Just Gaming* – the latter two both available in translation from Minnesota.

Georges Van Den Abbeele is associate professor of French literature at Miami University, Ohio. He has also been a faculty member at the University of California, Santa Cruz, visiting professor at the University of California, Berkeley, and a Mellon Faculty Fellow at Harvard University. Van Den Abbeele received his Ph.D. in romance languages and literature from Cornell University in 1981. He has contributed to *Diacritics, Esprit Créateur, French Studies*, and *Stanford French Review*.